Different Gospels

The **C. S. Lewis Centre** is an international network of Christians from many different churches and traditions. Despite their differences, they are united by their commitment to historic Christianity.

There are a number of ways in which we work to achieve our aims. These include:

Dialogue The Centre is a meeting point for Christians who would never normally talk to each other. We make it possible for people from a rich diversity of Christian traditions to engage in open, frank debate.

Education The Centre bridges the gap between the college and the pew by providing top-quality education for Christians in their local churches. This is done through seminars, workshops and conferences.

Research We carry out research into the relationship between Christianity and the modern world. We seek to develop a distinctively Christian voice in response to the critical issues of the day.

Publication The Centre generates a variety of publications, including the C. S. Lewis Centre books published by SPCK, video and audio tapes, and occasional papers. We also produce a quarterly journal, *Leading Light*.

For further information, write to: The C. S. Lewis Centre, c/o Dr Andrew Walker, Centre for Educational Studies, King's College London, Cornwall House Annex, Waterloo Road, London SE1 8TX.

Different Gospels
The New Edition

edited by

Andrew Walker

This revised edition first published in Great Britain 1993
Society for Promoting Christian Knowledge
Holy Trinity Church
Marylebone Road
London NW1 4DU

Originally published in Great Britain by Hodder & Stoughton 1988

Peter L. Berger's essay was originally delivered as the Erasmus Lecture, January
1987, in St Peter's Lutheran Church, New York City. It was published first in *This
World* 17 (1987), pp. 6–17, and then in Richard Neuhaus (ed.), *Apostate America:
The Triumph of Different Gospels* (Grand Rapids, MI: Wm B. Eerdmans, 1988). It
appears here, with only minor changes, by permission of Richard Neuhaus and
Peter L. Berger.
   R. J. Berry's essay, which appears here by permission of Macmillan Magazines
Ltd, is a revised version of his essay 'What to believe about miracles', which first
appeared in *Nature*, vol. 322, no. 6077, 24 July 1986, pp. 321–2, copyright © 1986
Macmillan Magazines Ltd, and was later also used as an appendix in his book *God
and Evolution* (London: Hodder & Stoughton, 1988).
   A version of Janet Martin Soskice's essay appeared in the August–September
1992 issue of *Priests and People*.
   Portions of Andrew Walker's essay have been used before, in his 'Resexing the
Trinity: The Spirit as Feminine', *King's Theological Review* 13.2 (1990), pp. 41–4.

British Library Cataloguing-in-Publication Data

A catalogue record for this book is available from the British Library

ISBN   0-281-04690-5   175292

Typesetting by David Mackinder, using *Nota Bene* software
Printed in Great Britain by Biddles Ltd, Guildford and King's Lynn

CONTENTS

CONTRIBUTORS

Peter L. Berger is Director of the Institute for the Study of Economic Culture, Boston University, Massachusetts

R. J. Berry is Professor of Genetics, University College, London

Gavin D'Costa is Lecturer in Theology, University of Bristol

James D. G. Dunn is Professor of Divinity, University of Durham

Colin E. Gunton is Professor of Christian Doctrine, King's College, London

Alasdair I. C. Heron is Professor of Reformed Theology, University of Erlangen, Germany

Gerard Loughlin is Lecturer in Religious Studies, University of Newcastle

Alister E. McGrath is Lecturer in Historical and Systematic Theology, Wycliffe Hall, Oxford

Lawrence Osborn is Co-ordinator of the Gospel and Culture programme

Thomas A. Smail is the Rector of Sanderstead, Surrey

Janet Martin Soskice is Fellow of Jesus College and University Lecturer in Theology, University of Cambridge

Alan J. Torrance is Lecturer-Elect in Systematic Theology, King's College London

Andrew Walker is Senior Lecturer in Theological Education, King's College London

Keith Ward is Regius Professor of Divinity, University of Oxford

INTRODUCTION

Andrew Walker

Different Gospels first appeared in 1988, on the twenty-fifth anniversary of C. S. Lewis's death, as both a tribute to the great defender of 'mere Christianity' and as an attempt, however inadequate, to continue his apologetic work. The book was enthusiastically reviewed and sold out in a few years. We felt that while we should meet the continuing demand for the book by republishing it, we should also radically revise, edit, and expand it in order to take account of the continuing changes in modern theology.

Society has also rapidly changed in the last few years. Since 1988 we have seen the spectacular collapse of Marxism, the War in the Gulf, and more famine in Africa. The continuing concern with impending ecological disasters and the growing problem of AIDS are again evidence that the world is not necessarily a safer place because communism has imploded. Capitalism, although the clear winner over centralized and planned economies, has entered its deepest recession since the 1930s, and with the rise of neo-fascism in Germany and the viciousness of 'ethnic cleansing' in former Yugoslavia there is a discernible jitteriness in the air as we approach the third millennium.

It is difficult to be certain which modern theologies will survive these years of anxiety and still be influential by the year 2000. Process theology, which promised so much a few years back, is already virtually dead. With the retirement in 1992 of its most sophisticated exponent, Schubert Ogden (1966), there would seem to be few prepared to continue its programme which owed so much to Whitehead (1979), Hartshorne (1983), and the optimism of the Enlightenment.

Bultmann made a considerable impact in the 1960s, but it is difficult to see his influence extending into the future as interest in his work, and in existentialism, has already waned (though see Alasdair Heron's essay). Liberation theology, which somewhat replaced Bultmann in many American universities, is itself somewhat in limbo since the demise of Marxist theory (though one can expect interest in

it to continue for some years in South America, Africa, and among
black seminarians in North America). That apparent Ozymandias,
Karl Barth, is clearly not down and out as once we thought, and
versions of neo-orthodoxy from Moltmann to the evangelicalism of
Fuller Seminary in California are clearly alive and well and look set
to survive well into the twenty-first century.

At the moment feminist theology (see Andrew Walker's and Janet
Martin Soskice's essays) is still a rising force, but it may be moribund
by the year 2000 if it surrenders to postmodernism. But will postmodernism replace all modernist thought, or does it flatter to deceive?
(See Gerard Loughlin's essay.) Perhaps postmodernism is really only
modernism gone sour, a disenchantment with the Enlightenment
rather than a new paradigm to replace it (cf. Harvey 1989 and
Jameson 1991).

The problem with speculating in this way, however, is that we are
living in a pluralistic world which is itself becoming increasingly
fragmented. For Christians, this fragmentation means that while for
some postmodernism is a pressing intellectual concern, for others it is
of no concern at all, for they have never heard of it. Many Christians
are still coming to terms with what is usually called 'liberalism' or
'modernism'. People still want to know whether the scriptures are
reliable (see James Dunn's essay), miracles are possible (see Keith
Ward's and R. J. Berry's essays), and whether the holy Trinity makes
any sense in the modern world (see Tom Smail's essay).

This concern is not a question of being out of date. Modern
pluralism, by definition, points to the fact that we live in a society
where different world-views coexist in blissful ignorance of each
other.

Although we now live in a 'global village' where world faiths rub
shoulders with each other, inter-faith dialogue is not even on the
agenda of many churches (see Gavin D'Costa's essay). Or again, a
new paganism is rampant in secular society, and yet Christian
denominations have little knowledge of this 'New Age' and outside
Catholicism and Anglicanism few churches have had experience of
Matthew Fox's 'creation spirituality', which is a hybrid of this new
paganism and (reinterpreted) classical strands of Christianity (see
Lawrence Osborn's essay).

Fox is an important figure to cite, for his influence has not been
felt, or even recognized, in the universities, but it is to be found
through bookshops, the ecological movement, and in those Christian

circles where spirituality seems to take precedence over theology. If we were to take popularity as a criterion for theological influence, then we would have to say that one of the major figures in the last decade has been the Californian charismatic John Wimber (1985, on whom see Wright 1993).

In this new edition of *Different Gospels* we do not pretend to cover every new theological and religious fashion, for it is neither intended to be a reader of modern theology nor a dictionary of contemporary Christianity. Its purpose is twofold. First, we wish to demonstrate that classical theology can be defended against modern criticisms; and, second, that the Christian tradition is deep and resourceful enough to launch a few counter-charges of its own against some of these criticisms, and also against some of the new theologies which seek to replace it.

The fact that some essays are eirenic in style and others more pugnacious in tone is a reflection of the broad range of writers who have contributed to *Different Gospels*. Our distinguished authors, who represent Catholic, Orthodox, and Reformed traditions, have been subject only to two editorial constraints: one, that their essays are accessible to a broad non-specialized lay audience; two, that we stand together as 'mere Christians'.

'Mere Christianity', Lewis once reminded us, is '. . . no insipid interdenominational transparency, but something positive and self-consistent, and inexhaustible' (Lewis 1971, 163). Lewis did not mean by this description Confessionalism, but he did mean historic Christianity – the apostolic faith, as reflected in the creeds and councils of the early Church, and in a high view of holy scripture.

THE ENLIGHTENMENT AND MODERNISM

There is perhaps one thing worth spelling out by way of introduction to *Different Gospels*, and that is the relationship between modern theologies and the philosophical Enlightenment. All the recent talk about postmodernism as a repudiation of, but nevertheless a parasite upon, modernism should prompt us to remember that it is this modernism which, until the last few years, has probably posed the greatest threat to classical theology. The *Oxford English Dictionary* tells us that modernism is 'a tendency or movement towards modifying traditional beliefs and doctrines in accordance with the findings of modern criticism and research'. To understand modernism is to recognize that it is a product of the philosophical Enlightenment, and it is the Enlightenment which forms the backdrop against which the battle of orthodox Christianity and modernist/postmodernist thought has been fought.

One of the problems with the word 'modernism' is that it evokes notions of contemporaneous or, at least, recent history. When people talk about liberalism in the Church, for example, they tend to identify it with the recent liberalizing tendencies in the larger society. In the 1960s, during the so-called 'permissive' era, when there were so many changes in social, moral and sexual behaviour, it seemed to some Christians then as if this new liberalism had spilt over into the Church. This was the view in America, with the publication of Thomas Altizer's *The Gospel of Christian Atheism* (1966) and his *Radical Theology and the Death of God* (1966), written with W. Hamilton, and also in England, in 1963, with the *succès de scandale* of John Robinson's *Honest to God*.

But in fact Robinson's book was a popular and bastardized pastiche of Rudolf Bultmann's demythologizing theology and Paul Tillich's existentialism which had been around since the Second World War (Bultmann 1953 and Tillich 1968). Altizer's thesis was even older, being an extreme (and rather silly) extension of nineteenth-century kenoticism (the belief in the renunciation of the divine nature at the incarnation).

More recently, in the 1980s, some conservative evangelicals in Britain were up in arms over the BBC's *Sea of Faith* series and Independent Television's *Jesus: The Evidence*, as if the devil had suddenly been let loose on an unsuspecting British public with a clutch of new heresies with which to bamboozle the faint-hearted and weak-minded (see Cupitt 1984 and Wilson 1984). It may very well be that television is more devilish than meets the eye (see Walker 1987, ch. 6), but the theology that was expounded in those programmes was neither new nor did it represent mainstream academic theology. What it did do, like so much of modernist theology, was to rework themes in nineteenth-century liberalism (in the sense of the German school of Ritschl and his followers). These themes were predicated upon Enlightenment presuppositions. Michael Goulder has rightly said that 'we are driving over the same course as our eighteenth-century forefathers, only at four times the speed' (Goulder and Hick 1983, 88).

It is perhaps a sobering thought that modernism began some three hundred years ago, yet this sobriety will help us to see that there is no new crisis in theology and the Christian faith, in the sense that some flood of alien gospels has suddenly and unexpectedly burst upon us. What has happened is less dramatic but perhaps more damaging. We have all been caught in a flow tide of change that has gradually but relentlessly eroded traditional and historic Christianity (the rhythmic lapping of the waves gently lulling us to sleep). Today we are waking up and seeing that the erosion of the centuries has worn away much of our heritage, until we now find ourselves cut back to the bare rock – the foundations – of the faith.

For some of us the shock of being awakened from our somnambulism and seeing for the first time the situation as it really is has had the same effect as if we really had just been caught in the icy deluge of strange gospels.

If we want to turn the tide (and not merely swim against it, as Keith Ward has suggested we may be doing, Ward 1986), we have to realize that we are called to 'earnestly contend for the faith' through mission and evangelism not only to our people, but also to our culture (Newbigin 1989). The presuppositions of our modern thought need to be baptized and cleansed in an altogether different fountainhead, and we must stem the poison streams flowing from the Enlightenment itself.

Of course we must acknowledge that there are 'healing waters' and life-giving tributaries that flow from that great source of modern knowledge also (see Colin Gunton's essay): the Enlightenment is not the origin of all our ills, any more than it is the watershed of all that is good in modernity. No doubt many of us are glad that we are living on this side of the Enlightenment. Not only has it brought us critical tools that have helped us to understand the universe and our social world more richly, it has also brought with it a new and vital vision of freedom and autonomy for human beings. The Enlightenment offered us the chance to be free from the tyranny of authoritarian political structures, free from a 'moral law' imposed from above, outside and against ourselves. It seemed to offer us freedom from a God who throughout the Middle Ages and the post-Reformation period had become increasingly autocratic and dictatorial (see Andrew Walker's essay).

But tragically, as Colin Gunton's essay demonstrates, the desire for freedom did not free us to be ourselves. Rather, it led to a more

terrible tyranny: the insistence – the demand – that we be free to
control our own destiny, knowledge and morality. Is not the Enlightenment another bright Eden where again, dazed by the glittering
angel, we believe with all our hearts that we can 'shuffle off this
mortal coil' and be as the gods? So, for example, the deists of the late
eighteenth century cast the transcendent and holy God out of the
heavens and immanentized him in nature or history. It seemed better
to bring God down to earth, or to heel – making him one of us, or we
part of him – than to tolerate his radical otherness. (Is not this
Hegel's solution to what he saw to be the tyranny of God?)

The freedom to be ourselves is indeed a gift from God; but to be
free is not to free ourselves from him like the prodigal son, who
demanded his inheritance from his father as a right (a right which was
not his to claim, as the father was not yet dead). The language of
rights becomes, after the Enlightenment, both the demand for justice
and the demand for self-determination. The demand for autonomy, to
be free from God, is also a demand to be free of each other, to be
our 'own man', free of community restraints and obligations. The
language of rights is the assertion of individualism (at least for Kant
and Locke in Europe, and Franklin and Jefferson in the New
American Republic). And so the failure to find a personal bond
between the collective and the individual has been one of the
dominant problems in advanced industrial societies, both socialist and
capitalist (again, see Colin Gunton's essay, and the comments in Alan
Torrance's essay about the individual and the community).

To identify freedom as both a positive gift of the Enlightenment
and yet also a gift that is tainted with a strident and selfish
assertionism, is to recognize that good and evil are often poured out
together upon the world. To return to our earlier extended metaphor,
we can say that the healing and poisonous streams from the Enlightenment flow out together, but by their very nature cannot join up
together. And it is here that we detect the dualistic flow of thought
that has provided both the greatness and the destructiveness of our
modern era.

It is a truism that much classical thought attempted a unitary grasp
of realities. The macrocosm and microcosm of Neoplatonism and the
eternal verities of Aristotelianism were common features of medieval
scholasticism. But if we take an example from traditional Christology,
we can see here that Christians faced with the absolute otherness of
God and his radical separation from his creatures nevertheless saw

that in the incarnation something unique, miraculous, hitherto thought impossible, had happened: spirit and matter, otherness and givenness, knowing and unknowing, subject and object were integrated into one indivisible unity. Putting it more theologically: God and humanity, creator and creature, joined together without confusion in the person of Jesus of Nazareth.

Enlightenment thought cannot conceive of (nor permit) such a unity, for it operates with a dualistic concept of reality: that which can be known in the phenomenal world (science and 'hard facts'), and that which exists in the noumenal world (of ideas) but which cannot be known objectively. Such a radical dualism, exemplified by Kant's *Critique of Pure Reason* (1787), leaves traditional metaphysics in one realm and history, experience and matter in another. At a stroke Jesus is torn apart, leaving us with his historical location and humanity to be investigated in the phenomenal world, but banishing his divinity to an unknown and unknowable shadowland of ideas.

So, since the Enlightenment we have a world 'split in two', a world in which we have both a measurable and quantifiable universe that is open to scientific investigation and a world which is not measurable, not quantifiable. In the unmeasurable world (later, the logical positivists were to say the meaningless world) room is made for faith, feeling, subjectivity, opinion and traditional metaphysics. In the empirical, measurable world there is no room for miracles, revelation or divinity. Such a dualism renders patristic thought untenable (see Alasdair Heron's essay), and with it the unitary thrust of Christian orthodoxy.

If Kant's thought led to the severing of the umbilical cord that bound the noumenal and the phenomenal, the majority of the writers in that by now notorious book *The Myth of God Incarnate* (Hick 1977) were simply following through that fatal manoeuvre to its final and deadly conclusion (see Alister McGrath's essay): God is not after all joined to his creatures in solidarity and love – though Hick, like others before him, is quite happy for God to be in all of us, as long as he is neither radically other than us nor uniquely joined to humanity in the person of Jesus.

But also stemming from Kant we do not merely inherit a dualism that divides physics from metaphysics, measurability from immeasurability: we inherit a commitment to what Kant (*Critique of Practical Reason*, 1788) wants to call 'autonomy'. This is the arena of thought and action which is under our personal control, and the

only sphere in which faith, moral action and practical reasoning can
legitimately be exercised. 'Heteronomy', on the other hand, Kant saw
as objectivized reality over and against our freedom as rational and
autonomous beings. It is not to be seen as synonymous with the
noumenal world (though they often overlap), because it is any source
of knowledge external to, and hence constraining, ourselves.
Heteronomy could be the dogmas of Christianity, the systematic
metaphysics of a Thomas Aquinas, or the laws of natural science in
the phenomenal realm.

And so, by implication, Kant's severance of the noumenal from
the phenomenal, and his insistence that we should look for morality
and faith in ourselves (autonomy), cut Christianity off from the objective revelation of God in Christ and raised the issue that the scriptures
themselves are over and against us until we assent to them and make
them our own. Kant remained a rationalist and an idealist, but in
opposing autonomy to heteronomy he opened up the possibility that
faith for us must now be predicated upon experience, personal
moralism, self-consciousness, emotion or will, but certainly not on
outmoded (and now cut off) metaphysics and tradition. And it is the
'father of modern theology', Schleiermacher (1821), who, accepting
Kant's strictures on the noumenal world, and yet wishing to avoid a
purely phenomenalist and heteronomous (empiricist and external)
basis for knowledge, opts to build a modern systematic theology on
experience rather than revelation (see Gavin D'Costa's essay).

Modernist theology proper takes its assumptions from Kant,
Schleiermacher and Hegel. Hegel at least saw the problem inherent in
Kantian dualism. He attempted to describe the whole of reality as a
synthesis of the objective and the subjective, the metaphysical and the
historical. Dialectic was an attempt to articulate the necessary
harmony of these apparent oppositions. As Gunton points out,
however, Hegel takes the radical otherness of God and brings him
into history as the *Geist* of progress who, like some Platonic
Demiurge, seeks to realize himself by coming to be. Conversely, we
find that we creatures – pictured as separated from God by nature in
the Christian schema of salvation – are now ourselves capable of
divinity, not because of what God in Christ has done for us, but
because we are potentially divine: we too can become part of the
divine spirit by virtue of being caught up in the process of the laws of
history moving towards their utopian consummation.

Tragically, Hegel, the apostle of freedom and synthesis, bound us – as Kierkegaard saw only too plainly (Kierkegaard 1941) – to a philosophy of unfreedom where men and women are subject not to the liberating divine Spirit, but to the iron laws of history (heteronomy). As every sociologist and student of socialism knows, Marx tried to turn Hegel on his head and ground his metaphysics in the concrete world of economy and society (but he could never shake off his Hegelianism): the totalitarianism of Marxist systems is inextricably bound up with the totalitarianism of Hegelian metaphysics.

But if Hegel at least saw the problem of the Enlightenment, it has been more typical in modernity that philosophical and theological thought have tended to oscillate between heteronomy and autonomy. Kantian dualism led to the horns of a dilemma, and few besides Hegel have attempted to grasp them both. Various thinkers have tried to hold on to either an idealism 'out there' – despite Kant's strictures on the noumenal (the English idealist T. H. Green comes to mind); or, more typically, the heteronomy of science. The positivism of Comte and the mechanistic determinism of Bernard probably had more of an effect on nineteenth-century thought (outside of Germany) than did Hegelianism. Positivism squeezed out free will and human imagination from reality and replaced them with laws of nature. In this respect positivism bound humankind by the iron laws of nature every bit as much as men and women were bound by the inexorable unfolding laws of Marxist history.

Science was so powerful because it was both phenomenalist (in the Kantian sense I have outlined here) and a source of dogmatic truths. Its very objectivity (its facticity and measurability) pushed the noumenal world even further away from consciousness. And yet the modernist search for authenticity from Schleiermacher onwards has tended to ignore heteronomy and ground its truth in experience and self-consciousness. Existentialism and Heideggerian (and Husserlian) phenomenology would be paradigm examples of this approach, though we also find both Ritschl in Germany and Tolstoy in Russia falling back upon moralism (albeit a moralism stripped of revelational and supernaturalist truths) in their search for authentic faith.

In practice, what has happened in all areas of intellectual thought, but particularly in theology, is that scholars have tended to accept the heteronomy of science and have taken it as given (how mechanistic and absolute was Rudolf Bultmann's trust in science, for example).

Having accepted that side of the Kantian dualism, they have then turned to autonomy (to the subjective sphere) in order to deal with those other issues of faith and destiny, and morals and beliefs, about which science has nothing to say (see R. J. Berry's essay).

But autonomy, lacking any objective standard, can provide no common ground for human society and morality. Indeed, it runs the risk of being seen as ultimately inauthentic – an illegitimate attempt to impose subjective meanings on a meaningless universe (see Nietzsche 1966). Interestingly, many French postmodernist writers come close not only to denying the legitimacy of autonomous thinking, but also to insisting that the autonomous 'self' is itself an invention of the Enlightenment.

MODERN SOCIETY AND THE END OF THE ENLIGHTENMENT PROJECT

Perhaps one could argue that while talk of dualism and modernity is all very well for intellectuals, it really has little or no relevance for the ordinary man or woman in the pew. But, on the contrary, it does. Dualistic patterns of thought permeate the whole of our culture, not just universities. We see a passionate concern for human rights and justice in our societies, but from what does it stem? What common standards of morality or rules of evidence can be invoked? Some people insist on public morality – and we still have a sort of civil religion that insists on a penal code and acceptable rules of social behaviour. But there seem to be no agreed standards of moral behaviour in private life.

I think that the public/private split in our modern societies is analogous to Kant's heteronomy/autonomy split. (But I do not mean to suggest here that there is any logical relationship between these two – more what Max Weber would have called an 'elective affinity'.) Public life is for society – which is seen to have its own 'needs' and functional prerequisites – and private life is for the self-fulfilment of individuals.

The public world is that objectified world 'out there'; it is a world of legal and rational activity, as exemplified in the banking system, city finance and the forces of law and order. On the other hand, there is the private world of leisure, the family, church, and voluntary associations. Here individual autonomy rules. Personal preferences, private moralities, relativistic philosophies and traditional beliefs jostle for attention. But this autonomous province is the land of opinion, not truth. The familiar riposte, 'But that's just your opinion!' is a tacit acceptance that one opinion is as good as another, and that truth (in the autonomous world at least, if not in the law courts!) means 'your truth' but not necessarily 'my truth'. Subjective relativism dominates in this world, so that it becomes taboo to insist that a truth such as the Christian gospel transcends our many versions of reality and truth-telling.

We might reasonably say that we are engaging here not only in theology, but also in what is usually called the 'sociology of knowledge' (the most distinguished proponent of which is Peter Berger, whose essay 'Different Gospels' lends itself to the title of this book). This is an important exercise, for it may very well be that the postmodern enterprise, while seemingly a philosophical repudiation of modernism, is also a sociological response to pluralism – to the autonomy of the private world run amok.

The fragmentation of what Marxists like to call 'late capitalism' – or what we might prefer to think of as 'modernity in an advanced state of decay' – can lead either to the deepest pessimism (MacIntyre 1985; Davidson and Rees-Mogg 1992), a gleeful playfulness (the 'art' of Jeff Koons, or Cupitt's theology, 1990) or defiant hope (see Gerard Loughlin's essay, and Steiner 1991). Whichever response we find the most appropriate, we all need to recognize that it is beginning to look as if what Jürgen Habermas called 'the Enlightenment project' has just about run out of steam: the dream of a unitary field of knowledge, or a universal critical rationality, is dying (though see Weinberg 1993). If this were not enough, the breakdown of society into public and private, the increasing specialization of knowledge, the rampant atomism of modern individualism, the hedonistic destruction of consumerism – all of these societal changes have facilitated the breakdown of communication and community in the modern world.

This collection of essays, coming as it does from different disciplines and from various theological standpoints, cannot pretend to be a seamless unity. We are ourselves heirs of the Enlightenment, and no doubt we too reflect the pluralistic fragmentation that dominates late modernity. Nevertheless, we are also 'mere Christians', and as such believe that there is a gospel, a 'meta-narrative', that transcends the dualisms of our contemporary society. In the light of this gospel, it seems to many of us that we have expected too much from the Enlightenment.

It is to be hoped that our culture has now become mature enough to sift the chaff from the wheat, and to hold on to only that which is life-giving and to discard the rest. We must accept that we cannot go back to the innocence of Eden (back behind the Enlightenment); but on the other hand we must recall that the timeless truths of the gospel never call us to look back, they call us instead to look *up* – we who have heard and responded to the gospel of hope are marching to Zion.

1
THE HOLY TRINITY AND
THE RESURRECTION OF JESUS

Thomas A. Smail

Many modern Christians do not know what to make of the doctrine of the Trinity. Although they profess it in their creeds and liturgies and in their hymns sing about the God who is Father, Son and Holy Spirit, three persons in one God, they would find it hard to explain why they said these things or what they meant by them. To say that God is somehow both three and one at the same time can easily look like a highly incomprehensible kind of metaphysical mathematics which is entirely remote from the biblical gospel, our own living relationship with God, and our life in the world.

The evidence suggests that an understanding of and an enthusiasm for the doctrine among clergy and ministers are in many cases not much higher. In a recent survey quite a lot of ordained leaders said they found Trinity Sunday the second most difficult day of the year – after Remembrance Day – to know what to say. All in all it does not look as if the central Christian assertion about God – that he is Father, Son and Holy Spirit – is either understood or cherished in pulpit or pew.

There are many reasons for this neglect. Undoubtedly the fault lies at least in part with the way in which the doctrine of the Trinity has sometimes been expounded in the past, in rarified terms of theological speculation which do indeed make it hard to see how it is connected with the New Testament gospel, so that it looks as if you could ignore or even drop it without losing anything from the vital heart of Christian faith.

But the chief fault certainly lies in the ways of thinking of modernity, which for the last two centuries and more have powerfully influenced the whole Western world, Christians included. Modernist thinking and trinitarian thinking do not easily combine. Biblical criticism, strongly influenced as it has been by modernist presuppositions, has eroded the authority of the scriptures and in particular has cast doubt on the authenticity of those texts on which the doctrine of the Trinity was traditionally based.

More generally, the prevailing tendency of all modern thinking, when it deals with God at all, is to rely upon reason and experience rather than upon the Bible and God's self-revelation in Christ to which it bears witness. If, as a child of modernity, I want to know what can be known about God, I will turn to my own rational processes or my own religious experiences rather than to what God shows me about himself through the prophets and apostles and supremely through Jesus Christ. I will believe as much of the Bible as agrees with my own understanding and my own experience, and dismiss the rest.

If the Bible and God's revelation in Christ are treated in that way, it is no wonder that the doctrine of the Trinity soon begins to look irrelevant. The only reason for believing in a trinitarian God is that it is that sort of God who reveals himself in Christ. It therefore follows that if we are not prepared to take the Christian revelation seriously, we shall not take the doctrine of the Trinity seriously either.

We are, however, living at a time when the presuppositions of modern thinking are being challenged by scientists and philosophers alike, so there is a chance to escape from a framework that devalues the Christian revelation and its trinitarian understanding of God to a new framework of thinking that puts them both at the centre once again. This has been happening in much of the theology of the last fifty years. Karl Barth on the Reformed side and Karl Rahner on the Roman Catholic side are two eminent Christian thinkers who evolved two very different theologies which nevertheless have in common the centrality of a trinitarian doctrine of God arising from and being a key to the understanding of the biblical gospel.

In this essay my purpose is to show the connection between the doctrine of the Trinity and the New Testament in relation to one of the central assertions of the New Testament, namely that on the third day the crucified Jesus of Nazareth rose again from the dead. I shall be trying to indicate that we can make full sense of the biblical account of the resurrection only if we see it as an act in which God reveals himself as Father, Son and Holy Spirit, each acting in a distinctive way but in the closest possible relationship and indeed unity with one another. The resurrection needs to be understood as the act of three divine persons who are one God.

Before we can proceed with that main purpose we must first, however, say what we mean by the resurrection. What we think actually happened at Easter will affect whether we think that the event contains a revelation of a trinitarian God. To take an extreme example, if Easter is only about the rising again of the faith of the disciples rather than about the rising again of Jesus, since such an event tells us nothing about Jesus it is hardly likely to tell us anything about God.

My own understanding of Easter, which there is no room to defend in detail here, is much more conservative and traditional. The gospel writers seem to me to ring entirely true when they portray the risen Jesus not as the subject of some ethereal vision, but as the same Jesus of Nazareth who died on the cross, totally transformed indeed, but still a real man who can be touched and handled in space and time, to whom all power has been given on earth as well as in heaven. One does not have to accept the historical accuracy of every detail of the gospel accounts to believe their central assertion of the continued bodily identity of Jesus and his divine-human lordship over the created world. It is such a realist understanding of the resurrection that, we shall be arguing, contains within itself a revelation of Father, Son and Holy Spirit.

It is also important for our purposes that we should understand the resurrection in an integrated and inclusive way. In other words it includes not just the discovery of the empty tomb on Easter morning and the appearances of Jesus to his disciples that followed, but also the ascension and exaltation of Jesus to the Father's right hand and the imparting of the Spirit to the Church. Under the influence of the Church's liturgical year, based as it is on Luke's timescale of events, we tend to think of resurrection, ascension and Pentecost as three events separated in time from one another, each with its own distinct significance. But we need to remember that John and many of the other New Testament writers draw into the closest theological association the three events that Luke holds temporally apart. For John the lifting up of Jesus to reign with the Father in his ascension is seen in the closest connection with his being lifted up on the cross to die and his being lifted up from the grave to live (John 12.32). For John also the Holy Spirit is breathed out upon the disciples, to equip them for their mission, on Easter evening and not fifty days later (John 20.22).

Paul and the writer to the Hebrews also think of Easter in this inclusive and integrated way. In the early Christian hymn that Paul quotes in Philippians 2, the resurrection as such is not mentioned, but simply assumed as part of the exaltation of Jesus, 'He . . . became obedient to death – even death on a cross! Therefore God exalted him to the highest place' (Phil. 2.8–9). The same thing happens in Hebrews, which has only one explicit reference to the resurrection (Heb. 13.20), but whose whole teaching depends on the fact that 'We . . . have. such a high priest, who sat down at the right hand of the throne of the Majesty in heaven' (Heb. 8.1). We are therefore on good New Testament ground when we deal with the whole Easter complex of events in this inclusive way. To do so will enable us to see that it is the whole Easter mystery, comprising resurrection, ascension and outpouring of the Spirit considered in its wholeness, that reveals God as Trinity. As we look at it in this way we shall see Father, Son and Holy Spirit in action, each in a distinct way and yet in the closest possible relationship and indeed unity with one another.

First, then, *as regards God the Father: it is consistently clear throughout the whole Easter event that it is the Father who is both the initiating source and the ultimate goal of all that happens in relation to the raising of the Son and the sending of the Spirit. It is from the Father that it all starts and it is to the Father that it is all to return.*

'Praise be to the God and Father of our Lord Jesus Christ! In his great mercy he has given us new birth into a living hope through the resurrection of Jesus Christ from the dead' (1 Pet. 1.3). That verse is typical of many others in different parts of the New Testament in which the resurrection is seen as the distinctive personal act of God the Father, his justifying vindication of Jesus in the face of his crucifiers. Men put him to death, but he appealed his case to his Father (Luke 23.46) and in response God said his own great Yes to all that Jesus had lived and died for by raising him from the dead. Walter Künneth has the weight of the biblical evidence behind him when he says, 'it is decisive to recognize that *God is exclusively the subject of the action in the resurrection of Jesus*' (Künneth 1965, 128). Jesus rises because he has been raised up by his Father, he acts because he has first been acted upon by God. He is the resurrection and the life (John 11.25), not in and by himself but because he has received this from the Father.

What is true of his resurrection is also true of his exaltation. He does not exalt himself – that would be against his whole character – it is his Father who exalts him to his own right hand. His Father's act is of course grounded in what Jesus has done. As Paul puts it in the

passage we have already quoted, 'he . . . became obedient to death –
even death on a cross! *Therefore* . . .' (Phil. 2.8–9). Nevertheless his
exaltation remains the distinctive personal act of God the Father,
'*God* exalted him to the highest place and gave him the name that is
above every name' (Phil. 2.9). The authority in heaven and on earth
that has been given to him (Matt. 28.18) is to be exercised in a way
that glorifies and serves the purposes of the Father who gave it (Phil.
2.11). In the end indeed, also according to Paul, that kingly authority
has to be surrendered back to the Father who gave it, so that God
may be all in all (1 Cor. 15.24–8). The primary agency of the Father,
as the ultimate source and goal of the resurrection and exaltation of
the Son, emerges as an emphasis that is persistent in the writings of
Paul and that characterizes the way in which all the other New Testament writers understand what Easter means.

The same emphasis is equally apparent when we turn to the post-
Easter outpouring of the Holy Spirit. Acts 2.32–3 is highly important
in this connection. Peter is speaking: 'God has raised this Jesus to
life, and we are all witnesses of the fact. Exalted to the right hand of
God, he has received from the Father the promised Holy Spirit and
has poured out what you now see and hear.' Here we have the clear
beginnings of a fully trinitarian understanding of what happened at
Pentecost. The Holy Spirit did not come on his own, he was poured
out by Jesus after and as a result of his resurrection and his exaltation
to God's right hand. Yet even Jesus is not the ultimate origin of the
newly poured out Spirit. He gives him only because he has first
received him from the Father. Here again the primacy and priority of
the Father are very clearly asserted and we are given good biblical
support for our attempt to understand the Holy Spirit in a fully
trinitarian way. Here is one point at least where Luke – who often
holds resurrection, ascension and Pentecost apart – begins to integrate
them theologically, and it is highly significant that he does so in such
a trinitarian way.

When we come to John's teaching about the coming of the Spirit,
we see the same trinitarian insights being worked out in a more
explicit and indeed sophisticated manner. We cannot do that teaching
full justice here, but must content ourselves with pointing to a few
significant verses.

In John 14.16–17 Jesus says, 'I will ask the Father, and he will
give you another Counsellor to be with you for ever – the Spirit of
truth.' Here both Father and Son are involved in the giving of the

Spirit. The giver is the Father, but he gives in response to the prayer
of the Son. So also John 15.26 (a verse that was at the centre of much
controversy in medieval times between Eastern Orthodox theologians
on the one hand and Western Catholic theologians on the other),
'When the Counsellor comes, whom I will send to you from the
Father, the Spirit of truth who goes out [proceeds] from the Father,
he will testify about me.' Here it is Jesus who immediately is going to
send the Spirit upon his disciples, but it is from the Father that he
sends him, it is from the Father as his ultimate source and origin that
he proceeds. To summarize, for John as for Luke the sending of the
Spirit is an act that involves in different ways both the Father and the
Son; in other words it is a trinitarian act. It is the Father who gives
the Spirit, but he gives him in the closest connection with the person
and the completed work of the Son (cf. John 16.7–8; 20.22).

As we have already hinted, it was disagreement about the part of
the Father and the Son in sending the Spirit that was a chief cause
of the division between the Eastern Orthodox and Western Catholic
Churches that came to a head in 1054, a difference that is still
reflected in the different forms in which these two bodies of
Christians say the third article of the Nicene Creed down to the
present day. In the Orthodox East they say, 'We believe in the Holy
Spirit, the Lord and Giver of Life, who proceeds from the Father';
and in the Roman Catholic and Protestant West they say, 'We believe
in the Holy Spirit . . . who proceeds from the Father *and the Son*.'
And because the words 'and the Son' are in Latin *Filioque*, the disagreement is commonly referred to as 'the *Filioque* controversy'.

If we compare the two competing positions with the teaching of
John we have just outlined, we can see that, as is so often the case on
such occasions, there are strong and weak points on both sides.

The East has the New Testament behind it in insisting that
ultimately and primarily the Spirit comes from and is sent by the
Father. To say he comes from the Father 'and the Son' is to obscure
that fact. At the same time the Eastern failure to say anything at all in
the creed about the Son's part in the sending of the Spirit is to leave
out what for John is a vital factor in the whole matter.

The West, on the other hand, is in line with John's teaching in
holding that the Son has an essential part in the sending of the Spirit,
but the formula it uses does not make it clear that the Spirit the Son
gives us is the Spirit that he himself has first received from the
Father. It is through the Son – and in no other way – that the Spirit

reaches us, but the one from whom he comes through the Son is the Father.

It is sometimes suggested nowadays that the old controversy could be ended in a way that is faithful to the New Testament and that guards the important points that both sides were making, if we all confess, 'We believe in the Holy Spirit, the Lord and Giver of Life, who proceeds from the Father *through* the Son.'

In this whole section, however, what we have been emphasizing is that everything to do with the resurrection of Jesus and the sending of the Spirit has its origin in God the Father. It is he who raises Jesus from the dead to his own right hand, and it is he who through his exalted Son sends the Spirit to the Church at Pentecost.

Now mainline Christian theologians have down the centuries maintained that, through Jesus Christ and in the Holy Spirit, God shows himself to us as he really is. As you can see what a man is like in his inmost being by how he reveals himself in his outward actions, so by contemplating what God does among us in human history, you can see what he is like in his own life and being from eternity to eternity.

Applying that principle, we can say that in God's action in the resurrection of Jesus we are shown a Father who sends his Son and his Spirit to us, and a Son and a Spirit who come from that Father and in their distinctive ways do his will, serve his purpose and glorify his name here on earth. So, according to that principle, if God is like that in his actions towards us, he is also like that in himself. God *is* Father, Son and Holy Spirit and, within his own divine life, the Son and the Spirit are what they are not from themselves or in themselves, but from the Father. He does not come from them, but they come from him.

In the resurrection of Jesus we see the Father giving life, power and glory to the Son and breathing out the Holy Spirit. That is what he does in his own life; the Father is the giver of life to the Son and the breather out of the Holy Spirit. In the Holy Trinity the Spirit and Son in their different ways owe their life and their being to him alone. Within the life of God, the Father is the source and origin of his Son and of his Spirit.

Second, *as regards the Son: the integrated Easter event that proclaims the primacy of the Father equally clearly proclaims what we may call the derived deity of the Son.*

When the Father raises his Son from the dead to his own throne, he is telling us something not just about himself, but about that Son, namely that he belongs not just with us on the human side of reality, but with God himself on the divine side of reality. Jesus of Nazareth who is our brother is also the eternal Son of God. It was chiefly in the light of Easter, and what followed after, that he was so revealed and proclaimed.

The New Testament writers, each in their own way, make it clear that it is to himself that the Father exalts his Son, because it is with himself, on the divine side of reality, that the Son eternally belongs. The name that the exalted Jesus is given is (again according to Paul in Philippians 2) the name that is above every name, the name *Kurios*, 'Lord', which is God's own name. The divine honours that according to Isaiah 45.23 are to be paid to the Lord Yahweh alone are now to be paid to the exalted Jesus. At his name every knee shall bow and every tongue confess that he is *Kurios*. Moreover, this confession of the divine lordship of Jesus, far from detracting from or being in competition with the glory of the Father, is actually the appointed way to glorify him.

Furthermore, the exaltation of Christ at his ascension is in this very passage seen to have astounding implications for the understanding of the being of God himself. The Philippians hymn makes it clear that the place and the name to which Jesus ascended are the place and the name that have from eternity belonged to him, that have always been his within the life of God himself. The historical exaltation of the Son is, in exact accordance with the principle that we were expounding at the end of the last section, read back into the being of God himself. Jesus is confessed as *Kurios* because that is what he is. The one to whom every knee bows and whom every tongue confesses (Phil. 2.10–11) is the one who is 'in very nature God' (Phil. 2.6). Or, to speak the language of Ephesians, 'What does "he ascended" mean except that he also descended to the lower, earthly regions?' (Eph. 4.9). His exaltation to God is seen to imply that his work and his person have their eternal origination within God's own life.

We can see the same process taking place within the other strands of New Testament Christology. In Hebrews the exalted high priest 'who sat down at the right hand of the throne of the Majesty in heaven' (Heb. 8.1) is also the eternal Son 'through whom [God] made the universe', who is 'the radiance of God's glory, and the exact representation of his being, sustaining all things by his powerful word'

(Heb. 1.2–3). The exalted Christ is again presented as one who shares the deity of the Father, but it is all the time taken for granted that his is a deity that is derived from and dependent upon that of the Father.

It is, however, in Johannine Christology that the connection between the resurrection and exaltation of Jesus and his eternal relationship to the Father is most clearly asserted. At the end of the gospel, as soon as Thomas is convinced about the resurrection, he confesses in the most unambiguous terms the deity of the risen Christ, 'My Lord [*kurios*] and my God [*theos*]!' (John 20.28). If Jesus is Lord and God in his resurrection and exaltation, that means for John that he is also, within the life of God himself, the eternal Son who is 'in the bosom of the Father' (John 1.18, RSV) and the Word (*Logos*) who is eternally with God and is himself God (John 1.1) and his partner in all his works (John 1.3). All this, however, is said on the clear assumption that it does not threaten the primacy of the Father. The Son is Son because on the one hand he is all that the Father is, he is of the very stuff of the Father's deity, but on the other hand all he is and all he has he owes not to himself but to the Father (John 5.19).

In these different ways the New Testament authors register their conviction that the exalted Christ reveals himself, in what he is and what he does, to be of the very being of God, and it is that distinctively Christian post-resurrection insight that generates a drastic revision in their whole understanding of God, which results ultimately in the developed trinitarian doctrine of the later creeds, but is present already within the New Testament itself at different stages of development.

There is of course no going back on the fundamental Old Testament faith that God is one, but that oneness is now seen in a different way. God is one not so much in the way that a solitary individual is one, but much more like the way in which a human family is one or a husband and wife are one flesh. It is a oneness that contains within itself the sort of relationship that Jesus had with his Father on earth, that he continues to have with his Father in his exaltation to heaven, and that he has always with his Father from eternity to eternity. Within the life of God there is one who is called Father and another who is called Son, two centres of personal being and action who relate to each other in mutual love and self-giving, as we see in the human life and death of Jesus. The Father is called Father because the Son derives all that he is from him, but the Son shares totally the divine nature of the Father: he is not a creature, but (as the creed puts it in an attempt to say the unsayable) 'eternally begotten of the Father, God from God, Light from Light, true God from true God, begotten not made, of one Being with the Father'.

That is the attempt of the creed to define what we have called the derived divinity of Christ, which says on the one hand that he is of the same being and nature as the Father, but nevertheless has that being and nature not in and from himself but from his Father. The risen Son of God shows himself to be not only our brother, but God's eternal Son, who is to us and does for us what only God can do. Yet at the same time he is to be differentiated from God the Father, as the one who is sent is to be differentiated from the one who sends him, the one who obeys from the one whom he obeys, the one who is raised from the one who raises him.

The doctrine of the Trinity depends upon our believing in the divinity of the risen and ascended Lord. That is why it has always been misunderstood and attacked by Jews and Muslims who could see in Jesus nothing other than a human prophet and teacher, someone not in any essential way different from those who went before him and those who came after him. There are also in our day liberal and radical Christians who dispute the New Testament estimate of Jesus and seek to understand him as a man in whom the Spirit of God resided as he does in all of us – only to a far greater degree – rather than as one who, as well as being wholly man and our brother, is also wholly God as God's Son.

On that modern radical view of Jesus there is of course no need for a trinitarian doctrine of God. Jesus so understood is man and not God. Whether we need a trinitarian doctrine of God or not depends on whether with Thomas and the vast multitude of Christians down the centuries and across the continents we will confess Jesus as Lord and God. It is impossible to go into the matter further here, except to register my own firm conviction that the confession of Jesus as divine Son made man is essential to the New Testament gospel, which soon falls apart without it. Only if he is God can he make an absolute claim on my obedience and worship. Only if he is God can he be the source of forgiveness, new life and salvation to those who believe in him. But if he is indeed God, then it takes something very like a trinitarian doctrine of God to express his relationship to his Father. In the end we all have to answer for ourselves his question, 'Who do you say I am?' (Matt. 16.15). The authentic Christian answer, which the Church has always given and goes on giving today, is: 'You are the

Christ, the Son of the living God' (Matt. 16.16). It is that answer, when it is worked out fully, that requires a trinitarian understanding of God.

So far we have spoken as if it was enough to talk of God the Father and God the Son – the Father who has divine life in and from himself, and the Son who has the same divine life in himself but has it from his Father. This is indeed the God who is at work and who reveals himself in the exaltation of Jesus. If we stopped there, however, we should speak only of a God who is two in one, in a *bi*nitarian rather than a fully *tri*nitarian way. We need now to remind ourselves that included in what we have called the integrated Easter event is what happened at Pentecost when, as a direct result of the resurrection and exaltation of Jesus, the Holy Spirit was poured out on the apostolic company. We need to ask ourselves now what we can learn from that about the relationship of the Spirit to the Father and the Son within the trinitarian life of God.

Our third and final thesis is therefore: *the integrated Easter event that reveals the primacy of the Father and the derived deity of the Son, also reveals the mutual interdependence of the Son and the Holy Spirit.*

The New Testament never delineates the distinct personhood of the Holy Spirit as clearly as it does that of the Father and the Son, but it says enough to indicate that in the great events of the life, death and resurrection of Jesus there is at work a third personal agent (usually identified as the Holy Spirit) who, as at the baptism of Jesus, comes from the Father to the Son to empower him for his work, and who at Pentecost and after comes to the Church to enable us to know and confess the Father and the Son and to participate in their life, love and power. The Spirit does his work in a way that draws attention not to himself but rather to the Father and to Jesus, and that is why he is the most difficult of the three to identify.

It is not possible here to deal with the rich New Testament teaching about the Spirit, so we must confine ourselves to his activity in connection with the resurrection of Jesus. Here we can see a twofold relationship. On the one hand it is through the activity of the Spirit that Jesus is raised, and on the other hand it is through the risen Jesus that the Spirit is sent to the Church at Pentecost.

To take the latter point first, the dependence of the coming of the Holy Spirit upon the resurrection and exaltation of Jesus is emphasized in many parts of the New Testament. We have only to recall Acts 2.33, '[Jesus] . . . has poured out what you now see and hear', and John 16.7, 'Unless I go away, the Counsellor will not come to you; but if I go, I will send him to you.' For Paul also the dependence of the work of the Spirit upon the work of Christ is so close that at some points (although not by any means always) he seems to identify the one with the other. According to 2 Corinthians 3.18, one of the central Pauline statements on this subject, the busi- ness of the Spirit is to transform Christians into the likeness of Christ, so that their lives as well as their lips proclaim that he is Lord (cf. 1 Cor. 12.3). In other words the Holy Spirit does nothing of his own that is apart from or beyond what Christ has done. He simply takes what is in Christ and so works in us that it becomes ours also. That is what is said explicitly in John 16.14–15: 'He will bring glory to me by taking from what is mine and making it known to you. All that belongs to the Father is mine. That is why I said the Spirit will take from what is mine and make it known to you.'

There is thus a dependence of the work of the Spirit upon the work of Jesus. In accordance with the principle that we enunciated earlier (that the way God acts among us reveals what he is eternally in himself), trinitarian theology, especially in the West, has therefore concluded that the Spirit comes eternally from the Son as well as from the Father. That is why the Western form of the Nicene Creed affirms that the Holy Spirit 'proceeds from the Father *and the Son* [*Filioque*]'.

We have already seen that this Western formula is open to criticism because it obscures the primacy of the Father over the Son in the sending of the Spirit. But even if we amend it to read '. . . who proceeds from the Father *through the Son*', it is still not entirely acceptable, because it suggests that there is a one-way dependence of the Spirit and his work upon the Son and his work. This is to leave out an important strand of New Testament evidence about the activity of the Spirit, as we shall now see.

The New Testament provides considerable support for the trinitarian statement that the Father raises the Son from the dead through the activity of the Holy Spirit (cf. Rom. 1.4; 1 Cor. 6.14; 1 Tim. 3.16; 1 Pet. 3.18). If that is so, then it is the Son who is dependent upon the Spirit in his reception of resurrection life from the Father, just as he was dependent upon the Spirit for his human birth from Mary (Luke 1.35) and for his endowment with messianic power in his baptism. For the New Testament writers the Father incarnates, empowers and raises up his Son through his Spirit. In the story of Jesus it is not just that the Spirit comes through the Son, but equally that the Son comes through the Spirit.

Thus the relationship between Son and Spirit that is brought to light at the resurrection of Jesus is not a one-way dependence of the latter upon the former, as Western trinitarian thought has often suggested, but rather a mutual interdependence of the one upon the other, the Son upon the Spirit and the Spirit upon the Son. The two-sided mutuality of that relationship is classically expressed in the words of John the Baptist in John 1.33: 'The man on whom you see the Spirit come down and remain is he who will baptise with the Holy Spirit.' At his baptism Jesus receives the Spirit and all that he brings from the Father for his own work; at Pentecost he sends that same Spirit from the Father to empower us in our work for him.

We may therefore conclude that, if the relationships between Son and Spirit in the eternal life of God are as they are revealed in the life and especially in the resurrection of Jesus, we need to speak of a mutual interdependence of the one upon the other and of the dependence of both of them upon the Father from whom they come and whose being and nature they share. The second-century theologian Irenaeus of Lyons put it well when he said that the Son and the Spirit are the two hands of God. As such they work in the closest coordination with each other and neither has priority over the other.

If we were therefore to amend the creed to reflect this relationship, we would need to say about the Spirit that 'he proceeds from the Father *through the Son*'; but we would also need to say about the Son that he is 'eternally begotten of the Father *through the Spirit*'. In that way what we say about the relationships of Father, Son and Spirit in God would more faithfully reflect what the New Testament obliges us to say about the relationships revealed in the life and in the resurrection of Jesus.

The primacy of the Father, the derived deity of the Son, the mutuality of Son and Spirit, these are the consistent patterns of trinitarian relationships that characterize the interactions of the three divine persons as portrayed in the Easter gospel. These three are one because they share the same being and nature, the same will and purpose in all that they do: they so give themselves, the one to the other, that they mysteriously interpenetrate and indwell one another in all that they do and are. This is what we mean when we speak of Father, Son and Holy Spirit, three persons and one God.

If we do our thinking about God within the presuppositions of modernity, we shall have little time for such trinitarian mysteries; but if, as Christians have always done, we defy the presuppositions of the thinking of our day and look to Jesus Christ – incarnate, crucified and risen – to learn what God does and who he is, then, as we have tried to show, we shall be led to the same insights as the first Christians and see that the God who raised Jesus from the dead has to be confessed in his triune glory as Father, Son and Holy Spirit, to whom indeed be glory for ever.

2
RESURRECTION AND INCARNATION: THE FOUNDATIONS OF THE CHRISTIAN FAITH

Alister E. McGrath

> The doctrine of Christ's divinity seems to me not something stuck on which you can unstick but something that peeps out at every point so that you'd have to unravel the whole web to get rid of it. (C. S. Lewis, letter to Arthur Greaves, 11 December 1944; Hooper 1979, 503)

For C. S. Lewis, the coherence of Christianity was such that it was impossible to eliminate the idea of the divinity of Christ without doing such damage to the web of Christian doctrine that the entire structure of the Christian faith would collapse. Far from being an optional extra, something which had accidentally been added and which now required removal, it was an essential and integral part of the authentically Christian understanding of reality. Modernism, however, has laid down two fundamental challenges to this view.

First, that it is *wrong*. Our growing understanding of the background to the New Testament, the way in which Christian doctrine has developed, the rise of the scientific world-view, and so on, force us to abandon the idea that Jesus was God in any meaningful sense of the word.

Second, it is *unnecessary*. Christianity can exist without the need for such obsolete and cumbersome ideas as God becoming man, traditionally grounded in the resurrection of Jesus Christ and expressed in the doctrine of the incarnation. In a world come of age, Christianity must learn to abandon these ideas as archaic and irrelevant if it is to survive.

In the present essay we wish to suggest that the only way in which Christianity is likely to survive in the future is by reclaiming its incarnational heritage as the only proper and legitimate interpretation of the significance of the history of Jesus of Nazareth.

It will be obvious that it is impossible in this brief essay to do justice either to the objections raised against the traditional understandings of the resurrection and the incarnation, or to recent responses to these objections. The present essay is concerned to indicate briefly the *ineffectiveness* of recent criticism of these doctrines, and the *inadequacy* of the proposed alternative explanations of the identity and significance of Jesus Christ. We begin by considering the objections raised against the resurrection and the incarnation.

OBJECTIONS TO THE RESURRECTION AND THE INCARNATION

THREE CRITICISMS OF THE RESURRECTION

The New Testament is permeated by references to the resurrection of Jesus of Nazareth. The consequences of this event for both the personal experience of the first Christians and their understanding of the identity and significance of Jesus himself dominate the horizons of the New Testament writers.

It was on the basis of the belief that the one who was crucified had been raised by God from the dead that the astonishing developments in the perceived status and identity of Jesus took place. The cross was interpreted from the standpoint of the resurrection, and Jesus' teaching was accorded reverence on account of who the resurrection disclosed him to be. Jesus was worshipped and adored as the living Lord, who would come again – not merely revered as a dead rabbi.

The tendency to 'think of Jesus Christ as of God' (2 Clement 1.1) is already evident within the New Testament. It cannot be emphasized too strongly that the most important developments in the Christian understanding of the identity and significance of Jesus Christ took place not during the patristic period, but within twenty years of the crucifixion itself.

1. *The first Christians were mistaken*
Of course, the modern critics of the resurrection point out, it was easy for the first Christians to believe in the resurrection of Jesus. After all, belief in resurrections was a commonplace at the time. The first Christians may have jumped to the conclusion that Jesus was raised from the dead, when in fact something rather different actually happened.

Although the crude charges of yesteryear (e.g., that the disciples stole the corpse of Jesus from its tomb, or that they were the victims of mass hysteria) are still occasionally encountered, they have generally been superseded by more subtle theories. Thus, to note the most important, the resurrection was really a *symbolic* event which the first Christians confused with a *historical* event on account of their uncritical presuppositions.

In response to this, however, it may be pointed out that in Jesus' day neither of the two contemporary beliefs about resurrection bore any resemblance to the resurrection of Jesus. The Sadducees denied the idea of a resurrection altogether (a fact which Paul was able to exploit at an awkward moment, Acts 23.6–8), while the majority expectation was of a general resurrection on the last day, at the end of history itself.

The sheer *oddness* of the Christian proclamation of the resurrection of Jesus in human history, at a definite time and place, is all too easily overlooked by modern critics, even though it was obvious at the time. The unthinkable appeared to have happened, and for that very reason demanded careful attention. Far from merely fitting into the popular expectation of the pattern of resurrection, what happened to Jesus actually contradicted it. The sheer novelty of the Christian position at the time has been obscured by two thousand years' experience of the Christian understanding of the resurrection – yet *at the time* it was wildly unorthodox and radical.

To dismiss the Christian understanding of the resurrection of Jesus because it allegedly conformed to contemporary expectations is clearly unacceptable. The suggestion that the resurrection of Jesus may be explicable as some sort of wish-fulfilment on the part of the disciples also strains the imagination somewhat. Why should the disciples have responded to the catastrophe of Jesus' death by making the hitherto unprecedented suggestion that he had been raised from the dead? The history of Israel is littered with the corpses of pious Jewish martyrs, none of whom were ever thought of as having been raised from the dead in such a manner.

2. *The New Testament writers used pagan and gnostic myths*
The second attack on the historicity of the resurrection of Jesus mounted in recent years is based upon the parallels between pagan myths of dying and rising gods and the resurrection of Jesus.

In the first part of the present century a substantial number of scholarly works appeared which drew attention to these pagan and gnostic myths. (Perhaps J. G. Frazer's *Adonis, Attis, Osiris* (1907) is the most famous of these in the English-speaking world.) And so it was argued that the New Testament writers were simply reproducing this myth, which was part of the intellectual furniture of the ancient world. Rudolf Bultmann was among many scholars who subsequently argued for such influence (deriving from the Mandaeans) upon the resurrection accounts and beliefs of the New Testament, and then proceeded to take the logically questionable step of arguing that such parallels discredited the historicity of the resurrection of Jesus.

Since then, however, scholarship has moved on considerably. The parallels between the pagan myths of dying and rising gods and the New Testament accounts of the resurrection of Jesus are now regarded as remote, to say the least. For instance, the New Testament documents with some care indicate the place and the date of both the death and the resurrection of Jesus, as well as identifying the witnesses to both. The contrast with the ahistorical narrative form of mythology is striking. Furthermore, there are no known instances of this myth being applied to any *specific historical figure* in pagan literature, so that the New Testament writers, had they utilized it, would have given a stunningly original twist to this mythology. (It is at this point that the wisdom of C. S. Lewis – who actually knew something about myths – must be acknowledged. Lewis intuitively realized that the New Testament accounts of the resurrection of Jesus bore no relation to 'real' mythology, despite the protests of some theologians who had dabbled in the field.) Perhaps most important, however, was the realization that the gnostic redeemer myths – which the New Testament writers allegedly took over and applied to Jesus – were to be dated later than the New Testament itself. The gnostics, it seems actually took over Christian ideas.

The challenge posed to the historicity of the resurrection by these theories has thus passed into textbooks of the history of ideas. But an important point must be made before we proceed any further. We have seen how allegedly responsible academic scholarship, regarded as competent in its own day, was seen to pose a serious challenge to a central aspect of the Christian faith. It was taken seriously by theologians and popular religious writers. Yet the sheer *provisionality* of scholarship seemed to have been ignored. Scholarship proceeds by evaluation of evidence and hypotheses, a process which takes decades, in which what one generation took as self-evident is often demonstrated to be in error. The fate of the resurrection myth is a case in point: in 1920 it was treated virtually as an established fact of serious and responsible scholarship; in 1993 it is regarded as an interesting, if now discredited, idea.

How many more such theories, which now seem to be persuasive and to pose a challenge to the Christian faith, will be treated as discredited and obsolete in fifty years time? For example, in *The Myth of God Incarnate* Michael Goulder (Hick 1977, 64–86) seriously expected Christians to abandon faith in the incarnation there and then on account of his ingenious, if improbable, theory about its historical origins! Christianity can hardly be expected to abandon its proclamation of the risen Christ as Saviour and Lord on such flimsy grounds – it has a duty to speak for two thousand years of history, as well as for an untold period in the future, in refusing to allow the short-term preoccupations of modernity to dictate its character for posterity.

3. There is no historical analogue to Jesus' resurrection
A third line of criticism of the historicity of the resurrection is due to the German sociologist Ernst Troeltsch (1972), who argued that, since dead men don't rise, so Jesus couldn't have risen.

The basic principle underlying this objection goes back to David Hume, and concerns the need for present-day analogues for historical events. Troeltsch asserted that since we have no contemporary experience of the resurrection of a dead human being we therefore have reason for supposing that no dead man has ever been raised. But of course, as Christianity has insisted that the resurrection of Jesus was a unique historical event, the absence of present-day analogues is only to be expected.

The most vigorous response to Troeltsch's criticism has been made by Wolfhart Pannenberg (1968), who points out that Troeltsch adopted a remarkably dogmatic view of reality, based upon his questionable metaphysical presuppositions, effectively dictating what could and could not have happened in history on the basis of his preconceived views. For Pannenberg the decisive factor in determining what happened on the first Easter Day is the evidence contained in the New Testament, and not dogmatic and provisional scholarly theories about the nature of reality. How, asks Pannenberg, are we to account for the New Testament evidence? What is its most probable explanation? The historical evidence liberates us from the kind of dogmatic metaphysical presuppositions about what can and what cannot have happened in history that underlie Troeltsch's critique of the resurrection, and allows us to return to the Jesus of history. And for Pannenberg the resurrection of Jesus is the most probable and plausible explanation of the historical evidence (McGrath 1986, 83–5, 161–76). Perhaps it lacks the absolute certainty which the more fundamentalist of metaphysicians seem to demand – but, as Bishop Butler so carefully demonstrated in his *Analogy of Religion* (1736), probability is the law of religious life, whether orthodox or deist (Ferreira 1986).

CRITICISMS OF THE INCARNATION

The doctrine of the incarnation has also come under sustained criticism recently. Many such criticisms of the incarnation, for example those expressed in *The Myth of God Incarnate*, demonstrate a regrettable tendency to concentrate upon objections to the *idea* of incarnation, rather than the *basis* of the idea itself. After all, the idea of God incarnate in a specific historical human being was quite startling within its first-century Jewish context, and a virtual impossibility within the Greek ontological framework underlying the patristic period, so that the question of what caused this belief to arise requires careful examination. Of central importance to this question is the resurrection itself, a subject studiously ignored (along with the major contributions to the incarnational discussion by Pannenberg (1968), Moltmann (1974), Rahner (1961–81), Kasper (1976) and others; cf. McGrath 1986, 161–203) by most of the contributors to *The Myth of God Incarnate*. The idea of incarnation is easy to criticize: it is paradoxical, enigmatic, and so on. But everyone already knows this, including the most fervent advocates of the idea! The question remains, as it always has been, is the incarnation a proper and legitimate interpretation of the history of Jesus of Nazareth?

The fact that something is paradoxical and even apparently self-contradictory does not invalidate it, despite what many critics of the incarnation seem to think. Those working in the scientific field are only too aware of the sheer complexity and mysteriousness of reality. The events lying behind the rise of quantum theory, the difficulties of using models in scientific explanation – to name but two factors which I can remember particularly clearly from my own period as a natural scientist – point to the inevitability of paradox and contradiction in any except the most superficial engagement with reality. Our apprehension of reality is partial and fragmentary, whether we are dealing with our knowledge of the natural world or of God. The Enlightenment world-view tended to suppose that reality could be totally apprehended in rational terms, an assumption which still persists in some theological circles, even where it has been abandoned as unrealistic elsewhere. All too many modern theologians cry 'Contradiction!', and expect us all to abandon whatever it is that is supposed to be contradictory there and then. But reality just isn't like that.

Logical contradiction may pose a less than decisive challenge to the principle of the incarnation, but it may immediately invalidate an incoherent argument. An example of such an argument apparently invalidated by logical inconsistency is that developed by one of the contributors to The Myth of God Incarnate, Frances Young, who argues (Hick 1977, 13–47) that the patristic development of the doctrine of the incarnation inevitably led to the 'blind alleys of paradox' and 'illogicality'. Having thus dismissed this doctrine for such reasons, she affirms that 'religion is destroyed without mystery – without paradox', as she develops her thesis that we must learn to live with unresolved contradictions. It would seem that paradoxes, illogicality and unresolved contradictions invalidate the patristic idea of the incarnation, but not the modern ideas which allegedly replace it! In fairness, of course, it may be noted that Professor Young's more recent writings are much more sympathetic to the idea of incarnation.

A more serious charge against the principle of the incarnation is developed by John Hick, who asserts ('argues' is not the mot juste) that the idea of Jesus being both God and man is logically contradictory (Hick 1977, 167–85). Quoting Spinoza, Hick asserts that to talk of one who is both God and man is like talking about a square circle. Hick's sensitivity at this point is difficult to follow, since he is already committed to the belief that all the concepts of God to be found in the world religions – personal and impersonal, immanent and transcendent – are compatible with each other. Indeed, such is the variety of the concepts of divinity currently in circulation in the world religions that Hick seems to be obliged to turn a blind eye to the resulting logical inconsistency between them – only to seize upon and censure this alleged 'inconsistency' in the case of the incarnation.

But Hick cannot be allowed to make this robust assertion concerning the logical incompatibility of God and man unchallenged, and his less than adequate knowledge of the development of Christology in the medieval period is clearly demonstrated in this matter. The fact that there is no logical incompatibility between God and man in the incarnation is demonstrated, and then theologically exploited, by that most brilliant of all English theologians, William of Ockham (McGrath 1984). Ockham's discussion of this point is exhaustive and highly influential, and has yet to be discredited.

More seriously, Hick seems to work on the basis of the assumption that we know *exactly* what God is like, and on the basis of this knowledge are in a position to pass judgement on the logical niceties of the incarnation. But this is obviously not the case! Hick may be saying that there is a logical problem involved with classical theism (a *philosophical* system) in relation to the incarnation – but this is merely to suggest that classical theism is not necessarily compatible with Christianity, a point which has been made with increasing force by theologians such as Jürgen Moltmann (1974) and Eberhard Jüngel (1983) in recent years. It is not to discredit the incarnation!

Hick may be in a position to say that God is totally unable to come among us as a human being, and that the incarnation is impossible on account of who and what God is – but if he can do so, he would seem to have access to a private and infallible knowledge of God denied to the rest of us! And do we really fully understand what is meant by that deceptively familiar word 'man'? Do we really have a total and exhaustive grasp of what it is to be human? Many of us would prefer to say that the incarnation discloses the true nature of divinity and humanity, rather than approaching the incarnation on the basis of preconceived ideas of divinity and humanity.

HISTORICAL AND CULTURAL RELATIVISM

In the present section of the essay we have sketched briefly some of the objections raised recently against the resurrection and incarnation of Jesus Christ, and indicated briefly the way in which they have been met. It has not been possible to do justice to either these objections or the responses to them, and all that we have had the opportunity to do is to note how resurrection and incarnation alike are 'bloodied but unbowed' through recent criticisms. But one final point may be made before moving on. All too often we are given the impression that something dramatic has happened recently which suddenly forces everyone of any intellectual respectability to abandon faith in these matters. We are told that in a world 'come of age' ideas such as resurrection and incarnation are to be discarded as pre-modern, perhaps as vestiges of a cultic idol. We are children of the modern period and must accept our lot, bequeathed by the Enlightenment, and make the most of it. But is this really the case?

If our thinking at any one time – such as the modern period – is so heavily conditioned and determined by the prevailing cultural and historical conditions, as the contributors to *The Myth of God Incarnate* in particular suggest, we must recognize that we are confronted with a near-total relativism of values and thought which discredits the New Testament on account of its first-century Palestinian context, and also discredits modern interpretations of the New Testament (including criticism of the ideas of resurrection and incarnation) on account of their twentieth-century Western context. Each and every historical idea is conditioned by its historical context, and cannot necessarily be regarded as valid outside that context. All possess relative, not absolute, validity. Logical consistency demands that criticism of the doctrines of resurrection and incarnation be acknowledged to be as historically conditioned as those doctrines themselves, and of no permanent or universal value. This scepticism has the virtue of consistency, but is unlikely to commend itself to most critics of the resurrection and incarnation, who appear to envisage their criticisms as establishing a new, more relevant and universal version of Christianity.

But what might this new version of Christianity be like? The inclusion of the word 'new' is deliberate and weighed: historically, Christianity has regarded both the resurrection and the incarnation as essential to its historical self-understanding, and any attempt to eliminate or radically modify them would seem to lead to a version of Christianity which is not continuous with the historical forms it has taken in the course of its development. In the following section, we shall look at the result of the elimination or radical modification of these two traditional ideas.

A CRITICAL ASSESSMENT OF 'NEW' CHRISTIANITY

Modernism asserts: (a) that Jesus was not God in any meaningful sense of the term; (b) that he was a man, like us in every way, but far superior religiously and morally; and (c) that everything which Christianity has wanted to say about the significance of Jesus can be said, and said well, without the belief that he was God as well as man. Let us see if this can actually be done.

On the basis of a number of important works reflecting the spirit of Enlightenment modernism, it is clear that a central idea congenial to the modern spirit is that Jesus reveals to us the love of God. It is frequently pointed out that the modern age is able to dispense with superstitious ideas about the death of Jesus (e.g., that it represented a victory over Satan or the payment of a legal penalty of some sort), and instead get to the real meat of both the New Testament (so movingly expressed in the parable of the prodigal son) and modern Christianity – the love of God for humanity. In what follows, I propose to suggest that abandoning the ideas of resurrection and the incarnation means abandoning even this tender insight.

This may seem an outrageous suggestion to make, but I cannot see how this conclusion can be avoided. How may the death of Jesus Christ upon a cross at Calvary be interpreted as a demonstration of the love of God for humanity? Remember, the idea that Jesus *is* God cannot be permitted, given the presuppositions of modernism. Once modernism dispenses with the idea of incarnation, a number of possible alternative explanations of the cross remain open.

1. It represents the devastating and unexpected end to the career of Jesus, forcing his disciples to invent the idea of the resurrection to cover up the totality of this catastrophe.

2. It represents God's judgement upon the career of Jesus, demonstrating that he was cursed by the law of Moses, and thus disqualified from any putative messianic status.

3. It represents the inevitable fate of anyone who attempts to lead a life of obedience to God.

4. It represents the greatest love which one human being can show for another (cf. John 15.13), inspiring Jesus' followers to demonstrate an equal love for others.

5. It demonstrates that God is a sadistic tyrant.

6. It is meaningless.

All of these are plausible, within the framework of modernism. The idea that the cross demonstrates the love of God for man cannot, however, be included among this list. It is not *God* who is dying upon the cross, who gives himself for his people. It is a man – an especially splendid man – who may be ranked with others in history who have made equally great sacrifices for those whom they loved. But the death of an innocent person at the hands of corrupt judges is all too common, even today, and Jesus cannot be singled out for special discussion unless he *is* something or someone qualitatively different from us.

A critic might, of course, immediately reply that Jesus is a higher example of the kind of inspiration or illumination to be found in all human beings, so that he must be regarded as the outstanding human being – and for that reason his death assumes universal significance. But this is a remarkably dogmatic assumption – that Jesus is unique among human beings in this respect! The uniqueness of Jesus was established by the New Testament writers through the resurrection (an assumption which modernism cannot allow), and the subsequent recognition that Jesus was none other than the living God dwelling among us. But this insight is given and guaranteed by two doctrines which modernism cannot allow. It would seem that modernists are prepared to retain insights gained through the traditional framework of resurrection and incarnation – and then declare that this framework may be dispensed with. It is as if the traditional framework is treated as some sort of learning aid which may be dispensed with once the ideas in question are mastered.

But this is clearly questionable, to say the least. If the traditional framework is declared to be wrong, the consequences of this declaration for each and every aspect of Christian theology must be ascertained. Discard or radically modify the doctrines of resurrection and incarnation, and the idea of the 'uniqueness' or the 'superiority' of Jesus becomes a dogmatic assertion without foundation, an assertion which many of more humanist inclinations would find offensive. We would be equally justified in appealing to other historical figures such as Socrates or Gandhi – as encapsulating the desiderata of Christian moral behaviour.

This point becomes more important when we return to the question of how the death of Jesus can be interpreted as a self-giving divine act that demonstrates the love of God for humanity. It is not God who is upon the cross: it is a human being. That point must be conceded by those who reject the incarnation. It may then be the case that God makes his love known indirectly (and, it must be said, in a remarkably ambiguous manner) through the death of Jesus Christ, but we have lost for ever the insight that it is God himself who shows his love for us on the cross.

What the cross might conceivably demonstrate, among a number of other, more probable, possibilities, is the full extent of the love of one human being for others. And as the love of human beings can be thought of as mirroring the love of God, it would therefore be taken as an indirect demonstration of what the love of God is like, in much

the same way that countless other individuals have given up their lives
to save their friends or families throughout history. But who did Jesus
die to save? None, save possibly Barabbas, can be said to have benefited directly from his death.

Furthermore, it would seem that modernism would like us to
understand Jesus' death as making some sort of religious point which
will enrich our spiritual lives. But this is not how the New Testament
writers understood his death (not least because they insisted upon
interpreting that death in the light of the resurrection, a procedure
regarded as illegitimate by modernists), and it is certainly difficult to
see how it would have cut much ice in the hostile environment in
which Christianity had to survive and expand in the first period of its
existence.

Had Jesus died in Western Europe in the modern period, such an
interpretation of his death might have had a certain degree of
plausibility – but the historical significance of Jesus' death was
determined by its historical context, and we are committing historical
errors which parallel those of the ill-fated nineteenth-century 'quest
of the historical Jesus' if we project modern cultural preoccupations
on to the event of the death of Christ. The interpretation which
modernism wishes to place upon the death of Christ is culturally
conditioned by the social and personal values of Western society, and
is imposed upon (rather than discerned within) the history of Jesus.

The traditional framework for discussion of the manifestation of
the love of God in the death of Christ is that of God humbling himself
and coming among us as one of us, taking upon himself the frailty
and mortality of our human nature in order to redeem it. To deny that
the lonely dying figure upon the cross is God is to lose this point of
contact, and to return to the view which Christianity overturned in its
own day and age – that 'God is with us only in his transcendence'
(Don Cupitt).

On the modernist view, a divine representative – not God himself
– engages with the pain and suffering of this world. It is his love,
not God's, which is shown. And to those who might think that this
difficulty may be eliminated by developing the idea of God allowing
himself to be identified with the dying Christ, it may be pointed out
that the exploration of this idea by Moltmann and Jüngel leads not
merely to an incarnational but to a *trinitarian* theology. In order to do
justice to the Christian experience of God through Jesus Christ, a
higher profile of identification between Jesus and God than function

is required – we are dealing with an identity of being, rather than just an identification of function: Jesus acts as and for God precisely because he *is* God.

A similar point may be made in relation to suffering. Twentieth-century apologetics has recognized that any theology which is unable to implicate God in some manner in the sufferings and pain of the world condemns itself as inadequate and deficient. The twentieth century witnessed previously unimagined horrors of human suffering in the trenches of the First World War, in the extermination camps of Nazi Germany, and in the programmes of genocide established by Nazi Germany and Marxist Cambodia. The rise of 'protest atheism' – perhaps one of the most powerful sentiments to which modern theology must address itself – reflects human moral revulsion at these acts. Protest atheism has a tendency to select soft targets, and there are few targets softer in this respect than a non-incarnational theology.

An incarnational theology speaks of God subjecting himself in the grim scene at Calvary to the evil and pain of the world at its worst, bearing the brunt of that agony itself. God suffered in Christ, taking upon himself the suffering and pain of the world which he created. A non-incarnational theology is forced, perhaps against its intuitive desires, to speak of a God who may send his condolences through a representative, but who does not (or cannot, for fear of being accused of logical contradiction?) enter into and share his people's suffering at first hand.

And for a modernist, highly critical of substitutionary theories of the atonement, God can hardly be allowed to take responsibility for the suffering of the world vicariously, through a human representative who suffers instead of and on behalf of God. In 1963, the English *Sunday Observer* publicized John Robinson's book *Honest to God* with the headline 'Our image of God must go'. The image that Robinson had in mind was that of an old man in the sky. But the 'image of God that must go' in the face of the intense and deadly serious moral criticisms of protest atheism is that of a God who does not experience human suffering and pain at first hand – in short, a non-incarnational image of God. Many of those who criticize the incarnation seem to realize the force of this point, and attempt to retain it, despite their intellectual misgivings. Perhaps in the end it will not be the protests of orthodoxy which destroy non-incarnational theologies, but protest atheism, which wisely and rightly detects the fundamental weakness of such a theology in precisely this respect.

A final point which may be made concerns the permanent significance of Jesus Christ. Why is he of such importance to the Christian faith here and now, some twenty centuries after his death? The traditional answer is that Jesus' significance lay in his being God incarnate; that in his specific historical existence God assumed human nature. All else is secondary to this central insight, deriving from reflection upon the significance of his resurrection. The fact that Jesus was male; the fact that he was a Jew; the precise nature of his teaching – all these are secondary to the fact that God took upon himself human nature, thereby lending it new dignity and meaning.

But if Jesus is not God incarnate, his significance must be evaluated in terms of those parameters which traditional Christianity has treated as secondary. Immediately, we are confronted with the problem of historical conditioning: what conceivable relevance may the teachings and lifestyle of a first-century male Jew have for us today, in a totally different cultural situation? The maleness of Christ has caused offence in radical feminist circles: why should women be forced to relate to a male religious teacher, whose teaching may be compromised by his very masculinity as much as by the patriarchal values of his cultural situation? And why should modern Western humanity pay any attention to the culturally-conditioned teaching of such an individual, given the seemingly insuperable cultural chasm dividing first-century Palestine and the twentieth-century West?

For reasons such as these a non-incarnational Christianity is unable convincingly to anchor the person of Jesus Christ as the centre of the Christian faith. He may be the historical point of departure for that faith, but its subsequent development involves the leaving behind of the historical particularity of his existence in order to confront the expectations of each social milieu in which Christianity may subsequently find itself. Jesus says *this* – but we say *that*. *This* may be acceptable in a first-century Palestinian context – but *that* is acceptable in a modern Western culture, in which we live and move and have our being. Jesus is thus both relativized and marginalized. Many non-incarnational versions of Christianity accept and welcome such insights – but others find them disturbing and perhaps unconsciously articulate an incarnational Christianity in order to preserve insights which they intuitively recognize as central.

CONCLUSION

In this essay we have briefly summarized the case for defending the resurrection and incarnation as proper and legitimate interpretations of the history of Jesus of Nazareth, and the case for rejecting alternative explanations as inadequate.

It is hoped that the contours of the case for arguing that the resurrection and incarnation are proper and necessary elements of the Christian faith have been sketched in sufficient detail to allow the reader to take his own thinking further.

We now end this essay with some final reflections.

Critics of doctrines such as the resurrection and incarnation tend to work on the basis of two presuppositions. First, that there exists a theological equivalent of precision surgery, which allows certain elements of the Christian faith to be excised without having any detrimental effect whatsoever upon what remains. Second, that by eliminating logical and metaphysical difficulties a more plausible and hence more acceptable version of Christianity will result. Both these assumptions are clearly questionable, and must be challenged.

To return to our surgical analogy, we are not talking about removal of an appendix (a vestigial organ that apparently serves no useful purpose), but of the heart, the life-pump of the Christian faith. Faith in the resurrection and incarnation is what kept and keeps Christianity growing and spreading. The sheer vitality, profundity and excitement of the Christian faith ultimately depend upon these. In a day and age when Christianity has to fight for its existence, winning converts rather than relying upon a favourable cultural milieu, a non-incarnational theology despoiled of the resurrection has little to commend it. It is perhaps significant that many critics of the resurrection and incarnation were themselves originally attracted to Christianity through precisely the theology they are now criticizing. And what, it must be asked in all seriousness, is the *converting power* of an incarnationless Christianity?

The history of the Church suggests that such a version of Christianity is a spiritual dead end. To recall the words of Thomas Carlyle: 'If Arianism had won, Christianity would have dwindled to a legend.' To its critics, incarnationless Christianity seems to be scholarly, bookish and devoid of passion, without the inner dynamism to challenge and conquer unbelief in a world in which this is essential for its survival. But this is where history will pass its own judgement, in that only a form of Christianity which is convinced that it has

something distinctive, true, exciting and relevant to communicate to
the world in order to transform it will survive.

3
THE NEW TESTAMENT AS HISTORY

James D. G. Dunn

Is the New Testament history? The question posed like that is obviously too compressed and needs to be restated more fully. Is the New Testament concerned with history? Does the New Testament consist of historical documents? Or better still: Were the writers of the New Testament documents concerned to record history? Does the New Testament provide good historical information?

The question, however, is still not clear. So much depends on this word 'history'. Indeed, the whole issue of the historical value of the New Testament hangs on this word. So we had better start by making clear what we do *not* mean by it.

THE NEW TESTAMENT IS *NOT* HISTORY

The New Testament is not 'history' if by that word we mean a wholly objective and literal account of 'what actually happened'. For one thing, most of the New Testament writings do not actually fit into any such historical category. Twenty-one of the twenty-seven documents in the New Testament fall into the category of letters; they record the beliefs and counsel of the authors, not a dispassionate account of events with which they had to do.

The claim has often been made in the past that the last of the twenty-seven, the Apocalypse (= Revelation) of John, should be understood in some such literal sense. But that is certainly wrong. As is characteristic of the apocalyptic writings of that period, Revelation uses symbolism and often bizarre imagery to express its message. There is sometimes clear allusion to recognizable events and figures contemporary with the author, but never in a straightforward, literal sense. Apocalyptic is the clearest exception to the rule that the literal sense of a text is preferable to a symbolic or allegorical meaning. So with Revelation the history it contains is presented in heavily coded form, which we would be unable to decode (to the extent that we can do so) on its own.

So the issue revolves primarily around the other five New Testament documents – the four gospels and the Acts of the Apostles. Here too it quickly becomes apparent that if 'history' is defined too narrowly the answer to our opening question has to be a No. For the very fact of *four* gospels, with their innumerable differences of detail, order and emphasis, shows at once that the writers cannot have been concerned merely with 'what actually happened'. Had the evangelists conceived of themselves merely as archivists or been motivated by an archaeological concern to record every item of the tradition in the strictest possible chronological and geographical correlation, we would have had one, not four gospels, or at least gospels which could be integrated without difficulty. Even the gospels therefore cannot be assumed to provide 'straight' history. Which leaves only Acts among the twenty-seven New Testament documents. And that was written by one of the evangelists! In short, any attempt to argue that the New Testament is history in a narrow sense is bound to fail.

Another ense in which the ew Testament is *not* history is that it is not *modern* history. For example, a modern historian would think it improper to attribute to a historical character a speech for which he or she lacked sound documentary evidence. And if only fragmentary or impressionistic 'ear-witness' testimony was available a responsible modern historian would so indicate. But in ancient historiography the dividing line between history on the one hand and poetry or rhetoric on the other was not at all so clear. Speeches were included to delight and impress the reader as much as to inform. The point can sometimes be exaggerated, as though all ancient historians felt wholly free to compose speeches as they liked and to attribute them to whom they liked. That is not borne out by the evidence and does not accord with what historians like Thucydides and Polybius claimed they were doing. Nevertheless it remains characteristic of ancient historical writing that a fair degree of what we may properly call 'artistic licence' was both accepted and expected as part of the historian's task and skill. In reading the speeches or sermons recorded by the first Christian history (Acts), therefore, this historical context, this understanding of what was proper and what could and would be expected, must be kept in mind.

We find another example of the danger of misreading the New Testament as modern history in the issue of whether the synoptic gospels can be called 'biographies' or not. The fact is that they are not biographies as we today define biographies. Although the gospels are set within a broad chronological framework, there is no real attempt to maintain a sustained chronological record: so many stories about Jesus are told without 'locating' them either temporally or geographically; frequently there are thematic rather than chronological groupings of teachings, parables and miracles. Above all there is no attempt made to trace out the development of the character of the hero (Jesus). But all that is simply to say that the gospels do not share the concerns of *modern* biographies.

They do however share many of the concerns of *ancient* biographies. At that time the conception of human character was much more fixed, so that the idea of development in character was not present to the thought. Rather the biographer's objective was to display the hero's character by recounting episodes relating to him and memorable things he had said. And this is just what we find in the synoptic gospels – Jesus portrayed in terms of event and word. To be precise, in terms of genre a gospel is distinctive; but the nearest parallel to a gospel is in fact the ancient *bios* or *vita* or biography.

All this means that if we come to the New Testament documents with distinctively modern questions in mind we are likely to be disappointed. If we insist on trying to co-ordinate the four gospels into a single narrative we will almost certainly get it wrong, for the simple reason that we do not know what is correct. If we insist that different versions and sequences of events have to be harmonized in order to be counted historical, we impose concerns on the gospels which the evangelists did not share, and may well miss the points which they wanted their readers to hear. If we insist that the speeches of Acts are not historical unless they were first spoken just as narrated, we impose limitations on Luke the historian which neither he nor those for whom he wrote would recognize.

In short, if we are to answer the question about the historical worth of the New Testament fairly we must avoid prejudging the issue by insisting on our own definition of 'history' and must beware of trying to squeeze the New Testament into a 'historical' mould which it was not intended to fit.

THE NEW TESTAMENT *IS* HISTORY

The New Testament is history, first of all, in the sense that those who wrote the documents which go to make it up were at one in their claim that Christianity was founded on events which actually happened. Actually, it is not quite fair even to put it like that. For most of the New Testament writers the facticity of Jesus' life, ministry and death was not an issue. No one doubted or disputed it. So no elaborate defence of the claim had to be mounted. That tells us something right away: the historicity of Jesus was simply taken for granted both by the writers of the New Testament and by those for whom (and presumably also against whom) they wrote. Likewise it would seem ludicrous to ask about the historical fact of the beginnings and initial growth of Christianity. The New Testament writings are themselves witness to that fact: the people who wrote these documents and the people for whom they were written hardly needed to be convinced of the historicity of Christianity's beginnings; they were part of it!

But where the claims made by the first Christians were a matter of dispute it is also true that the New Testament writers made a point of asserting their historicity. This is clear from the earliest period in the case of the claim that 'God had raised Jesus from the dead'. One of the earliest formulations in all the New Testament is Paul's account in 1 Corinthians 15 of the confession which he himself had first received (that is, within two or three years of the event). There he lists the various appearances of Jesus after his resurrection and makes a point of stressing that many of the largest group of witnesses were still alive (1 Cor. 15.6). In other words, any who might wish to question the confession could seek out the witnesses for themselves and hear their testimony first-hand. So too, later in the same chapter, he insists that the faith he proclaims is based on the firm fact of the resurrection of Jesus; without it both proclamation and faith would be empty and useless (1 Cor. 15.14). No wonder contemporary theologians who wanted to maintain that faith must be based solely on the preached word and not be made to depend on any historical fact thought that Paul had lost his way at this point. An equivalent emphasis on the fact that the first disciples were 'witnesses' of Jesus as risen from the dead is also a consistent feature of the Acts of the Apostles (Acts 1.8, 22; 2.32; 3.15; 5.32, etc.).

So too, when later on the reality of Jesus' life and death became an issue, we find a similar insistence on their historicity. John's gospel makes a point of stressing the real humanness of Jesus: to those who thought that material flesh was inferior and worthless, the evangelist states firmly 'the Word became flesh' (John 1.14). To those who found it hard to believe that the divine could die, he asserts with equal firmness that he was an eyewitness of Jesus' death (John 19.35).

Likewise the first letter of John insists on the concreteness of Jesus and dismisses any suggestion that he might not have been a real man (1 John 1.1–3; 4.2).

There can be little question then that the New Testament is history at least in the sense that the New Testament writers were concerned with the historical reality of the events on which Christianity's distinctive claims were based.

Thus far the claim being made is modest enough – that the New Testament writers were concerned to maintain the historical fact of Jesus' life, death and resurrection. But we can say a good deal more. For once again the very fact of there being so many gospels in circulation among and cherished by the earliest Christians tells us something: that the first Christians wanted to remember and retell stories about Jesus and things he had said. Sometimes students of the gospels in effect make a very odd assumption: that the material which goes to make up the gospels (I am thinking here particularly of the first three gospels) was not in circulation before Matthew, Mark and Luke first wrote it down. As though the first disciples of Jesus, who had been with him during his ministry, did not speak at all of their time with Jesus, and after the first Easter spoke only of his death and resurrection! As though Mark (usually taken as the first gospel to be written), and then the others, had to go to the disciples and drag the information from them so that it could go into circulation for the first time in the latter decades of the first century! The idea is little short of ludicrous. Of course the traditions which appear in the gospels were in circulation, most of them at least, before the evangelists wrote them down. Which is simply to say that the earliest Christian communities among whom these traditions circulated were concerned to *remember* Jesus.

All the available evidence points firmly in this direction. Let me summarize it briefly.

1. Consider first what we might call 'the sociology of groups' – the recognition that groups naturally try to identify themselves and to mark themselves off from other groups by emphasizing the distinctiveness of their beliefs, and that religious groups in particular tend to regard their founding traditions as especially important. Characteristic of such groups will be opportunities and rituals by which they will recall their members to these traditions and celebrate them together as part of 'group bonding' and demarcation. Clearly the ritual occasions of baptism and the common meal (Lord's Supper, Eucharist) played

an important part here, and there is no doubt that they were part of
Christianity from the first. But so too would traditions about things
Jesus had done and said. There must have been very few (if any) of
all those early converted to the new movement who were content
simply to celebrate the bare 'that' of Jesus' life, death and resurrection. Committed as they were to Jesus as 'Lord', they would
inevitably want to know more about this Jesus. Who can doubt that
the earliest material which now makes up our gospels served this
purpose (among others) of giving new converts an informed
understanding and picture of Jesus the Christ to whom they now
belonged individually and together?

2. This 'in the nature of things' deduction is confirmed by the
prominence given to teachers and tradition in the New Testament. As
far back as our records go, wherever there is talk of recognized
ministry among the Christian churches the teacher has an honoured
position and the importance of teaching is stressed (e.g., Acts 2.42;
13.1; Rom. 6.17; 1 Cor. 12.28; Gal. 6.6; Jas. 3.1). Paul, writing
within thirty years of Jesus' ministry, and often eager to stress his
independence from the mother church in Jerusalem, is equally
consistent in stressing the importance of tradition, of the continuity of
the tradition he made a point of handing on to his newly founded
churches (1 Cor. 11.2, 23; 15.1-3; Col. 2.6; 1 Thess. 4.1; 2 Thess.
2.15; 3.6). Again, who can doubt that among the traditions Paul
passed on to his new churches would be many of those we now have
in the gospels? Christian congregations around the eastern end of the
Mediterranean would have been odd indeed if they did not have a
common stock of stories and sayings of Jesus which they shared and
regularly celebrated for their mutual edification. Before the stories
and sayings were written down, part of the teacher's function would
be to serve as the oral repository of such tradition.

3. These deductions are also confirmed by the gospels themselves.
As already noted, the synoptic gospels conform in large measure to
the type of the ancient biography. That is to say, their purpose is to
portray Jesus by telling stories about him and relating his more
memorable sayings and parables. But this biographical character was
assuredly not stamped on the gospel material for the first time by the
evangelists. There are forms and groupings of material behind the
gospels which all New Testament scholars recognize, in principle at
least. And the gospels all, in greater or less degree, attest the
fascination which this Jesus exercised on those who rejoiced to be

known by his name – Nazarenes, Christians. Nor is it coincidental that the most consistent and common title for Jesus in the gospels is 'teacher' and that they all stress how much of his ministry consisted in teaching. It would be ludicrously inconsistent if those who passed on these traditions from the first were not concerned to present their teaching precisely as the teaching of Jesus. The Cynic philosophers of the time are closest to the first Christian preachers in their missionary concern and practice. One of the ways in which they spread their message was precisely by telling stories about Diogenes, their honoured founder. Again, who can doubt that the gospel material served a similar function among the first Christians from the first?

The picture we must grasp with historical imagination, therefore, is of Christian communities scattered round the eastern end of the Mediterranean, each with its stock of traditions about Jesus. The churches in Palestine would retain most of these traditions in Aramaic, their everyday language. Most of the rest would already have them in Greek, the most widely used language of the eastern part of the Roman Empire. So when Mark wrote his gospel he would be drawing on traditions which were already widespread. And though he was (most probably) the first to put them together in such an extensive way, most of the churches would be familiar with many of these traditions. The versions might be different, but they would recognize many of the stories and sayings which they too cherished. So too when Mark's gospel reached the churches where Matthew and Luke worshipped it would hardly be the case that this was the first time they had heard all these traditions. Their congregations too would already include many of the same traditions among their own stock of stories about Jesus. And evidently they had more, which Mark either had not known or had chosen not to use. And so Matthew and Luke wrote their gospels to give a more complete portrayal of Jesus. In each case we are talking of communal memories of Jesus' ministry, most of which must have been part of different congregations' heritage from their earliest days. And however much they may have been interpreted and elaborated in the telling and retelling, they would go back to eyewitness testimony and reflect a basic concern to remember Jesus and to draw inspiration and instruction from that remembering. In short, what we have in the synoptic gospels is basically Jesus as he was remembered in the earliest Christian congregations of Palestine and beyond.

The point is harder to argue in the case of the Acts of the Apostles, since we have only the one record, and since we cannot make the same assumption that the stories and speeches used by Luke would have had the same foundational and authoritative significance for all the churches as the traditions about Jesus. But there are various indications that Luke was a careful historian who for much of his narrative at least was able to draw on good and accurate eyewitness accounts. For example, the well known 'we' passages, which are a feature of his narrative from Acts 16.10 onwards, are best understood in terms of the conventions of the time as a claim to have been personally present on the occasions recounted. And, where we can test the details of the narrative, the accuracy is impressive – as, for example, his awareness that the city authorities in Thessalonica had a distinctive title, 'politarch' (Acts 17.6, 8).

Even with the speeches there are sufficient indications that Luke has sought out much earlier material and has incorporated it into the brief formalized expositions which he attributes to Peter, Stephen, Paul, etc. For example, the distinctive character of the speech in Acts 7 (Stephen's speech of defence), with its slanted review of Israel's history and its climactic attack on the temple (Acts 7.48 – 'made with hands' = idolatrous!), is best explained if Luke derived it from the group who made the break with the temple, before the law became an issue – that is, from the Hellenists, of whom Stephen was the most prominent. And the primitive presentation of Jesus in such passages as Acts 3.19–21 (where uniquely 'the Lord' is God and not Christ) and Acts 10.36–8 ('God anointed Jesus of Nazareth . . .') is likewise best explained if Luke was indeed drawing on material which had been preserved from the earliest days of the new movement, when Peter was in fact the chief spokesman.

This means that in terms of ancient historiography Luke has taken greater pains than many of his first readers would expect in order to present his material with as much authentic detail as he could. Like all historians, his presentation is slanted: he is a Christian and his portrayal is selective, as we might expect; he chooses to draw a veil over some of the strong disagreements in which Paul, his hero, was involved; his account of Paul's preaching does not always wholly match what Paul himself says; in describing the ministries of the first Pauline churches he probably uses terms which reflected his own time more than Paul's; and like all historians he most probably gets one or two details wrong (Acts 5.36). But even so, when all has been said and done, Luke comes across as one of the most reliable historians of his age, whose account can be credited with a high degree of trustworthiness.

In short, the New Testament *is* history, because the letter-writers were dealing with real historical situations, which are often reflected in their letters, and because Matthew, Mark and Luke were concerned to tell the story of Jesus and of Christianity's beginnings as these were actually remembered in traditions (oral and written) cherished within the first Christian communities.

THE NEW TESTAMENT IS *LIVING* HISTORY

In stressing the positive historical value of the New Testament, however, we must not think of the New Testament writers as always looking back to what was past, as though they were simply purveyors of *dead* history. On the contrary, what was so important about their remembering was the continuing vitality and relevance, particularly of their traditions about Jesus.

This is a further deduction which can be drawn from the diversity of the four gospels. Again and again, in the first three gospels especially, we have different versions of the same episode or saying of Jesus. In most cases there are some significant differences of detail, but the overlap is so extensive that the most probable conclusion is that they stem from memories of the same event or piece of teaching (e.g., Matt. 13.53-8//Mark 6.1-6; Mark 3.27-9//Luke 11.21-2 and 12.10; Matt. 6.9-13//Luke 11.2-4). The point is that such differences emerged because the material remembered was being used - used in teaching, preaching, apologetic, polemic, worship and evangelism. And as it was being used, so it was being adapted to that use - translated, differently grouped, explained to bring out a particular point, and so on. Hence the differences. There was nothing underhand or devious in this - simply a concern that what Jesus had said and done might speak with greater force to the situation addressed. This is not to undermine what was said in the previous section, simply to note that as the tradition of Jesus was reflected on and heard afresh in new contexts that hearing inevitably reflected something of those contexts.

We see other indications of this in the way Paul uses the tradition of Jesus' teaching. The fact that Paul refers to Jesus' teaching explicitly in only a small handful of cases is one of the most notorious

features of the New Testament. If the point was pursued with severe
logic, it might be taken to support the conclusion that Paul knew only
a small handful of sayings. But, as we have already noted, the
thought that Paul set up a whole series of churches without passing on
to them a solid core of traditions about Jesus is hardly credible and
runs counter to our other evidence. The better explanation lies in
recognizing a whole sequence of allusions to the teaching of Jesus in
the sections of his letters where he turns to ethical exhortation. This is
where we might expect the traditions of Jesus' teaching to make their
influence felt, rather than in the more heavily doctrinal sections. And
so we find – for example, in Romans 12.14, 18, 20; 13.8–10; 14.13–
14, 17, 19–20; 15.1–2, 8. Some of these are closer to traditions
preserved in the gospels, others less so. But they all express the
attitude which Jesus inculcated by his teaching (and by his life – the
example of Jesus is explicitly cited in Rom. 15.3, 5, 8). The reason
why Paul does not cite them as 'words of Jesus' is presumably
because he did not think of them as sayings spoken twenty-five years
earlier, but as 'the word of the Lord' there and then. Presumably he
also expected his readers to appreciate the authority of his counsel by
recognizing most of these same allusions. The same point is evident
in one of the cases where Paul actually does cite Jesus explicitly, but
adapts the teaching to the situation addressed (cf. 1 Cor. 7.15 with
Mark 10.11 and Matt. 19.9). The point is, Paul did not merely
remember the tradition of Jesus' teaching, he lived in it.

John's gospel is the most extensive example of tradition
remembered and elaborated. The points of overlap with the other
three gospels are sufficiently numerous for us to be confident that the
Johannine version of the Jesus tradition is rooted in the same earliest
memories of Jesus' ministry. But in John's case the whole process has
moved into a higher gear, as the extent of the differences from the
synoptic gospels makes clear. What we seem to have in the fourth
gospel is an extended process of reflection on typical events in Jesus'
ministry and on characteristic sayings which likewise go back to Jesus
(e.g., cf. John 3.3ff. with Matt. 18.3, and John 10.1–18 with Luke
15.4–6). But the extended meditations are the work of the author or
of the tradition which he used. In this case we most probably have to
recognize a good deal less of historical information than in the other
gospels. But that too should not be taken to undermine our earlier
conclusions. For John was probably less concerned to write history
than the others. It was no doubt his intention to present his gospel as

what it seems to be – meditations designed to bring out the full truth of Jesus as that was now seen to be in the light of all that had happened. And had he been pressed on the historical character of his narrative he would probably have been the first to point out that it was not his intention to provide such narrative. Here too Jesus is not merely remembered but experienced in all his significance, with various typical episodes and characteristic sayings from his ministry allowed to unfold the full sweep of their meaning for faith. In this case the history as such is largely hidden within the brightness of the living history.

To sum up: the New Testament *is* history – not mere history, and not history as opposed to theology, but history which provides a firm foundation for Christian beliefs about Jesus and a living history which can still speak with its original authority and power.

4
MIRACLES

Keith Ward

Some twentieth-century presentations of religious faith make it solely a matter of inner personal experience or commitment. But one of the clearest facts about religion is that, whenever religious faith becomes intense and living, miracles are widely claimed to occur. Miracles are not just inner experiences; they are outward and publicly observable events, closely connected with religious faith, which seem to go beyond the ordinary processes of nature. They are, in the strict and proper sense of the word, 'paranormal' occurrences. They show, in an outward and visible way, something of the spiritual character of reality, the fact that there are spiritual forces at work in the world as well as the unconscious material laws of nature which we nowadays take so much for granted.

Most claimed miracles are miracles of healing, when some illness is cured in a sudden and unexpected way which it is beyond the present powers of medical science to explain. Of course they would not be miracles unless it was believed that God or (in the case of faith healing) some mental or spiritual agency had caused the cure. What a miracle is claimed to show is the power of mind over matter. Matter, it is alleged, can be altered by some form of psychic influence – whether it is taken to be God himself, or some saint or holy person, or merely an unknown psychic power which some individuals apparently possess.

The healing miracles of Jesus are by no means unique in kind. Similar healing powers are claimed of many holy men, and the Old Testament prophets had such powers too. In the Christian tradition, and indeed in most religious traditions, miracles are not just said to be caused by God interrupting the natural order in a seemingly haphazard or arbitrary manner. Miracles are closely associated with holiness, with the possession of strong faith or a special sort of spiritual capacity. So we find that in the Indian religious traditions those who pursue the paths of yoga and spiritual discipline are expected to develop miraculous powers of various sorts – the ability to levitate, to stop the heart-beat for periods of time, or to seem to manipulate events around them. Yet they are encouraged to regard these powers as diversions from the real business of establishing a true relationship with God or perfect enlightenment, as it is variously described.

If we look at the case of Jesus, we find a similar phenomenon. He is reported to have had remarkable powers of healing; he practised exorcism; he could calm storms, walk on water and seemingly produce food out of nothing. Yet he refused to use these powers to convince everyone of his own spiritual status, and to some extent, according to Mark's gospel, tried to keep them secret. He certainly did not use miracles to prove his divinity – that was precisely one of the temptations in the wilderness which would have distracted him from his proper task.

It seems, then, on the New Testament understanding, that miracles are not proofs of God. They are more like natural and inevitable manifestations of holiness, of closeness to God. Some people, because of their intense love of God, are so filled with his presence that the imperfections of our physical bodies are made whole by their touch, and the internally destructive mental forces which possess us are driven out and replaced by the integrating power of forgiveness and love. If Jesus was uniquely close to God, then one might expect that his miracles would be especially clear and vivid; and so the gospels say they are.

Not all the biblical miracles are of that sort, though most of them are. There are also the major miracles which mark the beginning and end of Jesus' life, the virginal conception and the resurrection. These were not brought about by some power of Jesus himself. They are unique interventions by God in human history which establish the utter uniqueness of Jesus himself and provide the vindication of his mission as the anointed one of God. Such miracles, as direct acts of God in history, are also recorded in the Old Testament – the rolling back of the Red Sea (or 'the sea of reeds' in Hebrew) being the clearest example. On the Christian view, God is always in some way active in history. These miracles are wholly extraordinary and indeed unique historical events which help to accomplish the purpose God has for the world.

It was these miracles which gave rise to David Hume's famous definition of miracle as a violation of a law of nature by a God (Hume 1748, 114). The Bible did not see it quite like that, for its authors had little idea of laws of nature in our modern sense. But it was clear that these events ran contrary to general expectations and that they were seen by the faithful as directly willed and brought about by God. These acts again surround specific prophetic figures – Moses, Elijah and Elisha – but they are not primarily thought of as produced by those persons via some power of their own. God acts in direct and wonderful ways to free his people from Egypt and bring them to the promised land. He is recorded in the pages of the Old Testament as causing floods, destroying walls, causing earthquakes and storms, causing the sun to stand still and armies to be thrown into irrational panic. It is the Lord who fights for Israel and defeats her enemies in quite astonishing ways.

Biblical scholars differ in the view they take of such records. At one extreme the accounts would be accepted much as they stand. There was a physical pillar of cloud and flame going before the Israelites in the wilderness. There was a cloud of light filling the temple and fire consuming the sacrifices. For is not God the Lord of all nature, so that he can cause it to change in any way he pleases? At the other extreme many of these accounts would be seen as legends. Perhaps they are poetic metaphors which have been later turned into 'facts' – thus the stars did not really fight for Joshua, and the sun did not really stand still. Rather, very significant events in the history of Israel have been dramatized by giving accounts of these celestial phenomena, trying to show that the very powers of nature themselves fought on behalf of Israel.

It is probably true to say that most scholars would accept that there are elements of exaggeration and fictionalization in the Old Testament narratives. For instance, the flood at the time of Noah did not really cover the whole earth, and the ten plagues at the time of the Exodus were not quite so dramatic and drastic as they are portrayed. But the question remains: Did God guide the Israelites to Canaan and act in special ways to ensure their inheritance of his promises?

Whatever view one takes of the particular details of the Old Testament wonders, the Bible as a whole would hardly make sense if it is not true that God acts in history to accomplish particular purposes. That indeed is the testimony of the prophets, that God judges and blesses his people; that he has a specific calling for the Israelites; and that he will ensure that his promises are fulfilled. The life of Jesus makes sense only when it is seen as a fulfilment of the prophecies of the Old Testament. If Jesus was indeed the fulfilment of prophecy, then God had ordained what would happen and had in time brought it to pass. So the biblical testimony is that God acts in history in particular and unique ways – ways which are not repeated anywhere else on earth.

Of course, that does not by itself entail that miracles occur. Perhaps God always acts in ways which are not very extraordinary. But that seems very unlikely when one reflects on the claims a little further. If God is thought of as acting, as bringing things about for a purpose, then an analogy is being drawn with human persons. When human beings act intentionally they do not have to perform miracles, and their actions are not usually thought of as 'violating the laws of nature'. If I want to write this essay, I will sit down and start to type. What happens in the world – the state of affairs consisting in my typing – will be caused by my purpose. If a physicist wished to explain this state of affairs, he could no doubt do so. But if he considered only the laws of physics and nothing else, he would always miss out something important. He would miss out my purpose, about which physics would tell him nothing; and he would miss out my awareness of what I was doing, and how that affects the whole process of thinking and typing. I am, for instance trying to construct a logical and coherent argument. Yet no number of laws of physics will even mention the rules of logic or explain how arguments proceed. The physicist can tell you only about the 'hardware' of the programme, if you like. The whole personal dimension will be missing.

Now the physicist's account of my actions may be complete in its own terms. But it will still miss out all the elements I take to be most important about my actions, and so in that sense the physical account will be an incomplete explanation. It will provide only part of the story of what is going on in the world. Now it is possible that some extra-terrestrial physicist, who was not human, might come to earth and give a physical account of all human actions, without realizing anything about consciousness, thinking, purposes and so on. He might think we were all robots. Then he might think that he had completely explained human behaviour. But we would know that he was wrong; the most important elements would still be missing.

In a similar way, when a contemporary scientist looks at the universe he may be able to explain what happens in terms of laws of physics, biology, chemistry, and so on; and he may think that is all there is to it. Yet it might still be true that God – a personal agent with consciousness, purpose and thought – is in fact acting in the world to realize his purposes. The scientist might miss out this dimension altogether, and then he would have missed out the most important thing about the world. But he might never notice what he had done, because the account seems complete to him, just because he has no direct access to the mind or purposes of God.

However, I have glossed over a very important question about this analogy. To go back to the human case, is it true that the existence of consciousness, purpose and thought makes no difference to what happens on the purely physical level? Suppose there were no thought, purpose or awareness at all. Would precisely the same things happen, in accordance with the laws of physics alone? That seems a very strange idea, because it means that our thoughts really make no difference at all, that they are totally irrelevant: we think it makes a difference what we think; but in fact it does not. That view seems to me too strange to accept; it would mean that we lived under a permanent illusion about our own causal efficacy. Our belief that we can think and so cause differences to the world is so strong, deeply rooted and important that it would take an overwhelmingly strong argument to show that we were mistaken. No such argument exists; so we are quite reasonable in thinking that our thoughts make a real difference to the world. If so, there is here a further sense in which the account of physics is incomplete. Not only does it miss out one dimension of being, but it cannot explain all that happens solely in terms of the laws of physics. For if only those laws operated, without any human action, things would not be precisely as they in fact are. That is to say, the laws of physics alone cannot predict correctly what will happen in the world. Thinking makes a real difference.

We still would not say that thinking violates the laws of physics; that seems silly. What we should say is that the laws of physics state what will happen, if and only if no other influences operate to alter the situation. However, thinking is precisely another influence; it alters the situation; so the laws of physics are not broken. They are supplemented by further causal influences with which they do not directly deal. It is not that they cease operating, it is just that other factors – other sorts of causal influence – modify the way in which they operate in these specific cases.

If we now think about the actions of God again, we would similarly expect that his purposes and actions will make a difference to the world. Things will be different than they would have been if

God had not had certain purposes and put them into effect. So there
will be some events in the physical universe which the physical
sciences alone cannot completely predict. These divine purposes need
not violate the laws of physics, because, in the way I have suggested,
they can supplement these laws, adding a new causal factor which
modifies the way those laws operate in particular cases. Would these
instances be called miracles? At first sight it seems not. Just as human
actions are not miraculous, so divine actions need not be miraculous.
However, we have to remember at this point that whereas there are a
great many human beings there is only one God. Because there are
many human beings, we take human action to be fairly commonplace.
We expect people to reflect, to have purposes and to cause changes in
their immediate environments. Because we expect them we do not call
such changes miraculous; they occasion no surprise. But the actions
of God are not commonplace in the same way. So if the acts of God
cause changes in the universe which would not have happened in
accordance with the laws of physics alone, those changes might be
called miraculous. They are, after all, caused by a supernatural
agency and are not wholly accountable for by using the scientific laws
we have available.

In one sense all the acts of God are miraculous. But it would be
silly to call them miraculous, because they are usually not particularly
amazing and may even be undetectable. It may seem strange to
suppose that the acts of God could be undetectable, but it is obviously
true. We can say that something is an action if it brings about some
physical state of affairs in accordance with some intention. Intentions
themselves are not observable by others. We may have some intention
for the whole of our lives, while nobody even discovers what it is.
We may conceal it perfectly, and I suppose that the most successful
spies, especially those who are double-agents, do so. Normally, of
course, we judge a person's intentions by what they do. And although
that is not always a good guide, since people may not always do what
they want, we do have their bodily behaviour to observe, and that
helps us to judge their intentions.

God, however, has no particular observable physical body. So we
cannot pick out some piece of observable behaviour anywhere in the
universe and say, 'That is the behaviour of God's body; from it we
can at least hazard a guess as to his intentions.' Suppose, then, that
God has the intention that some state of affairs should come about,
and it does come about. As observers with no direct access to the

mind of God we would not know that he had such an intention, and we would not know that he had brought it about, as opposed to its coming about by physical laws or by someone else's actions. We could never be sure of that, because we can never observe any divine body acting so as to bring a state of affairs about. If we do not know either what God wants or what he does to bring it about, it is obviously true that we do not know exactly when God is acting. He may have purposes we know nothing of – and he may ensure they are brought about in ways of which we are wholly ignorant – but we would never know.

I may be thought to have taken things too far. If we can never know when God is acting, isn't the whole idea of divine action irrelevant? There are two things to say in reply to this question. First, it might be very important that God is acting, even though we can never know it. For what we attribute to good luck or coincidence might in fact be due to the action of God. And it would be very important if God did act to ensure that in the end our lives attained the purpose he willed for them. Second, it is of course an exaggeration to say that we can *never* know when God is acting. All I suggested was that many of the acts of God are undetectable. The physical universe is so complex, so many different factors operate at any one time – the free decisions of others, the laws of the sciences, and perhaps other as yet unknown laws too – that we could not be expected to pick out God's contribution with any certainty.

Christians, however, believe that the whole point of revelation is that God should show what his major intentions are, should show how he acts in general and should make at least some of his particular actions clear. I said earlier that we have no direct access to the mind of God. That is true, unless God himself provides such access by telling us his purposes. That, in the religious sense, is the point of miracle; it is an extraordinary happening – so extraordinary that we can take it as a revelation by God of his nature and purposes. It seems to me that if there is a personal God who has a purpose for the world, we should expect there to be some miracles in this sense. It would be very odd if God never made his purpose clear at all and left his existence to be wholly a matter of guesswork.

It is true that God does not make his existence quite unambiguously clear – atheism is still a possibility for human beings. So revelation is not something which convinces everyone beyond reasonable doubt, as it could have been. If God had just wanted to convince everyone of his existence, he could certainly have performed such a miraculous act – the stopping of the sun in full view of everyone, with perhaps a message written in the clouds, would probably do. Miracles are not proofs in that sense. Furthermore, it is important to remember that they do have a religious element about them. That is, they express something of God himself and call for a response of faith.

A consideration of the central miracle of the Christian faith, the resurrection of Jesus, will make this clearer. Jesus could presumably have appeared to the Sanhedrin or to Pontius Pilate. He could have made his risen life perfectly indubitable by walking openly in Jerusalem and then ascending into heaven before a packed assembly of the priests and Pharisees. But he did not. He appeared almost secretly to the apostles, behind closed doors or in the solitude of Galilee. He left them in no doubt of his resurrection; but he was not concerned to establish it to the satisfaction of those who had crucified him.

It seems, then, that the resurrection is a testimony of faith. It is not given as a clearly attested very odd happening. It is rather that it is an objective event which transforms the understandings and lives of the apostles as it vindicates the life and teachings of Jesus, showing that he did not end defeated by his enemies. It is certainly wholly extraordinary; but it occurs only in the context of faith. Within that context it has the function of making the divine purpose clear, of testifying to the authenticity of the life of Jesus as a revelation of that purpose. God makes his purpose clear to those who respond to him in faith. Miracle is neither a proof for the uncommitted nor a purely subjective event in the mind. It is, as recorded in the gospels, an objective event which confirms faith and helps to shape it further. Those who are not devoted to God by a commitment of repentance and hope will see only a very odd event; or perhaps they will miss it altogether and hear of it only from others. But those who seek the kingdom and the new life it brings will find the purpose of God expressed in an event so unexpected and yet so 'right' – the defeat of death itself by the power of God – that it will confirm for them the commitment which might otherwise have been thrown into doubt by the crucifixion.

We might see miracles, then, as confirmations for faith of the purposes of God and also as revelations of his nature and will. If so, this helps to answer a question which is often put to those who believe in miracles: Why does God not act miraculously more often, to save his people from suffering, for instance? Do alleged miracles not seem arbitrary and much too rare? If God can heal disease, why does he not intervene much more to eliminate cancer or diabetes?

When such questions are asked there is a particular picture of God at work which makes them seem sensible and real. God is seen as an all-powerful person who would seek to eliminate suffering wherever it occurred. Being all-powerful, he can of course eliminate it whenever he wants to. So it becomes completely inexplicable that he allows suffering to happen at all. It is even worse if he sometimes acts to heal people, for there then seems to be no reason why he heals some people and not others – or why he should not heal everybody.

It is most important to see that this is a picture of God which is almost wholly misleading; and it is not at all the biblical picture of God. When we read the book of Job we have to remember that it was the friends of Job who tried to explain suffering as a punishment for sin imposed by a powerful God. Their explanations are all rejected; and in the end Job finds that he must simply bow before the overwhelming mystery and majesty of God, confessing his own nothingness before the creator of all things. Part of the message of this strange book is that we cannot explain the acts of God as if they were those of some very powerful human person – as if we could judge him morally for his goodness. God is the source of all beings, and they exist only in total dependence upon him. We cannot understand why things are as they are; but we can know that all things derive from God. We can also know that God calls us to obey and love him, and promises the joy of his presence if we do so. The biblical view is that God is almighty – all things depend solely on his power. And God is one who brings punishment on those who hate him, but shows love to those who love him and obey his laws (Exod. 20.5–6). We might put this another way by saying that God allows those who choose the way of pride and hatred to bring themselves to destruction, but he guides those who are penitent to the way of eternal life.

It is futile to set ourselves up in moral judgement of the creator. If we really see – as Job did, in the end – that we depend wholly for our existence upon God, and that he offers us eternal life, then it is no use complaining that he should not have created suffering. Suffering is an integral part of this world; without it, we would not be. God offers us final deliverance from suffering; but he does not simply remove it; for to do so would be to change the structure of the world itself.

I am not trying to justify the existence of suffering, as though I could offer some explanation of why it exists. Only God knows why it exists; but we can say that it arises from the divine being itself and that it seems to be implicit in the nature of at least this creation (there may be others, but we know nothing of them). Does it limit the omnipotence of God if suffering, or the possibility of suffering, is necessarily implicit in his own being? In some abstract logical sense, no doubt it does – God is then unable to do everything that can be consistently stated in some proposition. There will be things God cannot do – create this world without any suffering in it, for instance. Yet God may be almighty in the very real sense that there is no being which could logically have more power than he has; there is nothing which has some source other than or opposed to God himself. Moreover, one might add that God is able to bring overwhelming good out of the suffering that exists, even though, since it is necessarily involved in the very nature of this creation, he is unable to remove suffering altogether.

This seems to me a possible notion of God. It seems to be more like the biblical idea of the imageless God who rides the clouds of storm and thunder as well as liberating his people through earthquake and pestilence than it is like the philosopher's idea of a God who would never permit any suffering to exist. The point is that there may be necessities in the world of which we understand nothing. It may be true that God cannot just eliminate all suffering without destroying the world as we know it.

But does that mean that God should never perform miracles, that he should never eliminate suffering? It seems to make sense to say that God will not destroy the structures of the world he has created. He will not just arbitrarily break some of the physical laws on occasion, as David Hume (1748) seems to suggest. When he acts, it will be in response to the prayer and faith of creatures. The structure of the world may, after all, be such that faithful response to the creator does open up new possibilities of unique change, a transformation of the everyday which enables it to show the divine purpose which underlies it. We need to see the physical universe as a multi-layered whole, able to generate new levels of meaning which can transform the lower levels at critical points. Thus the physical level gives rise to the biological when physical elements become organized in functional wholes. The biological gives rise to the conscious level. Then purposes and perceptions affect the patterning of both biological and physical levels. May there not also be a spiritual level at which human beings relate to the spiritual forces which surround them? If we look at the biblical miracles, we find that they occur when some prophet or person of deep faith so establishes a relationship to God that .they become vehicles of his purposes. Around them, we might say, the material world becomes more transparent to the spiritual. It is at such points that miracles occur, opening the physical world to spiritual powers.

Seen in this light, miracles are not just rare and arbitrary violations of physical laws by God. They are points at which the dynamic power of God breaks into the world in manifestation of his purposes; and that power is released by faith, by the relationship to God attained by Abraham, Moses, Elijah, the prophets and, most fully, by Jesus. These are not so much violations of laws as manifestations of a higher law of the spirit, taking natural objects beyond their normal modes of operation. Often this is manifested in healing, whether physical or mental. But one should not think of God just deciding to heal John and not Mary, when he could easily have healed both. Rather, healings occur as part of the natural processes of the world when and in so far as they become transformative points, points where the power of the Spirit breaks in through prayer and faith. God does not contradict the nature he has created. He fulfils it when it is brought to the point at which it is ready for such fulfilment.

Miracles are from faith and for faith. They occur when faith has brought a particular moment of history to the point at which it can embody the divine power. And their purpose is not primarily to eliminate suffering, much less to prove the existence of God to all. It is to show that suffering is not final defeat, to confirm the purpose of God to save, to make whole those who turn to him in penitence and faith. For Christians, the greatest miracle of all is the raising of Jesus from the dead. This miracle was from faith; for the whole life of Jesus had been one of total devotion to the will of the Father, and his life was in itself a prefiguring of that wholeness of being to which all are called. And it was for faith; for it assured the apostles that their discipleship had not been in vain. The way of Christ was still the way of the cross – pain was not eliminated. But victory was assured; and that is the Christian gospel, which makes faith powerful and effective for salvation.

Miracles are very important for the Christian religion; if Christ was not truly raised from death, then Christian faith is vain. A Christian faith without miracles is like a house without foundations. It may look very fine; but it will not stand for long. So it is important to have some idea of what miracles are, and to know whether they can occur. I have suggested that, in the broadest sense, a miracle is an extraordinary event, inexplicable on the known laws of physics, which is caused by some paranormal mental power or some spiritual agency. In this sense, holy men may perform miracles, as may demons or spirits of various sorts, if they exist. In a rather narrower sense, a miracle is such an event which is caused by God, the one and only creator of all things. Many such miracles are recorded in the Bible; and even if some of these records are legendary, or contain elements of legend, the overwhelming testimony of the Bible is that God has acted in such ways at various times.

There seems no reason at all why, if he exists, God should not act in such ways, and arguments against the very possibility of miracles seem wholly unconvincing. The real questions, therefore, are why God should perform miracles; and why, if he does, he performs them so rarely. I have suggested that if there is a God with a purpose for this world, he will continually be modifying the operation of physical laws in order to realize his purposes. Such actions will normally be undetectable, since we have no way of observing God's actions. However, a good reason for performing a miracle would be to reveal at least the general divine purpose for the world. Thus the resurrection of Jesus reveals God's purpose to raise us from death and give us eternal life. We could hardly have known that otherwise, or have had good reason for thinking it was true, without some sort of divine confirmation. Nevertheless, in so acting, the biblical records suggest that God is both responding to a faith which opens the world, at a particular point, to the power of his Spirit; and he is speaking to a faith which will allow itself to be conformed to the purpose so revealed.

Miracles are neither arbitrary nor are they proofs of God's existence or decisions to eliminate suffering. When the way is prepared they reveal God's purpose to those who desire to conform their lives to it. The miracle of the resurrection was prepared by a long history of faith and hope in Israel, culminating in the willing response of Mary to the birth of Jesus and the perfected life of Jesus himself. It showed the purpose of God to redeem humanity through the community of the Church. And it is not only rare but unrepeatable precisely because what it shows is the uniqueness of God's saving activity in Jesus. I conclude that at least the outlines of an intelligible account of miracles can be given. Christians may reasonably claim that the miracle of the resurrection, though wholly extraordinary and inexplicable in terms of physical laws as we know them, is a wholly natural manifestation of the power and purpose of God. It shows God's purpose for the whole human race and is the reasonable foundation of a life committed to God, whose will is that we shall all be raised with Christ in glory.

5
MIRACLES:
SCEPTICISM, CREDULITY OR REALITY?

R. J. Berry

A few years ago I was one of fourteen signatories of a letter to *The Times* (13 July 1984) about miracles. All of us were professors of science in British universities; six were Fellows of the Royal Society. We asserted:

> It is not logically valid to use science as an argument against miracles. To believe that miracles cannot happen is as much an act of faith as to believe that they can happen. We gladly accept the virgin birth, the Gospel miracles, and the resurrection of Christ as historical events . . . Miracles are unprecedented events. Whatever the current fashions in philosophy or the revelations of opinion polls may suggest, it is important to affirm that science (based as it is upon the observation of precedents) can have nothing to say on the subject. Its 'laws' are only generalisations of our experience.

An article in the leading science periodical *Nature* (19 July 1984, p. 171), although accepting our statements on the nature of scientific laws, dissented from our conclusion about miracles on the grounds that they are 'inexplicable and irreproducible phenomena [which] do not occur – a definition by exclusion of the concept . . . the publication of Berry et al. provides a licence not merely for religious belief (which, on other grounds, is unexceptionable) but for mischievous reports of all things paranormal, from ghosts to flying saucers'.

Subsequent correspondents disagreed. For example, P. G. H. Clarke (*Nature*, 11 October 1984, p. 502) objected that 'your concerns not to license "mischievous reports of all things paranormal" is no doubt motivated in the interest of scientific truth, but your strategy of defining away what you find unpalatable is the antithesis of scientific'. Donald MacKay in the same issue emphasized that

for the Christian believer, baseless credulity is a sin – a disservice
to the God of truth. His belief in the resurrection does not stem
from a softness in his standards for evidence, but rather from the
coherence with which (as he sees it) that particular unprecedented
event fits into and makes sense of a great mass of data . . . There
is clearly no inconsistency in believing (with astonishment) in a
unique event so well attested, while remaining unconvinced by
spectacular stories of 'paranormal' occurrences that lack any
comparable support.

The credibility of belief in miracles has resurfaced in *The Nature
of Christian Belief* (1986), a report of the Church of England bishops
produced in response to the controversy about statements made by one
of their number, David Jenkins, the Bishop of Durham. *The Times*
(6 June 1986) commented on it: 'Did the two key miracles at the
centre of the Christian faith, the Virgin Birth and the Resurrection,
really happen? . . . The exercise has established one thing clearly:
that belief in miracles, at least where they are central to the faith, is
thoroughly intellectually respectable . . .'
It would be easy to decry the criteria or standards of truth accepted
by the bishops, but their integrity is presumably not in doubt. It is
more profitable to enquire whether miracles are really credible, and,
if so, what are the circumstances where they might be expected.

THE BASIS AND BREAKABILITY OF NATURAL LAW

A distinguished physicist-turned-clergyman has written:

In an earlier age, miracles would have been one of the strongest
weapons in the armoury of apologetic. A man who did such things
must at the very least have the power of God with him. Jesus
himself is represented as using this argument when he said, 'If it is
by the finger of God that I cast out demons then the kingdom of
God has come upon you' (Luke 11.20). For us today, by one of
those twists that make up intellectual history, miracles are rather
an embarrassment. We are so impressed by the regularity of the
world that any story which is full of strange happenings acquires
an air of fairytale and invention. (Polkinghorne 1983, 54)

The historical twist referred to by John Polkinghorne was an
inevitable consequence of the separation of observation (or test) from

interpretation, which is the essential feature of what we call science. Before the sixteenth century, 'how' and 'why' questions were answered in much the same way: acorns fell to the ground so that new oaks might grow; rain came so crops might flourish and people feed, and so on. The realization that the same event could be interpreted in more than one way led to an emphasis on mechanism, and therefore on the uniformity and predictability of natural events, with a consequent restricting of divine activity to the ever-decreasing gaps in knowledge. God became unnecessary, except as a rationalization for the unexplainable (Coulson 1955).

By the seventeenth century, scientists were using the 'laws of nature' in the modern sense, and the physical and (increasingly) the biological worlds were regarded as self-regulating causal *nexi*. God was merely the 'First Cause', and could intervene in the world only by breaking or suspending the 'natural laws'. Locke and Hume used the determinism of Newtonian physics to argue that natural laws were inviolable, and therefore that miracles could not happen (Brown 1984, 42–6, 80–6). Their conclusion seemed to be vindicated in the nineteenth century when the Darwinian revolution purged from biological systems the simple notion of purpose and created pattern. And as Don Cupitt says, 'religion was more badly shaken when the universe went historical in the nineteenth century than it had been when it went mechanical in the seventeenth century' (Cupitt 1984, 58). The futility of believing in a god unable to do anything exposed the problem that spurred the English bishops to reaffirm that miracles could happen (Harris 1985).

MIRACLES AND MECHANISMS

Defenders of miracles have tended to descend into an unconvincing mysticism or an assault on determinism. A few decades ago, it was fashionable to claim that physical indeterminancy gave God enough freedom to control events. Biological indeterminancy is a live debate now, particularly in sociobiology (Berry 1984, 102–6). For example, R. C. Lewontin (an American geneticist who would be unlikely to argue that miracles are common or important) strongly attacked the reality of biological laws beyond

> very special rules of comportment or particular physical entities
> . . . If we are to find biological laws that can be models for social
> laws, they will surely be at the level of laws of population, laws of

evolution, laws of organisation. But it is precisely such laws that are absent in biology, although many attempts have been made to erect them. (Lewontin 1985, 21)

However, the case for miracles does not depend on indeterminancy, since the intellectual orthodoxy stemming from Hume's underlying thesis is not as strong as it is usually made out to be. C. S. Lewis pointed this out succinctly:

> of course we must agree with Hume that if there is absolutely 'uniform experience' against miracles, if in other words they have never happened, why then they never have. Unfortunately we know the experience against them to be uniform only if we know that all the reports of them are false. And we can know all the reports to be false only if we know already that miracles have never occurred. In fact, we are arguing in a circle. (Lewis 1977b, 106)

Exposing the fallacy of Hume's attack on miracles also reveals that it is based on an unjustified assumption, that events have only a single cause and can be fully explained if that cause is known. This is logically wrong. For example, an oil painting can be 'explained' in terms either of the distribution of pigments or the intention and design of the artist; both explanations refer to the same physical object, but they complement rather than conflict. In the same way, a miracle may be the work of (say) a divine upholder of the physical world rather than a false observation or unknown cause. Such an interpretation does not depend on any irruption into a causal network, since the determinism of the machine is only one of the levels of the phenomenon (*sensu* Polanyi 1969).

'Complementary' explanations of causation are excluded only by making the reductionist assumption that a single identifiable cause is the sole effect operating in a particular situation. This assumption is common, but unnecessary and restrictive. The Nobel laureate Peter Medawar has dissected this clearly:

> That there is indeed a limit upon science is made very likely by the existence of questions that science cannot answer and that no conceivable advances of science would empower it to answer. These are the questions that children ask – the 'ultimate questions' of Karl Popper. I have in mind such questions as: How did everything begin? What are we all here for? What is the point

of living? Doctrinaire positivism – now something of a period piece – dismissed all such questions as nonquestions or pseudo-questions such as only simpletons ask and only charlatans of one kind or another profess to be able to answer. This peremptory dismissal leaves one empty and dissatisfied because the questions make sense to those who ask them, and the answers to those who try to give them; but whatever else may be in dispute, it would be universally agreed that it is not to science that we should look for answers. There is then a prima facie case for the existence of a limit to scientific understanding. (Medawar 1984, 66)

As far as miracles are concerned, this means that they are impossible to prove or disprove on normal scientific criteria; we accept the possibility of their occurrence by faith, and equally deny them by faith. Even if we know or deduce the mechanism behind a miracle, this does not necessarily remove the miraculous element. For example, the Bible tells us that the Israelites crossed the Red Sea dry-shod because 'all that night the Lord drove the sea back with a strong east wind and turned it into dry land' (Exod. 14.21); the significance of the miracle lies in its timing and place rather than its actual occurrence.

IMPLICATIONS

The act of faith that denies the possibility of miracles is a straight-forward reductionist judgement. Miracles by themselves are always susceptible to an explanation other than the miraculous (even if they have physical manifestations, such as 'spontaneous' healing or the empty tomb), so the value of the reductionist assumption can be best tested by its implications. These were spelled out with depressing clarity in the nihilism of Jacques Monod (1971), and comprehensively answered by W. H. Thorpe (1978), who expounded a version of the dualism of Sherrington, Eccles and Popper, which is kin to the complementarity espoused above (MacKay 1979a; MacKay 1979b).

There are implications of embracing a reductionist determinism which impinge on two recent controversies; creationism and the definition of human life.

Creationism is largely an insistence that God made the world in a particular way, without using 'normal' evolutionary mechanisms. Part of this claim stems from a restricted interpretation of the Bible, but it has the effect of prescribing that God acted in an interventionist

fashion. Notwithstanding, it is entirely consistent with both evolutionary biology and Bible texts to maintain that God worked
'complementarily' with genetic processes so that the world is both a
causal outcome of mutation, selection, and so on, but *also* a divine
creation. The creationist position is at odds with both scientific and
theistic understanding (Midgley 1985; Berry 1988).

Individual human life has a physiological and genetic continuity
with that of other humans (and indeed other animals); the *value* of
individual life lies not in genetic uniqueness (cancers and
hydatidiform moles are also genetically unique), but in being (in
Christian language) 'made in the image of God'. This *imago* is not a
physical entity, and it is a category mistake to confuse it with genetic
coding or mental function. Notwithstanding, defenders of the
inviolability of the early embryo make this precise mistake. The
imago is a non-biological attribute, and there is no logical or
scriptural reason for assuming that it is present from conception
(Rogerson 1985, 85). If this simple point was realized, the ethical
debate over developments in human reproduction could proceed more
sensibly.

The conventional view of miracles is that they depend on
supernatural intervention in, or suspension of, the natural order.
Some theologians have been over-impressed with scientific
determinism, and have attempted a demythologized (miracle-free)
religion. This endeavour is now unfashionable, but it is worse than
that; H. R. Nebelsick has characterized it as a speculative device
imposed on unsuspecting persons 'based . . . on false presuppositions
about both science and the "scientific world-view"' (Nebelsick 1984,
239). This is no help to scientists, and an interventionalist God will
always be an embarrassment to us.

I believe that the interpretation that miracles are a necessary but
unpredictable consequence of a God who holds the world in being is
more plausible and more scriptural than deist interventionism. This
does not mean that apparent miracles should be approached with any
less objectivity than we would employ for any scientific observation;
our standards of evidence should be just as rigorous. Those who deny
the possibility of miracles are exercising their own brand of faith; but
it is based on a questionable assumption, and one which creates
problems with its implications, never mind historical problems with
the empty tomb and such like. Miracles in the New Testament are
described as unusual events which are wonders due to God's power,

intended as signs. Confining oneself wholly to this category (leaving aside the question of whether other sorts of miracles occur), this makes at least some miracles expectable and non-capricious, and independent of any knowledge of their mechanism.

In his exposition of the 'Two Cultures', C. P. Snow described the scorn of the one for the other as intellectual Ludditism (Snow 1975, 21). Miracles are examples of events which may easily be denied by an illegitimate reductionist Ludditism; scientific reality will be hindered in the process. A doctrinaire disbelief in miracle is not 'more scientific' than a willingness to accept that they may occur. Some years ago Sir George Porter, a former President of the Royal Society, London, wrote:

> Most of our anxieties, problems and unhappiness today stem from a lack of purpose which was rare a century ago and which can fairly be blamed on the consequences of scientific inquiry . . . There is one great purpose for man and for us today, and that is to try to discover man's purpose by every means in our power. That is the ultimate relevance of science. (*The Times*, 21 June 1975)

He was not writing specifically about miracles, but his argument applies. Miracles are not inherently impossible or unbelievable, and acceptance of their existence does not necessarily involve credulity, but does involve recognizing that science has limits.

6
THE SPIRIT AS LORD:
CHRISTIANITY, MODERNITY AND FREEDOM

Colin E. Gunton

I

Two successive television programmes broadcast in the autumn of 1986 provide the theme for this paper. The first was a performance of Beethoven's ninth symphony: a monument, as the announcer reminded us, to the great achievements of the human spirit. The second took us to the English landscape, and its incomparable beauties. And yet what were the images which remained in the mind? The rape of peatlands by automatic excavator in the interests of quick profit; and a litter of plastic bags. On the one hand, the glories of modern achievement, set free by the great movement of European humanism; on the other, some of its by-products, the sheer tawdriness and destructiveness of which surround us on every side.

Modern civilization is a mass of such contradictions. Juxtaposed are a naïve belief in progress and a deep pessimism, sometimes in the same person; or the technological achievements and wealth which would civilize, but which seem incapable, sometimes, of building an attractive block of offices. The contradictions are in large part anthropological, as the illustrations from the autumn's television reveal only too well, for they are a function of the anthropocentrism of the age. On the one hand, we have claimed a kind of divinity for the human race – like the psalmist, but in a very different way, elevating ourselves to be near the angels. On the other, we have turned ourselves into mere consumers, knowing the price of everything and the value of very little. On the one hand, we are humanists; and, on the other, have lived in a century that is the most destructive of human life there has ever been, and bids fair to destroy even more. It can also be said that an age dedicated to the advance of human freedom has produced, indeed, democracies, but at the same time a clutch of tyrannies of scarcely paralleled viciousness.

The purpose of these introductory remarks is not to belittle our times – to remind us of our ethical infancy – so much as to ask whence such an astonishing turn of affairs could come to be, in which contradictions which make Christianity's deepest paradoxes a model of rationality are comfortably assimilated (by Christians as well as by others) with scarce an awareness of their absurdity. The answer – and it gives a reason why Christians should beware of claiming innocence or superiority in the matter – is to be found in large part in our own theological history. Modern humanism is to a great extent a reaction against the form Christianity took during its apparently most flourishing phase. Because the Christian Church has for much of its history behaved in contradiction of both the words and manner of life of its Lord, our era has come to believe that to glorify God can only be at the cost of our humanity. And so the contradictions of the age have developed: by glorifying ourselves instead, we attempt to become what we are not. But that is to anticipate a fuller telling of the story.

The problem is set out in Dostoyevsky's story of the Grand Inquisitor in *The Brothers Karamazov* (1880). Those who know the story will remember that it tells of a return of Christ, not in glory but in a humanity that is yet recognizable, at the height of the Inquisition. He is hauled before the Grand Inquisitor, who tells him that he was wrong. The Church knew better, and has therefore found it necessary to improve upon his work. Jesus brought freedom, but in view of the fact that people were not ready for this freedom, it has been replaced by miracle, mystery and authority. The underlying suggestion of this part of Dostoyevsky's tale is that the Church transformed the faith of free believers into an oppression. The point is hardly a new one, and can be (and frequently has been) made too much of. But there is enough truth in the complaint to account for the development of the modern reaction against Christendom. Against a God who is the personification of power and imposed authority, the modern movement, represented especially by the Enlightenment, asserted, and to a large extent justifiably asserted, the necessity of human freedom.

The problem is that the freedom which was demanded was not always the freedom of the gospel, and for a number of reasons. First, it was regarded not as a gift to be received but as a possession to be grasped. That which had been usurped by an authoritarian institution was, hardly surprisingly, demanded as a right by those from whom it had been taken. Second, the freedom that was demanded tended to be conceived individualistically, of the claim of my rights against yours, my freedom to do what I want with my own life and the world.

Third, it tended to be a freedom of dominion, of control, in marked
contrast to the dominion of Genesis 1—2, where the human race is
called to cultivate a garden in partnership with the beasts, not as their
absolute disposer. Put the three features together, and you gain a
picture of humankind as absolute lord, arrogating divine powers in an
abstract way, grasping at divinity. The root of the contradictions of
modernity is thus a contradiction of life: the attempt to be what we
are not.

It was Søren Kierkegaard who, in intellectual engagement with
Hegel, isolated the theological heart of the matter. Hegel's response
to the crisis of the modern world was a work of genius. He realized
only too well that the collapse of the once unified medieval
civilization would bring in its train a fragmentation of culture and
society. Unlike some nineteenth-century theologians, notably in
England, however, he did not view the Middle Ages nostalgically, as
a model to be imitated, but saw in them and in some features of post-
Reformation thought alike an unacceptable authoritarianism. In that
respect, whatever the totalitarian outcome of aspects of his thought,
Hegel was a philosopher of freedom, a thoroughly modern man. His
daring response to the crisis brought on by the Enlightenment was to
attempt to reshape Western culture by the use of central Christian
categories, particularly those of spirit and incarnation. But the
Christian categories were at the same time transformed in such a way
that instead of moving away from the modern tendency to divinize
humankind, Hegel brought it to a kind of apotheosis.

He did this in two ways. The first was a transformation of the
concept of God. In place of a transcendent creator – thought to be the
enemy of freedom by virtue of his otherness – Hegel developed the
notion of a God who realized himself within the world of space and
time: an immanent deity, coming to be in the dialectical movement of
history. The second was to draw the corresponding Christological
conclusions from the revamped theology. What had Christianity
traditionally thought? That Jesus of Nazareth was God made man for
our salvation. Hegel fought to retain what he saw to be the elements
of truth in that doctrine, but he was more interested in its general
possibilities for a philosophy of culture. The God-man becomes a
symbol of a possibility inherent in humanity – a freedom to be
realized by ourselves – and therefore a call to all to realize their
divinity. To put it the other way round, God is to come to be as the
result of humankind's realization of its inherent divinity.

Kierkegaard realized that Hegel and his successors – the 'relevant' and modernizing churchmen of liberal Denmark – were simply using Christianity as the means by which to 'baptize' the emerging liberal society. By the fact that he called the phenomenon 'Christendom' he showed that he was aware of the pedigree of the programme: it was precisely what had been done with Christianity before, and so was continuous, for all its appeal to freedom, with the programme of the Grand Inquisitor. Looking forward, he showed that its consequences were ultimately authoritarian and totalitarian. Equally importantly, however, he penetrated, particularly perhaps in *Training in Christianity* (1850), to the theological question underlying the new theology. To teach the divinity of the lowly, suffering Jesus is one thing – and authentic Christianity; to teach the inherent or even potential divinity of us all is paganism, and the opposite of Christianity.

Kierkegaard is not always fair to Hegel, but he is basically right, especially in view of what some of Hegel's successors on both the left and the right have since made of him. For it is our grasped divinity that is the problem, and leads directly to the contradictions of modernity. It must also be remembered that Hegel is not alone, and that the company he keeps is equally influential. Before Hegel, Kant's moral philosophy had moved towards a position in which human moral decision was given a function which in effect placed it in the place of God ('knowing good and evil'). Similarly, Hegel's great contemporary, the theologian Schleiermacher, though in many ways different, developed a Christology whose outcome is in effect the same as that of Hegel. Jesus is the man whose religious experience represents a virtual existence of God in him, and is as such the possibility and example of our incipient divinizing. The shared danger is that to seek the divine too soon and too immanent to the present human condition is to lose the human. By another path, accordingly, we return to the place where we began: the contradiction of our essential reality in the attempt of the finite to exercise the prerogatives of the infinite.

II

What has come to be called 'modernist' theology takes its assumptions, essentially, from the combined influence of Kant, Schleiermacher and Hegel. It is not, of course, all of a piece; nor

should it be possible for anyone writing after the Enlightenment to
be unaffected by the movements of truth in the modern rejection of
authoritarian forms of Christianity and of political order. The
complaint is not against the aim of the modernity, but against the fact
that its outcome has been the opposite of that intended. The old
authoritarianism has not been driven out, but has been replaced with a
new one. If, therefore, there is to be opposition to modernity, it must
be made not in the name of some obscurantist authority, but because
its end product has not been liberation but a deeper slavery. If this is
so, the appropriate response is not a return to the past, but a quest for
the possibility of freedom: in this case, the freedom which is the
promise of the gospel and the gift of the Spirit. The devil can be
driven out only by putting something better in its place. To be sure,
theological papers do not often drive out devils, but they can do the
preliminary work of questioning assumptions. Certain of the working
assumptions of much modern theology militate against the freedom
that is the gift of God the Spirit. What are they?

The first is the assumption that 'modern man' is a different kind of
person from all who went before. Here, if the divinity of the human
mind is not always asserted or supposed, something like it is often
near to the surface: that we *necessarily* see things more clearly (for
example) than did they who wrote the Bible and most theology up to
the modern era. The chief objection to such an assumption is that it
does justice neither to the achievements of the ancients nor to the
fallibility and finitude of the moderns. It makes the modern age an
idol, and blinds us to the continuity of our humanity with that of
other times. Equally seriously, it introduces a savage rent in the
tradition. One of the positive lessons we have learned from modern
thought is to appreciate the movement of thought and culture from
one generation to another. To know our place in the tradition is
possible only if there are no artificial breaches. Modernity must be
rooted in its past if it is not to be treated as something above
criticism.

The second assumption that is often made is that any God about
whom we may speak must be discernible as a feature of the general
structure of our world: he must be conceived immanently. The
obverse of this dogma – and it is a marked feature of Mr Cupitt's
writings – is that any God conceived to be other than the world as its
creator and redeemer is necessarily the foe of human freedom: if we
are to be free, we must be free from the authority of the *other*. There

are, to be sure, various versions of this dogma which relate us closely
to the problem of the Grand Inquisitor. Some would hold that we may
speak of God only as a symbol of certain possibilities inherent within
us; others would allow speech of a divinity who qualifies or works
within the general (evolutionary) order of things, as for example
G. W. H. Lampe in *God as Spirit* (1971). The general direction,
however, is held in common. The otherness of God is a positive
menace to human flourishing, and the more we involve him in the
processes of history and evolution the better. Hell is not only other
people, but the otherness of God.

Closely linked with that second assumption is a third, this time
about the nature of human freedom. To be human is, on this account,
to be an autonomous individual, the creator of one's destiny and the
decider of one's ethics. The authentic human person is the one whose
decisions are made on the basis of no 'external' authority, certainly
not that of tradition or Church (even though some moderns are
willing to concede to the state – as in some way incorporating
individual freedom – an authority beyond that ever claimed by the
Church). The way this emerges in modern theology is to be observed
in its Christology. Modernist Christology has ceased to see Jesus as
the incarnate Word, the human agent of a divine redemption, coming
from the Father and dying for us. In that respect, it has followed the
lead of Kant, Schleiermacher and Hegel. In its place, we have Jesus
the example of autonomous humanity, an autonomy expressed in
various ways: existentialist, moralistic, political. The underlying
assumption is that for Jesus to be divine is the same thing as for him
to express a divinity which is inherent in our humanity. The
ambiguity intrinsic to this dogma was well expressed by the words
placed by *Private Eye* on the lips of one of the essayists of *The Myth
of God Incarnate*: 'Jesus was no more divine than I am.'

As has already been hinted, the greatest danger presented by the
uncritical adoption of the assumptions of the age is of a collapse into
new forms of authoritarianism. They are about us all the time: religious fundamentalisms of Bible, experience or tradition; political fundamentalisms of left and right. One welcome refuge from the storms
of a life lived in contradiction is the safe haven of some apparently
secure and tested 'orthodoxy'. But that is to return to the equal and
opposite contradiction, to place one's faith equally in a divinity
which can be identified with some finite institution or form of words.
If theology can do no better than that, it had better leave the battle

to more determined combatants. It seems to me, however, that the
problem, like all real problems, is at root theological, so that the
challenge must not be evaded.

III

We have so far observed two features of the intellectual landscape of
our time. The first is that the modern age, in its justified rebellion
against authoritarian religion and politics, has generated a nest of
contradictions. I have argued that the source of the contradictions is
a failure to distinguish between finite and infinite. For the finite to
behave as if it were infinite is to live a contradiction. Our modern
world is living out that contradiction today. The second is that
the theology known as modernist – that which accepts the main
assumptions of the dogma of modernity – is unable to find a way out
of the contradictions because it operates on essentially the same
assumptions. To question questionable assumptions, however,
requires a viewpoint from which the landscape can be surveyed. Is
there one?

Because we cannot jump out of our conceptual skins to a place
where we can operate with a total freedom from presupposition, we
must be grateful that there is no absolute division between
modernism and some supposedly pure orthodox standpoint from
which *ex cathedra* pronouncements can be made. In most of us there
is a continuing conversation between two sides – that which would
accept the good things of the modern world and that which is wary of
all who bring gifts. Moreover, it is possible to see the history of
theological thought since the dawn of the modern era as a continuing
conversation in which elements of a tradition stretching deeper into
the past continually make their presence felt. (After all, one of the
contentions of this paper is that it is wrong to accept at face value
modernism's claim that there can be a completely new start.)

The crucial move is to show that even on the ground marked out
by modern ideology there are questions to be asked and distinctions
to be drawn which are not always brought to the surface. Let us
therefore take, as our paradigm the question that has already occupied
us as the central one for modern humanism: freedom and autonomy.
Modernism is right to hold that the two are inextricably related. To be
free is to live according to the law of one's being. It is to be and to
do, freely, that which belongs to us rather than that which is the

alien behest of another. Where, then, is to be found the difference between the freedom which is grasped at, and which draws ineluctably to contradiction, and what is here being claimed to be the freedom of the gospel?

'Where the Spirit of the Lord is, there is freedom' (2 Cor. 3.17). The dispute within theology about freedom is at bottom a dispute about who the Spirit is and how he operates. All Western theology, pre- and postmodern alike, has tended to conceive the Spirit as a force operating within a person and qualifying in a right direction that person's life and activity. Pre-modern thought, particularly in what we now call the Catholic tradition, tended to channel that Spirit through ecclesiastical institutions, calling down upon itself in the process often justified accusations of attempting to control and limit the free activity of God. In rebelling against such a conception, modernity secularized the action of the Spirit, which in the process became not so much a distinct divine *hypostasis* as a possession inherent within the life of the individual or of modern culture. That which had been claimed as the possession of the institution became the equally confidently grasped qualification of the individual or of modernity as a whole. It is no accident that *spirit* was so central a category for the immanentist thought of Hegel.

The mistake of both these tendencies (for they are only tendencies, whose extremes have been outlined here) was to identify the Spirit too closely with immanent human realities. Here, too, we must discern a failure to maintain the essential distinctness of finite and infinite. The Spirit is not the automatic qualification of anything finite, whether Church or individual. He is the Spirit of the Lord, the distinct but inseparable person of the Trinity. First of all he is the other, who proceeds in eternity from the Father: in Irenaeus' terms, one of the two hands of God. The sin of the West – Church and modernity alike – has been against the true otherness of the Spirit, against his true infinity and freedom, in an attempt to institutionalize or assimilate his work to some finite reality or work.

It was Kierkegaard who, following in the steps of Tertullian, stressed (especially in the early works written under the pseudonym of the sceptic Johannes Climacus) the essential paradox of Christianity: that in Jesus Christ time and eternity, man and God, are given together in a way that baffles reason. Kierkegaard stressed the paradox to the point of contradiction, but his contention remains that this makes for greater truth, greater respect for the way things are, than the logical and immanentist blandness which characterizes the work of so much recent Christian apologetic. In this paper, however, I have tried to isolate and expound another paradox of time and eternity, the pneumatological. It is only the otherness, the eschatological transcendence of the Holy Spirit, his irreducibility to anything human, which sets us free. Such a claim is paradoxical for a number of reasons, but largely because it appears to take away our autonomy, our apparent need to realize our own humanity. (On modernist assumptions, it appears to be not a paradox but a contradiction, because any autonomy that is *given* rather than *taken* will contradict assumptions about what it is to be human.)

But 'where the Spirit of the Lord is, there is freedom'. Why? It is a fact of our being that we are truly ourselves when we are constituted by our relation to the other. There are many levels at which this must be understood. The first is the most obvious. It is no surprise that the chief casualty of the rationalism of the Age of Reason was the Christian doctrine of salvation and its associated doctrine of sin. If there is already a divine Spirit within me, if to be human is to be at least potentially divine, salvation consists in realizing my reality on my own. Against this, classic Christian teaching (as it is to be found in Paul and in representatives of both East and West such as Athanasius and Augustine) is that apart from redemption in Christ and its realization through the Spirit there is no true humanity. It is only by the agency of God's two hands, Son and Spirit, that what is fallen, stained and alienated from its true being may be lifted up and restored. We need the other in order to be redeemed.

That first level, however, cannot stand on its own, if only because to assert it is simply to produce a counter-assertion to the modern claim that such a redemption is simply not needed. One positivism cannot be vanquished by the naked assertion of another. Rather, we must penetrate deeper, to show that it is not simply a question of fallenness, but that our being as human people is adequately encompassed neither by modern individualism nor by its *alter ego* collectivism. We begin, however, with the development of the point about the need for redemption. It is only an apparent paradox to say that to be myself I must be freed from myself. To set myself up as the centre of the world – as we all attempt in different ways and at different times – is to place myself out of the reach of my fellows and therefore to deny the possibility of human community. In particular, it is to attempt to live as if I do not need my neighbour in order to be

as I really am. Hell, therefore, is other people only because it is first
of all myself.

In what sense does such a way of being deny our human reality?
John Macmurray in his important *Persons in Relation* (1961)
demonstrates that human persons are what they are only by virtue
of what they receive from and give to each other. Children are
constituted by their relations first with their mothers, then with a
wider and ever-growing circle. Such relatedness is not accidental, but
the centre of what it is to be human. There are no persons who
'happen to have' relationships with others, although that is the way in
which moderns frequently talk. Persons are what they are in their
relations. In that sense, both heaven and hell are other people. We
unmake as well as make each other's personhood. Common to both
sides of that matter – the making and unmaking of each other as
persons – is a denial of naïve doctrines of individualism and
autonomy. We cannot extricate our being from that of others. If there
is to be a genuine doctrine of autonomy, of living according to the
law of our being, then it must embrace what Daniel Hardy (1989) has
called our sociality: our being in relation as determinative of our
created reality.

Macmurray's insights are profound because they derive ultimately
from theological sources. It is an element of the Christian doctrine
of the Trinity, recently spelled out in John Zizioulas' *Being as
Communion* (1985), that God is what he is as a communion of
persons. The three persons constitute each other as persons, receive
from and give to each other what they are, and only as such are one
God. It is, in the terms of this paper, only through their otherness
to and distinctness from each other that they are able to be mutually
constitutive. Their being consists in their free communion of giving
and receiving: that is the *autonomy* of God, his inner orderedness in
free relations.

To seek a genuine alternative to the inadequacy of Western
theology, both ancient and modernistic alike, we must attend to
the implications of such a trinitarianism. If God *is* only in the free
communion of distinct persons, how is our own freedom to be
conceived? Two points should be made. The first follows from the
more recent argument of the paper: we are free not when we extricate
ourselves from each other as individuals or when as in totalitarianism
we compel each other to be free – for there lies the way of treating
others as things – but when, in analogy with the trinitarian

hypostases, we freely share in the constituting of each other as *particular* persons. The tragedy of the historical Christian Church is that this dimension of its life has been reduced to a minimum. Particularly since the developments consequent on Constantine's legislation, it has often operated as an institution to which otherwise unrelated individuals come for salvation. The effective community has too often been, despite the rhetoric of service, a male caste, devoted to maintaining its privileges rather than to the creation of genuine community of women and men. There have been whole classes whose function has been to give rather than to receive, and vice versa.

Here once again we see the moment of truth in the modern rebellion that is characterized by the story of the Grand Inquisitor. The outbreak of feminist protest (merely secularizing though it must sometimes appear) is only one manifestation of a historical series of revolts against a system which has effectively denied community, particularly in rendering some – lay as well as women – largely passive rather than actively free. We shall finally overcome the modernist threat to Christianity not by berating its follies, manifold as they are, but by the practical faithfulness of building communities in which the free otherness-in-relationship of all particular persons may be given leave to grow.

The second point follows from the wider theological framework of the paper. Human community is the community of finite and fallen human beings: therefore the freedom to be with and for each other has to be received ever and again as gift. It is only as God is our other that this can take place. Here we must take leave of one of the dogmas of modernity. The modern tendency to conceive God as immanent is not our liberation but our enslavement. The closer the world is tied up with the immanence of God, the more it loses its otherness and therefore its autonomy and freedom to be itself. The doctrine of the incarnation is not the principle of a general immanence, but of a particular immanence realized and set free by the Spirit. It was only by virtue of his relation to this other that Jesus realized his divine and human calling.

The Spirit's activity in freeing Jesus to be himself – as is instanced in the temptation narratives – provides a model for human liberation in general. Jesus' particular calling was to be one kind of Messiah rather than another: to be in a certain definite relationship to the people of Israel, and so ultimately to the whole of humanity. Human freedom, so far as we can speak of it in general, is that which enables people to be constituted as *particular* persons in free and social relationships. This is not expected to happen only in the Church, for the Spirit is the free Lord; but the Church is there to embody the kind of freedom in community which is God's will for human life everywhere. That is why we must say that only where the Spirit of the Lord is, is there freedom. The Spirit is the Father's liberating otherness, realizing in our present the life of the age to come. Without that, there is no freedom, only enslavement to the finite. That is the paradox of freedom.

The argument of this paper is not a plea for paradox for its own sake, but for an acceptance of the nature of human finitude and the limits of human achievement and control. The 'paradoxes' of Christianity are truer to what we are than the manifest existential contradictions of modern ideology. Freedom is freedom when it is received as a gift, from God and from each other, not when it is grasped as an inherent divinity. This freedom takes shape at the human level in mutually constitutive relations with the other. The shame of the Church is its failure in so much of its own life to realize this freedom. Its glory is not its institutional success, but its calling to reflect the divine light that shines in the face of Jesus Christ. That is the work of the Spirit who is Lord.

7

WHAT IS WRONG WITH BIBLICAL EXEGESIS?
REFLECTIONS UPON C. S. LEWIS' CRITICISMS

Alasdair I. C. Heron

C. S. Lewis was well known for his regular attacks on the use of the Bible by academic biblical scholarship, which he regarded as all too often tiresome, trivial and blinkered, overladen by historicism, short-sighted in its understanding of the message of the Bible, and therefore incapable of unfolding that message in a way that could catch and set afire the imagination of people in the twentieth century.

As a Christian working in the field of literature, Lewis was convinced of the power of the Christian message to shape and inform thought, imagination and life today and tomorrow as well as yesterday. His more academic publications were less coloured by this concern, for he was careful to distinguish between his personal and theological interests and his responsibilities as an Oxford don and, later, a Cambridge professor of English Literature. But it was his implicitly or explicitly theological writing that won him his place as a major advocate of Christian faith in the twentieth century. The liveliness of his style, the incisiveness of his analysis and the imaginative resources on which he so powerfully drew combined to make him one of the most influential Christian writers of his day.

What did Lewis have against his contemporary world of biblical exegesis? His complaint was that it all too often tended to reduce the Bible and its message to a dead letter. It had learned, and learned well, to treat the biblical texts as objects of scientific, archaeological, historical and literary analysis – and in the process rendered itself incapable of listening to them with awe, astonishment and appreciation. The world of the biblical exegetes had become cold and empty – empty of miracle, empty of revelation, empty of imagination. It was a world in which no 'distant strains of triumph' could be heard, a world in which it was no longer seriously believed that the Church was on the march against the gates of hell, 'terrible as an army with banners' – whereby Lewis saw this army quite simply as made up of perfectly decent, normal and ordinary people who do not accept, refuse to believe in, and therefore constitute the most serious threat to Satan's drive for world-domination.

In Lewis' eyes, it was this very world of the everyday which is ever and again 'surprised by joy', illumined by transcendent light, a world of pilgrims looking forward 'till we have faces', a world of 'ordinary' people who precisely in their ordinariness are surrounded by intimations of grace, who are (or ought to be) on the way 'higher up and further in', but who are threatened and sometimes overcome by selfishness, meanness, arrogance and despair – a world, as he described it in *The Great Divorce* (1946), in which we are on the road either to the solidity and substance of heaven or to the last gnawing emptiness, the self-consuming insubstantiality of hell.

Lewis was above all a student of *literature*, though his early studies had been in philosophy. Unlike some other literary critics, however (most notably his Cambridge counterpart, F. R. Leavis), his interest in literature was not primarily *historical*, *social* or *political*. Literature presented itself to him as the art which at its best and highest is concerned with the profoundest depths and highest calling of human nature itself. He was and remained to the end of his days a Romantic, radically opposed to the reduction of literary criticism – or theology – to mere historicism or to a political or ideological programme. His thought was fed and his imagination nourished by the medieval allegories of love, by Milton, Bunyan and George Macdonald – and by the Bible.

Lewis' opposition to what he took to be the programme of contemporary biblical exegesis was especially sharply formulated in reaction to the influence of Karl Barth and, even more, Rudolf Bultmann. In neither case, certainly, does it seem that Lewis was very well informed at first hand on their concerns; Barth in particular had much more in common with Lewis (or vice versa) than Lewis ever realized. (Dorothy Sayers could have taught him better!) But Lewis' especial *bête noire* was Bultmann's 'demythologization' of the New Testament (Bultmann 1953).

Lewis' own view of the issue can perhaps best be understood in the light of his own personal history as illustrated by a conversation some sixty-five years ago with his friend J. R. R. Tolkien, a convinced Roman Catholic and, like Lewis, an enthusiastic student of the old Norse sagas. (Lewis and Tolkien were later to found the 'Inklings', a group of dons and their friends who met regularly in the Thirties in Oxford to hear papers, among them some of Tolkien's preliminary studies for *The Hobbit* and *The Lord of the Rings*.) At the time of this conversation Lewis was an atheistically-inclined agnostic, having abandoned his Ulster Protestant faith some years before. Tolkien tried with all the argumentative power at his command to persuade Lewis that the Christian faith was true precisely because it answered all the longings incorporated in the innumerable myths giving expression to the strivings of humanity after a profounder destiny than the world as it exists appears to promise. Lewis' answer then was: 'Myths are lies, even though breathed through silver.' When, not very much later, Lewis was reconverted to Christian faith, this brought a turn of 180 degrees in his attitude to 'myth'. From then on 'myth' signified for him a literary and imaginative category and form deliberately designed and intended by divine purpose to engage our human imagination in willing response to the message of the gospel.

Paradoxically enough, this contributed to Lewis' estrangement from Tolkien in later years. Tolkien was deeply committed to what he called 'subcreation', the imaginative construction of a literary world which might indeed reflect the reality of the actual world as seen through the double prism of Nordic mythology and Roman Catholic dogma, but at the same time constituted a fresh 'subcreative' achievement. He demanded that others too should be as serious as he in the work of 'subcreation', and found Lewis' Narnia stories deficient by this standard. Lewis, by contrast, sought to rearticulate the classical themes of Christian faith together with *motifs* from the sagas and classical mythology as speaking to people of every age and era. He was less interested in constructing fictional 'alternative worlds' than in drawing on the resources of ancient myth, the gospel and contemporary imagination to hammer home the message that everyday human life is besieged by God and the devil. His writing is in intention the reverse of escapist; even when he goes on to develop conceptions of 'other worlds', as in the Narnia series of children's books or the *Out of the Silent Planet* trilogy, it is always *this* world that he is concerned with, *this* world as illuminated in the light both of ancient myth and of the biblical message.

It is not surprising that Lewis reacted so negatively to Bultmann's attempt to demythologize the New Testament. Lewis himself was not best placed to appreciate Bultmann's motives in advancing this programme, which he first formulated in 1941 in an address to a meeting of representatives of the German Confessing Church. The Confessing Church was confronted at that time with the massive challenge of German National Socialism, with its mythological and ideological programme and its apparent success in breaking and reshaping the mould of national, political and military history. Lewis' reaction took no account of this; it bore less upon the original German context of the programme than upon its influence in English biblical and theological scholarship. The net result of the appropriation of Bultmann's ideas in academic theology in England after 1945 seemed to Lewis to run out into the sand of a total evacuation of biblical meaning, a dissolution of theological substance, an abdication of evangelical conviction, and a failure of Christian imagination.

Were Lewis' diagnosis and reaction justified? Or were they, as some would have it, simply those of a disappointed, cross-grained and bad-tempered outsider – albeit one possessing rare gifts of literary communication? Whatever might be said here about Lewis himself, it is hard to resist the conclusion that he had put his finger upon a weakness of *some* Anglo-Saxon theology and exegesis which has become even more apparent in the last twenty years. The kind of biblical scholar in mind here might be one who has picked up a smattering of German New Testament exegesis (usually at second hand), who is profoundly impressed by the fact of the Enlightenment (without necessarily knowing much about it), and who is therefore convinced that the New Testament has little or nothing to say to the people of the modern era. His (or her) primary convictions as Lewis understood them might be paraphrased as follows:

The Bible is an ancient collection of documents which is to be studied in theological faculties because the churches require the same. This gives us something to do, and justifies the drawing of our salaries.

Our chief responsibility is to make clear to theological students that the Bible possesses no authority, is a highly doubtful and arbitrary collection, and is in any case far remote from the concerns and interests of human life today. For the Bible was written before the Enlightenment and is therefore wholly *passé*, indeed meaningless, for the modern world.

If, occasionally, we nevertheless find it appropriate to stress the authority of the Bible, it is only to make clear that the entire tradition of Christian dogmatic theology is not biblically secured. This enables us to use the Bible (in which we do not really believe, but in which others do) as a means to undermine their confidence in the faith of the Church.

We continue to engage in our learned study of the biblical writings because that is our job, because progress in research holds out the hope of academic and ecclesiastical advancement, and because we might otherwise become unemployable.

This is, of course, a caricature, though some pretty close approximations to it can be found alive and well in various corners of the British academic and ecclesiastical establishment. Nevertheless, it would be grossly unfair to apply this caricature to more than a minority of our present biblical scholars or to give the impression – as Lewis was on occasion not above doing – that the whole enterprise of critical biblical scholarship had gone to seed in this fashion.

In much the same way, Lewis' *The Abolition of Man* (1943) takes as its target a thoroughly insignificant book which few would ever have heard of if Lewis himself had not attacked it for its reduction of ethical and aesthetic appreciation and judgement to expressions of subjective feeling. Yet Lewis had rightly detected that what that book articulated was a much more widespread attitude, shared by many others; and it was the attitude, and the book as symptomatic of it, not the book in itself, that primarily concerned him. Similarly, Lewis was certainly less than fair to the majority of British biblical scholars in his strictures on their biblical scholarship, yet did at the same time point to real dangers deserving serious attention.

Bultmann's programme of demythologization of the New Testament was not intended to empty the New Testament or the message of the gospel of meaning for the people of the twentieth century, but to open up that meaning afresh. To that end, Bultmann employed an *existentialist* interpretation: he sought to ask what meaning and implications *for human existence* are conveyed in mythical patterns of thinking and speaking, and to uncover these in their abiding relevance for his contemporaries. In this, however, his interest remained *theological*: the really important question was that of the challenge of human existence under the word of God, the gospel of the crucified Jesus of Nazareth.

Bultmann's immense appeal to younger German theologians in the generation following the Second World War stemmed in part from the fact that this programme offered a new beginning and a new orientation to those who had been caught up and swept along in the firestorm of Nazi ideology and the nightmare of the Third Reich, with its consequences of national collapse and crushing defeat. But it was also possible, as examples from both Germany and Britain show, for others to take up the call for demythologization simply as showing the New Testament to be largely irrelevant today and to present their own 'existentialist' programmes, purged of any discernible theological or evangelical content or interest.

This is what Lewis seems chiefly to have had in mind in his attacks on Bultmann and New Testament scholarship generally. Certainly, there remained fundamental differences between Lewis and Bultmann, above all in their attitudes to 'myth'. For Bultmann, 'myth' was a form of pre-critical thinking which was no longer viable in the modern world; for Lewis, it was an essential form of communication, belonging ineradicably to divinely created human nature as such. There are good grounds for holding that here Lewis came far closer to the truth of the matter than Bultmann; and Lewis' attacks on post-Bultmann New Testament work must be seen in this light. But the fact remains that Lewis was less concerned with Bultmann's own programme than with what he detected as its reception and application in the habits of thinking of some British biblical and theological work. And here he could be devastating in his criticism – devastating in a way reminiscent of the nineteenth-century Oxford theologian H. L. Mansel. Mansel's *Phrontisterion*, a satirical lampoon on contemporary trends in academic theology, included the following lines on the most prominent 'left-wing' Hegelians in Germany:

> Theologians we,
> Deep thinkers and free.
> From the land of the new Divinity;
> Where critics hunt for the sense sublime,
> Hidden in texts of the olden time,
>   Which none but the sage can see.
> Where Strauss shall teach you how Martyrs died
> For a moral ideal personified.
> A myth and a symbol, which vulgar sense
> Received for historic evidence.
> Where Bauer can prove that true Theology
> Is special and general Anthropology.
> And the essence of worship is only to find
> The realized God in the human mind.
> Where Feuerbach shows how religion began

From the deified feelings and wants of man,
And the Deity owned by the mind reflective
Is Human Consciousness made objective.
   Presbyters, bend,
   Bishops, attend;
The Bible's a myth from beginning to end. (Reardon 1980, 225)

Lewis' reservations on the same subject are most fully spelled out
in the address 'Fern-Seed and Elephants' (originally delivered to
theological students in Westcott House, Cambridge, and
posthumously published in *Fern-Seed and Elephants and Other Essays
on Christianity*. The following quotations are taken from the 1977
edition by Collins Fount; this essay is given there in pp. 104–25).
The title is Lewis' own reminting of Jesus' remark about those who
'strain out a gnat but swallow a camel' (Matt. 23.24), who are
obsessed with minutiae and lose sight of all larger issues. He wanted
to impress upon his hearers 'how a certain sort of theology strikes the
outsider' (p. 104). The reason:

> The minds you daily meet have been conditioned by the same
> studies and prevalent opinions as your own. That may mislead
> you. For of course as priests it is the outsiders you will have to
> cope with . . . The proper study of shepherds is sheep, not (save
> accidentally) other shepherds . . . I am a sheep, telling shepherds
> what only a sheep can tell them. And now I start my bleating.
> (pp. 104–5)

Lewis goes on to distinguish

> two sorts of outsiders: the uneducated, and those who are educated
> in some way but not in your way. How you are to deal with the
> first class, if you hold views like Loisy's or Schweitzer's or
> Bultmann's or Tillich's . . . I simply don't know . . . But that is
> your headache, not mine. (pp. 105–6)

Lewis himself claims 'to belong to the second group of outsiders:
educated, but not theologically educated' (p. 106). The rest of the
address is the attempt of one highly educated, erudite and informed
literary scholar to convey to a group of generally far less educated,
erudite or informed theological students four 'bleats' about the way in
which 'the work of divines engaged in New Testament criticism' is
accepted as 'the authority in deference to whom we are asked to give

up a huge mass of beliefs shared in common by the early Church, the Fathers, the Middle Ages, the Reformers, and even the nineteenth century' (p. 106).

First, says Lewis,

> whatever these men may be as Biblical critics, I distrust them as critics. They seem to me to lack literary judgment, to be imperceptive about the very quality of the texts they are reading . . . A man who has spent his youth and manhood in the minute study of New Testament texts and of other people's studies of them, whose literary experience of those texts lacks any standard of comparison such as can only grow from a wide and deep and genial experience of literature in general, is . . . very likely to miss the obvious things about them. (pp. 106–7)

After giving some illustrations of what strikes him as wooden literary insensitivity on the part of certain New Testament critics, he concludes: 'These men ask me to believe they can read between the lines of the old texts; the evidence is their obvious inability to read (in any sense worth discussing) the lines themselves. They claim to see fern-seed and can't see an elephant ten yards away in broad daylight' (p. 111).

'Now for my second bleat. All theology of the liberal type involves . . . the claim that the real behaviour and purpose and teaching of Christ came very rapidly to be misunderstood and misrepresented by His followers, and has been recovered . . . only by modern scholars' (pp. 111–12). Lewis offers a parallel from the tradition of philosophy in which he himself had been trained: 'One was brought up to believe that the real meaning of Plato had been misunderstood by Aristotle and wildly travestied by the neo-Platonists, only to be recovered by the moderns. When recovered, it turned out (most fortunately) that Plato had really all along been an English Hegelian' (p. 112).

Another illustration of the same tendency is supplied from his own field of literary criticism: 'every week a clever undergraduate, every quarter a dull American don, discovers for the first time what some Shakespearian play really meant' (p. 112). But:

> I see – I feel it in my bones – I know beyond argument – that most of their interpretations are merely impossible; they involve a way of looking at things which was not known in 1914, much less in

the Jacobean period. This daily confirms my suspicions of the
same approach to Plato or the New Testament. (p. 112)

The third complaint is directed against the assumption that neither
miracles nor genuine prophecy can have occurred in the fashion
reported in the New Testament. This, Lewis insists,

> is a purely philosophical question. Scholars, as scholars, speak on
> it with no more authority than anyone else. The canon 'If
> miraculous, unhistorical' is one they bring to their study of the
> texts, not one they have learned from it. If one is speaking of
> authority, the united authority of all the Biblical critics in the
> world counts here for nothing. On this they speak simply as men;
> men obviously influenced by, and perhaps insufficiently critical of,
> the spirit of the age they grew up in. (p. 113)

Lewis' 'fourth bleat', however, is his 'loudest and longest'
(p. 113). It is that all

> this sort of criticism attempts to reconstruct the genesis of the
> texts it studies; what vanished documents each author used, when
> and where he wrote, with what purposes, under what influences –
> the whole *Sitz im Leben* of the text. This is done with immense
> erudition and great ingenuity. And at first sight it is very
> convincing. (pp. 113–14)

But Lewis himself is not convinced. He instances the attempts
of reviewers to reconstruct the genesis of his own books and those of
others – attempts which according to his impression show 'a record
of 100 per cent failure . . . And yet they would often sound – if you
didn't know the truth – extremely convincing' (p. 115). 'The
"assured results of modern scholarship", as to the way in which an
old book was written, are "assured", we may conclude, only
because the men who knew the facts are dead and can't blow the
gaff' (p. 117).

Lewis recognizes that it may seem absurd 'to compare every
whipster who writes a review in a modern weekly with these great
scholars who have devoted their whole lives to the detailed study of
the New Testament' (p. 117). His riposte is, first, that respect for
the *learning* of the great biblical critics does not necessarily entail the
same respect for their *judgement*. Second, if the biblical scholars
are more learned than the 'mere reviewers', the latter have the

overwhelming advantage of dealing with works written in their own culture, their own day and their own language. In addition, the development of the study of English literature casts major doubt on some of the techniques – such as the extrapolation of hypothetical sources – used in biblical study. 'The huge essays in my own field which reconstruct the history of *Piers Plowman* or *The Faerie Queene* are most unlikely to be anything but sheer illusions' (p. 117). 'The confident treatment to which the New Testament is subjected is no longer applied to profane texts . . . Everywhere, except in theology, there has been a vigorous growth of scepticism about scepticism itself' (p. 119). Indeed, 'I do not wish to reduce the sceptical element in your minds. I am only suggesting that it need not be reserved exclusively for the New Testament and the Creeds. Try doubting something else' (p. 22) – such as, he implies, 'the assured results of modern scholarship'.

This brief summary of his 'four bleats' could perhaps give the false impression that Lewis simply rejected the application of critical literary and historical scholarship to the New Testament. He did not do so, but believed he could distinguish between more and less appropriate methods and procedures:

> We are not fundamentalists. We think that different elements in this sort of theology have different degrees of strength. The nearer it sticks to mere textual criticism, of the old sort, Lachmann's sort,[†] the more we are disposed to believe in it. And of course we agree that passages almost verbally identical cannot be independent. It is as we glide away from this into reconstructions of a subtler and more ambitious kind that our faith in the method wavers; and our faith in Christianity is proportionately corroborated. The sort of statement that arouses our deepest scepticism is the statement that something in a Gospel cannot be historical because it shows a theology or an ecclesiology too

---

[†] Karl Lachmann (1793–1851) was a pioneer in textual criticism of classical and Old German literature, notably the *Niebelungenlied*. He also published the first critical edition of the New Testament to be based primarily on ancient manuscripts rather than the received text of previous printed editions, with the aim of recovering the form of the text current in the late fourth century. His comparison of the contents of the three synoptic gospels, showing that Matthew and Luke agree on the order of events only where they share the material with Mark, paved the way for the hypothesis that Mark had been used as a source by the other two.

developed for so early a date. For this implies that we know, first
of all, that there was any development in the matter, and secondly,
how quickly it proceeded . . . I could not speak with similar
confidence about the circle I have chiefly lived in myself. I
could not describe the history even of my own thought as
confidently as these men describe the history of the early
Church's mind. (p. 121)

Or, as he remarks a little earlier:

> Dr Bultmann never wrote a gospel. Has the experience of his
> learned, specialized, and no doubt meritorious, life really given
> him any power of seeing into the minds of those long dead men
> who were caught up into what . . . must be regarded as the central
> religious experience of the whole human race? (p. 118)

Bultmann's answer to the challenge would doubtless have been that
his existential interpretation was intended precisely to discern and
broadcast what that 'central . . . experience' had been and remains
even in the modern world. But the main focus of Lewis' attack as just
outlined was the interest of Bultmann and other New Testament
scholars in tracing 'the genesis of the texts', in the belief that this was
the key to a proper understanding of them, along with such axioms as
'If miraculous, unhistorical' or 'The New Testament is the work of
the primitive Church.'

Now that we have followed Lewis so far, however, it is perhaps
time to consider how this attack is to be evaluated. It certainly
requires a differentiated appreciation, one which distinguishes the
strengths and weaknesses of different strands in his argument. It has
already been indicated that Lewis was not well placed to understand
or appreciate the special concerns of Bultmann (or Barth), though he
had read and could quote them. It should also be sufficiently obvious
that this writer is profoundly sympathetic to Lewis' contribution to
presenting Christian faith and hope in terms adapted to catch and
claim the imagination and commitment of people of the twentieth
century. However, proper appreciation involves critical reception of
ideas and arguments, albeit not of the kind that strains at gnats in
order the better to swallow camels. But Lewis' paper does put a
couple of camels – or elephants – on the menu.

   1. Lewis seems to imply that source-analysis of the biblical texts is
a useless diversion from proper engagement with them, an exercise in
hypotheses of a methodologically questionable sort.

2. Similarly, he puts a large question mark against all attempts to trace the development of thought and theology in the primitive Church, as reflected in the New Testament.

Both reservations are buttressed mainly by appeal to Lewis' own experience of work in the field of English literature, not by appeal to work done in the field of biblical scholarship, on which Lewis comments only – and very selectively – as a critical outsider. There is a good deal to be said on the other side!

First, it was critical literary and historical study of the Bible that delivered some of the main impulses to the critical study of other literature as well. Biblical study has benefited from techniques and approaches developed in work on other literature – but the reverse has also been the case: biblical study has pioneered the field of historical literary criticism.

Second, the very character of the biblical documents – the existence of four different gospels, for instance, or the sheer quantity of the letters claiming to be by St Paul – is itself a challenge to analyse and consider how this complex body of literature came into being, how the different documents are related, what stages of development in early Christian teaching and witness they may reflect, how far and in what ways they can best be understood against that background of development and controversy.

Third, we do as a matter of fact possess far more witnesses to the New Testament tradition in the form of manuscripts and papyri than to any other body of literature from the ancient world. Yet these sources themselves provide a host of variant readings, parallel yet different accounts of incidents and sayings, diverse but related formulations which cry out for careful analysis and comparison in the attempt to recover, so far as may be possible, the reliable original wording or to trace what lost sources may underlie the texts transmitted to us.

In short, Lewis' strictures upon the historical-critical study of the biblical material do less than justice either to the integrity of the enterprise as seriously undertaken or to the insights it offers into the history of the emergence of the biblical documents. There is a qualitative difference between, for example, Wellhausen's detection of different strands in the Pentateuch – following such clues as the two accounts of the creation in Genesis 1.1—2.4a and 2.4b–25 – and the attempts of Shakespearian scholars 'to cut up *Henry VI* between half a dozen authors and assign his share to each' (p. 110). The

former is serious literary, historical and theological scholarship, the
latter may well be mere literary dilettantism. But the triviality and
questionability of the latter is no proof of the inadmissibility of the
former.

Or, to take another example from the field of New Testament
study: we have no good reason today to reject the very considerable
evidence that St Paul did not write either Ephesians or the Pastoral
Epistles and that these represent two different appropriations and
expressions of Paul's legacy, long years after his death, not his own
writing. We can in fact learn far more about the dynamics of the
emergence of the biblical documents if we accept such patterns of
historical development and articulation than if we persist in insisting
upon Moses' authorship of the Pentateuch or Paul's authorship of all
the letters ascribed to him. And it is no service to the work of serious
biblical scholarship to dismiss all such enquiries as if they were
nothing more than pretentious guesswork, as Lewis seemed inclined
to recommend.

Here, in fact, lies both the strength and the weakness of Lewis'
argument. By temperament and training he was more philosopher and
literary critic than historian. His desire was not, except incidentally,
to understand the past 'as it was' or to track historical developments
for the sake of their interest for the historian. He was therefore ill-
equipped to appreciate the interest of historical-critical biblical study.

But if that was in one sense a weakness, it also enabled him to
sense the difference between a purely historical approach to the Bible
and the interest of Christian faith in reading the scriptures. And that
difference is surely important. Why, for example, do Lewis' Narnia
stories have the power to address and engage children who have never
heard of theories of *Heilsgeschichte* and would not understand them if
they had? Why does great literature in general have an appeal and an
interest for the sensitive reader quite different from that of the scholar
who is merely interested in analytical dissection of the same? Why, if
not that God's word is also able and keen to use the powers of human
imagination, baptized imagination, to discern and proclaim the gospel
of mercy and of judgement? Why, if not that there are more avenues
to confrontation with the sublime realities of which the Bible speaks
than mere archaeological busyness with the history of the emergence
of the biblical texts? The interest of historical-critical biblical
scholarship is not invalid, but it is also not the be-all and the end-all.

It can indeed become a distraction from the thing more important still.

Is there, then, something radically wrong with the approach and intention of contemporary biblical exegesis? Lewis is only one of many critics who have insisted that there is, though the critics are far from sharing the same views either as to diagnosis or as to remedy, as three other, rather different, examples can illustrate.

The profoundest theological thinker we have had in Britain in the last decades, Professor Thomas F. Torrance, is at least as critical of the reduction of biblical research and interpretation to a merely historical and archaeological discipline as Lewis was. His main line of counter-argument is, however, rather different from that of Lewis. Torrance (1969) maintains that the proper task of theological enquiry has to do with the objective probing of reality, that theology is itself in the proper sense of the word a *scientific* discipline – and one, moreover, which is called to subject its methods, forms of questioning and provisional conclusions, indeed its whole structure of thought and interpretation, to the same kind of rigorous objective control and testing as is expected in the natural sciences.

Taking his cue from Karl Barth, Torrance insists on the critical, scientific nature of theology; he goes beyond Barth, however, in tracing the interconnections in the history of thought between Christian dogmatic thinking and the development of the other modern sciences. This has led him to unfold a powerfully dynamic conception of the meaning of Jesus Christ as the central axis of the entire interaction between God and the created universe and, from that, a new perspective upon the history of the development of classical Christian dogma which is both critical and constructive, for example, in questioning traditions and habits of theological thought in the Eastern and Western churches to find how far they conform to the fundamental import of the gospel that God became man in the person of Jesus Christ in order to reconcile all things to himself.

Torrance's criticism of the enterprise of modern critical biblical scholarship is that it generally neither raises nor attempts to grapple with these methodological, theological and dogmatic issues, but remains largely set in a pattern of historical, literary and archaeological investigation which in its essentials was programmed by the flowering of historical scholarship in the nineteenth century. This is not to deny that these researches are *also* important; it is to question whether they exhaust the responsibility of biblical scholarship. Torrance challenges biblical researchers to think not merely *historically* or in terms of literary criticism or archaeological research, but *theologically* and *dogmatically* (i.e., scientifically), in the light of the real object of their work: the historical self-revelation of God in the person of Jesus Christ, incarnate, crucified and risen, who is the second person of the Trinity, the firstborn of all creation, the head of the Church, the prototype of redeemed humanity, and our future judge. In other words, he urges biblical scholars to take seriously the central message of the New Testament itself, and suspects that they do not always succeed in doing so, that in all too many cases, indeed, they have not even begun to try.

The second example is of a rather different sort. In recent years there has been a rising tide of conservative evangelical attacks on the entire undertaking of historical-critical biblical scholarship as at best misguided, at worst a betrayal of the Bible itself. The beginnings of this movement lie in the nineteenth century with the movement known as fundamentalism. Its concern was to recall Christians to the 'fundamentals' of the biblical faith, as opposed to the corrosive acids of modern thinking, especially since the Enlightenment of the seventeenth and eighteenth centuries.

One especially vociferous offshoot of this movement in recent years has been the 'creationist' movement in the United States. Its programme is the introduction of a biblical conception of the process of creation, based on Genesis 1—2, as an alternative *scientific* model to the theory of evolution. That well illustrates the general approach of the attack on historical-critical study of the Bible more broadly characteristic of conservative evangelicalism, though most conservative evangelicals would not perhaps be prepared to go quite so far as the creationists. All nevertheless have in common a conviction that no approach to the Bible can be appropriate which treats it simply as a historical collection of documents, to be analysed, interpreted and explained simply by the application of the same methods by which other historical materials are analysed, interpreted and explained. This seems to them to put the truth of the biblical witness in question, and therefore to be a theological dead end.

The third example is very different again. One of the targets most frequently singled out for attack by some conservative evangelicals is the 'theology of liberation', represented chiefly (though not only) by theologians in the Third World. It is not possible here to sketch all the forms which this approach has taken in the last twenty years. Let me cite just one example of acute contemporary relevance: the approach of some theologians in South Africa. Their theological opposition to the policy and politics of apartheid may be summed up in the programme: 'We believe that the Bible is true; from the story of the Exodus onwards it is the message of God's liberation of his people, yesterday, today and tomorrow.' For theologians and church leaders such as Beyers Naudé, Desmond Tutu or Allan Boesak, the Bible and the gospel speak directly to the South African situation, a situation of structural injustice and oppression. They and other Third World theologians have little patience with what they see as the comfortable academic pursuit of literary and historical biblical study and dogmatic theological enquiry lacking in any kind of social or political resonance.

Liberation theology poses hard questions to theological and biblical work as conducted in the cloistered academe of First World libraries and seminars. In particular, it raises the question whether a purely literary and historical study of the Bible does not all too easily serve to blunt its challenge and promise, to make the ears of the scholars and of their hearers dull to the calling of the Lord and the promise of his grace, his judgement and mercy as bearing directly on the economic, social, political and racial ordering of society.

Each of these three critical attacks on current modes of biblical scholarship raises many different issues which cannot be adequately explored here. My own sympathies lie more with the first and third than with the second – but also with Lewis, whose strictures upon much contemporary biblical and exegetical work as lacking alike in imaginative power and theological and human seriousness are even today not without relevance. The trends he criticized are still alive and well; they may be illustrated from a paper by an English New Testament scholar which I recently read. The argument of the paper may be summed up as follows:

1. Loyalty to the principles of the Reformation requires that we affirm the authority of the Bible over all later theological and dogmatic development.

2. That means today that only those New Testament sayings which can reliably be traced back to Jesus himself possess authority.

3. Given the paucity of such sayings we are faced with the question whether we should continue to assert the authority of the Bible in general and the New Testament in particular, or cast around for some other basis for our theology.

4. It is questionable whether the patristic model – i.e., the doctrine of the Trinity – is the best or only one available to express the threeness of God to which the New Testament witnesses.

5. The patristic model drew upon the patterns of thought developed in Hellenistic philosophy. Since the Enlightenment, however, these patterns have become meaningless.

These theses might at first appear to be entirely reasonable; in their own way, indeed, they are just that: *reasonable*. The programme of the paper could equally well have been formulated in the eighteenth century, in the Age of the Enlightenment. Its appeal to the authority of the Bible reduces to an appeal to what historical study can tell us about the sayings of Jesus. In the process it irons out what most serious New Testament study of the twentieth century has been concerned to emphasize: that the witness of the New Testament is to the gospel of the crucified and risen Jesus Christ, not simply to 'the historically indisputable sayings of Jesus'. The last two theses reduce, it hardly needs to be said, to a provincial rejection of the greater part of the history of Christian thought.

Precisely here lies the weakness of *some* prominent recent British biblical and theological scholarship; it is insular, shallow and unaware of wider connections and responsibilities, theological, ecumenical, social and political. It is largely uninformed on all but a small segment of the history of Christian theology and exegesis. It goes its own way, concerned only with its own questions. That it does so is largely the product of structural and institutional conditioning: the development in particular of the English universities and the Anglican Church has not always been such as to encourage profounder theological enquiry. It has often been adapted rather to promote a kind of serene dilettantism in the field of theology.

Another factor also deserves to be mentioned: the rise and rise of the media-orientated theologian. At least in England it is possible to become prominent by presenting oneself as a theological *enfant terrible*, preferably by demolishing this or that biblical or dogmatic foundation or by 'taking leave of God'. By comparison with other recent escapades of this sort the paper presented by our English New Testament scholar is mild stuff. But in principle it is of the same weave. It is a confession of bankruptcy, exegetically and theologically.

As I was drafting this paper I happened to come upon an article by the President of the British Academy, Sir Randolph Quirk, in *The Independent* of 12 November 1986. After discussing the teaching of English grammar and the advantage of learning foreign languages, he concludes: 'After all, it is not only in the pages of Anthony Burgess that we are warned of "the monoglot Englishman, unworthy to enter any comity of nations, tied to one tongue as to one cuisine, and to one insular complex of myths".' This would seem to score a direct and devastating hit on the theological trends just mentioned.

In conclusion, however, I would emphasize that the trends singled out here for attack – which are very similar to those that Lewis held up to scorn a generation ago – are not typical of all biblical scholarship and exegesis, whether in Britain or elsewhere. But they have been prominently displayed in recent years, especially in certain quarters in England. And the extremes to which they lead can serve to highlight the dangers lurking in a purely historical-critical approach to the New Testament if unaccompanied by theological sensitivity and prejudiced by a foreshortened view of the history of Christian thought. Our best theologians and our best biblical scholars are not guilty of this narrowness, but there are others, and they are not without influence.

The root cause of the problem lies in the branching-off of the various theological disciplines from each other in the last three centuries, so that exegetes, historians and dogmatic or practical theologians all too often work *alongside* but not *with* each other. The separation of the disciplines has been made necessary by the development of biblical and theological scholarship since the seventeenth century; no one today can hope to be comprehensively informed and expert in the technicalia of all the different fields, particularly so far as front-line research is concerned. But this makes it all the more needful that continuing dialogue should take place between the disciplines involved in the academic theological programme. We need historically and theologically informed exegetes just as we need exegetically and theologically informed historians and exegetically and historically informed theologians. All of these, individually and together, have their part to play. And all of them can

perhaps gain by also paying sympathetic attention to a figure such as
C. S. Lewis and his strictures upon the reduction of theology to a
purely academic, *historical* discipline. Theology has more serious
matters to attend to than mere academic games; not only biblical
scholars need on occasion to be reminded of that.

8
DIFFERENT GOSPELS:
THE SOCIAL SOURCES OF APOSTASY

Peter L. Berger

This is not a sermon. It is, as advertised, a lecture.[†] A sermon is an act of proclamation of the gospel by an individual who has been ordained to preach. That is a very solemn business indeed, one to which I have neither claim nor aspiration. I am not a preacher; I am a social scientist. I exercise a vocation that deals, not in proclamation, but in empirical enquiry, which by its very nature is tentative, probabilistic and open to falsification. Most of what I have to say in this lecture is based on many observations as a sociologist with an interest in American religion. I see no reason, however, to limit myself to doing sociology of religion. I am also a Christian; as such I find myself constrained to relate my understanding of the world to my faith, and I will attempt to do this in the latter part of the lecture. It is with this intention, and definitely not to suggest a sermon, that I begin with a passage from the New Testament.

The apostle Paul wrote to the Galatians as follows:

> I am astonished that you are so quickly deserting him who called you in the grace of Christ and turning to a different gospel – not that there is another gospel, but there are some who trouble you and want to pervert the gospel of Christ . . . As we have said before, so now I say again, If any one is preaching to you a gospel contrary to that which you received, let him be accursed. (Gal. 1.6–7, 9, RSV)

The theme of this passage is apostasy. People, especially those of a conservative bent, have the tendency to think that their own age has unique evils. To some extent, I suppose, this is a correct perception. Every age has a distinctive genius, for evil as well as good, and our

---

[†] Professor Berger's contribution was originally delivered as the Erasmus Lecture, in St Peter's Lutheran Church, New York City, in January 1987.

age has produced evils that can safely be called unique. But apostasy – the substitution of different gospels for the gospel of Christ – has been a constant in the history of the Church. It was there right from the beginning, as the letter to the Galatians (along with many other portions of the New Testament) serves to remind us. The essence of apostasy is always the same: seeking salvation, not in the grace of Christ 'heard with faith', but rather in what Paul calls 'the works of the law'. The specific contents of apostasy, the details of 'works-righteousness', vary from age to age. This lecture is a reflection about apostasy in our own age. As a social scientist I have certain analytic tools allowing an attempt to understand the mundane context of the 'different gospels' of the age. As a Christian I must also make some moral and theological assessments.

Let us do some sociology.

For historically well-known reasons (elaborated, among others, by H. Richard Niebuhr (1929) in the book whose title I have paraphrased here), there has always been a close linkage between religion and culture in America. This is a culture whose values and institutions, even whose aesthetic style have been crucially affected by Protestantism. Thus there is a direct line from the Puritan covenant, through the 'half-way covenants' of a disintegrating Puritanism, to the various secularized notions of American exceptionalism – all having in common the idea that, somehow, American society has a unique and putatively sacred mission. To be sure, there have been dissenters from this vision (within Protestantism and from without) and some American groups have never shared it, but its pervasiveness in American history to this day is remarkable, especially in comparison with societies having a more sober conception of themselves. In due course Catholics, Jews and others have come to participate in this quasi-covenantal vision, but, not surprisingly, the major Protestant denominations have had the most intimate connection with the culture. American civilization is a distinctively Protestant product; conversely, American Protestantism is a distinctively powerful case of so-called *Kulturprotestantismus*.

Sociologically, however, one can describe this religio-cultural unity more precisely. Here again H. Richard Niebuhr (building to some extent on Max Weber) is helpful: it is not culture in general that has been the partner in this marriage with religion; it is a specific *class* culture. The class, of course, is the bourgeoisie, lately called the middle class, that creator and carrier of capitalism which had to struggle against older classes in Europe, but which had hardly any serious competitors in America (except, though even that is debatable, in the ante-bellum South). America, from the beginning, was a bourgeois society – not, of course, in the sense that all Americans were middle class, but because this society was shaped by middle-class values and institutions without having to overcome antecedent aristocratic or peasant cultures. As both Weber and Niebuhr showed, Protestant morality and Protestant social arrangements were highly instrumental in this construction of a bourgeois world. Not only did Protestantism inspire the culture of the great American middle class, but it served as the very effective mobility machine by which people from the lower reaches of society, generation after generation, were assisted in *moving into* the middle class. Religiously (and, of course, sincerely so) lower-class individuals were washed in the blood of the Lamb, in one great revival after another. But in the process they also learned to wash their feet and to wash out their mouths – that is to act and speak in accordance with middle-class norms, and *ipso facto* to acquire habits and attitudes conducive to upward mobility in a relatively open class system. Already John Wesley observed (and was troubled by) the fact that Methodists had a pronounced tendency to start out poor and end up rich; Weber and Niebuhr would have had no difficulty explaining to him why this was happening.

As recently as the 1950s this class-specific 'culture Protestantism' was very much alive and well. The so-called mainline denominations existed in a by-and-large happy symbiosis with middle-class culture; lower-class sects and churches were continuing to grind away their time-honoured mobility machinery; and (as Will Herberg astutely observed at the time) Catholics and Jews had very largely joined this all-American celebration. To be sure, there had been a good deal of secularization in the contents of this common American faith, both in its social and its personal ethics (President Eisenhower embodied the former modification, Norman Vincent Peale the latter), and many of the harder theological contents of the various traditions had been softened, relativized (or, as John Murray Cuddihy has put it, 'civilized'). The main point, though, is that there was little tension between the major religious groupings and the cultural milieu in which they found themselves. They existed (if I may use a term I employed in my first writings about American religion) in an 'okay world': America was okay; the middle-class way of life was okay; indeed, it had become difficult to distinguish between the religiously sanctioned virtues and the values propagated by politicians, civics teachers and therapists. If I am to recall one *locus classicus* in the portrayal of this religio-cultural symbiosis (a critical one, of course), it would be William Lee Miller's essay 'Piety Along the Potomac' (published in *The Reporter* magazine in 1954); his 'The Gospel of Norman Vincent Peale' (*Union Seminary Quarterly Review*, 1955) would round out the picture in its more personal aspect.

Looking back on this period thirty years later one can easily say that the situation today is very different. So it is, in many respects. It is all the more important to understand that, in many respects, the situation hasn't changed that much.

I would argue that one of the most important developments of the post-Second World War period in America (and incidentally in other Western societies) has been a *bifurcation of the middle class*. This is the so-called 'New Class thesis', an idea that, interestingly, has been held in common by observers on the right and the left of the political spectrum. Thus Irving Kristol, the *doyen* of neo-conservatism, and Alvin Gouldner, the late neo-Marxist sociologist, have both written about the 'New Class', pretty much agreeing on its empirical characteristics; Kristol thinks that this class is bad news, while Gouldner hoped that it would bring about very desirable changes in the society. When observers with diametrically opposed ideological views agree on an empirical assessment, this gives good grounds for surmising that the assessment is close to reality. What is the reality in this case?

The underlying process is technological and economic: in our type of advanced industrial society an ever-shrinking segment of the labour force is needed to keep material production going. This frees up, indeed compels, the growth of an occupational sector that is geared to miscellaneous services (economists call this the 'quaternary sector'). Within this sector there is what has been called the 'knowledge industry', and within *that* there is a very peculiar activity, devoted to the production and distribution of what may be called symbolic knowledge. The 'New Class' consists of the people who make their living from this activity. These are the educators (from pre-school to university), the 'communicators' (in the media, in public relations, in a miscellany of propagandistic lobbies), the therapists of all descriptions (from child analysts to geriatric sex counsellors), and, last but not least, substantial elements of the bureaucracy (those elements concerned with what has been called 'lifestyle engineering') and the legal profession. They are, of course, a minority of the working population, but, because of their power in key institutions that provide the symbols by which the society understands itself, their influence is much greater than would be supposed by their numbers. Whether one calls this group a 'class' or not is a matter of sociological conceptualization; I use the term because I think it helps to clarify what is going on.

It is a class because it is a group with a distinctive relation to what Marx called the 'mode of production'. It is a *rising* class, and as such it finds itself in conflict with the class that previously controlled the societal areas into which it is moving. That class, of course, is the *old* middle class, still centred in the business community and the traditional professions. The conflict between the two middle classes, I believe, serves to explain many otherwise strange features of recent American politics – notably the fact that many economically and culturally privileged people have moved into strong, sometimes virulent opposition to key American institutions and values. The new knowledge class is generally left-of-centre. This fact, I think, can very largely be explained by the vested interests of this class, which, to put it very broadly, stands to gain from a shift of power from business to government. Thus this class has a vested interest in domestic policies that expand the welfare state and in foreign policies that de-emphasize military power. I regret that I cannot elaborate on this assertion here, but, be this as it may, the most relevant point to be made here is that the new class (like all classes, of course) has distinctive cultural characteristics. Again, I would argue that many of the socio-cultural conflicts today, from the environment to the sphere of sexual intimacy, must be understood as symbolic expressions of an underlying class conflict. Thus we know that class is the most reliable predictor of an individual's stand on such matters as nuclear energy, abortion or the gamut of items on the feminist agenda. By their bumper stickers you shall know them: it is not difficult to guess the class affiliation of individuals whose automobiles sport messages like 'US out of Central America', 'Save the Whales' or 'ERA Now', as against 'Nicaragua is Spanish for Afghanistan', 'Register Criminals not Guns', or 'Abortion is Murder'. The former, of course, is likely to be a fully accredited member of the new knowledge class; the latter may be an unrepentant bourgeois, or he or she may belong to that working class which (contrary to all Marxist theories) is now one of the staunchest carriers of traditional bourgeois culture.

The religious fall-out of this *Kulturkampf* is all too visible. The mainline Protestant denominations still contain (probably dwindling) numbers of old-middle-class and working-class individuals. But (and this is a decisively important fact) their clergy, officials and intellectuals have (understandably enough) identified almost completely with the culture and *ipso facto* the political agenda of the new middle class. A very similar process has been under way in the Roman Catholic community. Contrary to what was predicted by Jeffrey Hadden in his still-interesting book *The Gathering Storm in the Churches* (1969), laypeople who dislike the new-class rhetoric assailing them in these churches have put up remarkably little resistance; instead, they have quietly moved out. Some have joined the ranks of the unchurched; others have helped to swell the impressive numbers making up the great evangelical upsurge. And the latter too makes much more sense in the light of class analysis: to a large extent it may be seen as part of the 'bourgeois insurgency' (the apt phrase is by Richard Neuhaus), which is the movement of resistance by the old middle class and much of the working class against the political and cultural power grab of the new class. In this perspective, the New Christian Right is the mirror image of the mainline leadership in the ongoing class conflict.

What I am saying here is that, appearances notwithstanding, there has been no basic change in the relations between religion and culture, and between religion and class, in America. What *has* changed is the class system and its cultures. But, as always, most of American religion (and especially Protestantism) faithfully reflects the class culture in which it finds itself. As before, there is very little consciousness of the class location of one's own cultural and ideological propensities. *Kulturprotestantismus* prevails, eagerly emulated by many non- (or should one say neo-) Protestants. American society continues to be pluralistic and broadly tolerant, and one should not overestimate the degree of polarization. There are many people and entire groups who manage to live quite comfortably detached from all this political and cultural conflict. All the same, there are two class armies arrayed against each other on a sizable number of cultural battlefields. Increasingly, major religious organizations are serving the function of military chaplaincies in these armies, doing what chaplains have always done on battlefields – solemnly blessing the banners of their side and assuring the troops that their cause is God's.

Mainline Protestantism has suffered a good measure of decline. The future course of the aforementioned class conflict will largely determine whether this decline will continue, and I would not want to make predictions here. But one point should be made: if the mainline churches continue to decline, it will *not* be because of their alleged 'prophetic ministry'. It is hardly 'prophecy' if one says exactly what people in a particular social milieu want to hear. The decline will not be the result of 'speaking truth to power', but rather of backing the wrong horse in a game of power politics.

Needless to say, this sociological analysis could be greatly refined and elaborated. Of necessity, have been exceedingly sketchy here. I would strongly emphasize, however, that the analysis is 'value-neutral'. *All* religious and moral affirmations occur in a social context; to point out what this context is by no means prejudges the validity of the affirmations. I, for one, find myself unable to identify fully with the agenda of either side in the current conflict. Still, *morally speaking* (and leaving aside both cultural tastes and theological convictions), I find the new-class agenda the more reprehensible of the two. It seems to me that the most pressing moral issues of the present age are the avoidance of nuclear war, the survival of freedom and the alleviation of misery. These goals, I believe, depend upon the maintenance of a balance of power based on American military strength and upon the institutions of democratic capitalism; I further believe that the much-maligned bourgeois culture, albeit modified, continues to be a better vehicle for sustaining a decent society than its current competitors. Therefore, if pushed to make a moral choice between the 'bourgeois insurgency' and the new-class agenda, I opt for the former (even if I have to dissent from some planks of the platform). Put simply, I fail to see the moral superiority of an ideology committed to unilateral disarmament, a vague socialism and an assault on the family. I have elsewhere written at length about my reasons for this moral position and for the right-of-centre politics that follow from it. That, however, is not my purpose here. I mention it for two reasons. First, I will in what follows maintain that, in making a theological assessment, one can say the same things about those who would make a 'gospel' of a right-wing agenda and those who do this with an agenda of the left; I am *not* suggesting a symmetrical *moral* equivalence. And second, I want to make my own political position clear, precisely because what I have to say theologically is meta-political; indeed, I would say *exactly the same*, speaking theologically, if I located myself on the other side of the political divide.

Let us now do some theology. (For those of us who are not theologians, the warrant for doing this lies in the priesthood of all believers. Or, to put it in more mundane terms, theology is too important to be left to the professional theologians – especially seeing what they have done with the business of theologizing in recent years!)

Paul wrote to the Galatians: 'A man is not justified by works of the law but through faith in Jesus Christ. [Even] we have believed in Christ Jesus, in order to be justified by faith in Christ, and not by works of the law, because by works of the law shall no one be justified' (Gal. 2.16, RSV).

Faith in the gospel of Christ is constitutive of the Church. The Church is the community that embodies this faith. Apostasy occurs when any other content is deemed to be constitutive of the Christian community. At that point, the community becomes something other than the Church of Christ. Of all the so-called 'marks of the Church', the central and indispensable one is that the Church proclaims the gospel, and not any other message of salvation. Compared to the true gospel, all these other messages appear as 'works of the law', as manifestations of 'works-righteousness'. These allegedly salvific messages, of course, differ greatly in different periods of history. Thus it requires a considerable effort on our part to enter into the dispute over the status of Jewish law in the Galatian community; however important one may deem the dialogue between Judaism and Christianity in our own time, I think it is safe to say that it will have to be couched in very different language and that the specific problem of the Galatians is not our problem today. The underlying question, though, has not changed at all: Is it the gospel of Christ that constitutes the Church, or is it a 'different gospel'?

It seems to me that we face precisely this question in American Christianity today – nothing less – and it is an awesome question. Compared to this question, the different moral and political options available to us pale, not into insignificance (because Christians are in the world and responsible for the world), but into what Dietrich Bonhoeffer called 'penultimacy': the ultimate question is the question of salvation. Thus the issue I want to address now is *not*, emphatically not, the substitution of one cultural or political agenda for another.

Rather, it is the issue of placing *any* such agenda into the place that is reserved to the gospel in the faith and the life of the Church.

Allow me to explicate this point in somewhat personal terms. My own politico-cultural positions have much to do with the insights I believe myself to have gained over the years of working as a social scientist. While, by definition, these insights have no inerrancy and are always open to revision as new empirical evidence comes up, I am reasonably certain that I understand some things about the modern world. Thus, when I go to church or read church publications, I am irritated when I am confronted with statements that I consider to be empirically flawed. I don't go to church in order to hear vulgarized, 'pop' versions of my own field. The irritation deepens when these terrible simplifications are proclaimed to me in tones of utter certitude and moral urgency. Bad analysis obviously makes for bad policy, and here I am not just intellectually irritated but morally offended. For example, when, in the name of the 'preferential option for the poor' (a phrase with which, in principle, I have no quarrel), policies are presented as moral imperatives which, in my understanding, are likely to increase rather than reduce poverty (such as all the socialist and quasi-socialist panaceas proposed for the Third World by liberation theologians – and Third World development has been my major concern for the better part of my career as a sociologist), then I am more than irritated: I am constrained to make the moral judgement that what goes on here is profoundly irresponsible. Being human, I am sure that I would be less irritated, and less offended, if what I heard in church were, in my understanding, more competent analysis and more responsible politics. *Nevertheless*, not for one moment am I advocating here that *my* analysis and *my* politics should be substituted for the left-of-centre rhetoric rampant in our churches today (I am speaking, of course, of the mainline Protestant and Catholic churches). *Neither* side's agenda belongs in the pulpit, in the liturgy or in any statements that claim to have the authority of the gospel. *Any* cultural or political agenda embellished with such authority is a manifestation of 'works-righteousness' and *ipso facto* an act of apostasy.

This theological proposition, over and beyond all prudential moral judgements or political options, 'hits' in all directions of the ideological spectrum; it 'hits' the centre as much as the left or the right. 'Different gospels' lurk all across the spectrum. No value or institutional system, past or present or future, is to be identified with the gospel. The mission of the Church is not to legitimate any status quo *or* any putative alteration of the status quo. The 'okay world' of bourgeois America stands under judgement, in the light of the gospel, as does every other human society. Democracy or capitalism or the particular family arrangements of middle-class culture are not to be identified with the Christian life, and neither is any alternative political, economic or cultural system. The vocation of the Church is to proclaim the gospel, not to defend the American way of life, not to 'build socialism', not even to 'build a just society' – because, quite apart from the fact that we don't really know what this is, all our notions of justice are fallible and finally marred by sin. The 'works-righteousness' in all these 'different gospels' lies precisely in the insinuation that, if only we do this or refrain from doing that, we will be saved, 'justified'. But, as Paul tells us, 'by works of the law shall no one be justified'.

In the face of all these 'different gospels', the true gospel is *liberating*. As Paul puts it: 'For freedom Christ has set us free; stand fast therefore, and do not submit again to a yoke of slavery' (Gal. 5.1, RSV). It seems to me that this liberating power of the gospel has two aspects. The first, of course, is the liberation from sin and death that is Christ's work for us. This liberation is at the heart of the gospel, indeed *is* the gospel. While it affects everyone who believes it in a very singular way, its import is cosmic, transcending all the structures of this world. What is more, this liberation is available only to faith; it cannot be proved or demonstrated except by faith. I would contend, though, that there is, as it were, a lesser liberation brought about by the gospel – lesser only if compared with the world-shattering cataclysm of Christ's victory over sin and death – and this is the liberation from the bondage of mundaneness. This lesser liberation, unlike the first, can be perceived even short of faith; it is, if you will, an empirically available liberation. *The gospel liberates by relativizing all the realities of this world and all our projects in this world.*

We know – not by faith but by reason – that everything in this world is bound to perish. All men are mortal, and so are all the societies they create, even the most attractive ones. It is foolishness to act as if any one of the social constructions of men possesses ultimate importance or even reality. We can also know – and this knowledge is one of the major if bitter fruits of the modern social sciences – that our projects in the world almost never yield the results we intend.

Our actions regularly escape us, turn against us; all too often, they fail precisely in succeeding. This bitter truth is the common insight of allegedly successful conquerors and revolutionaries. History, which is the sum-total of all human projects in this world, has no rationally discernible direction – only faith can perceive in it the unfolding of God's hidden purpose. Empirically, history is an unending repetition of cruelty and madness: the gospel liberates because it opens up to the eyes of faith a reality *beyond* history. The currently fashionable politicalization of the gospel, especially the one ironically called 'liberation theology', restores us to the yoke of slavery that is imprisonment in history and imprisonment in the typically tragic web of our own projects in history.

I can already hear the muttered responses to what I have just said – accusations of 'other-worldliness', more appropriate perhaps to Buddhism than to Christianity; instructions about the concrete, historical character of biblical revelation; a brief lesson on how Christians are supposed to be in the world not escape from it. Need I say it? Believe me: *I know all these things*. I am always amused when clerical types, who only yesterday emerged from some pietistic underworld to discover politics and sex, take it upon themselves to lecture *me* on worldliness: *the world is my proper vocation* – I know it fairly well; I especially know it in its modern and modernizing structures; I spend most of my days weltering in the affairs of this world – *I don't need you to tell me about worldliness!*

Of course Christian faith is 'worldly', in the sense that this world is believed to be God's creation, and history the arena of his redemptive actions. Of course the Christian is called upon to act in this world (or perhaps one should say, *most* Christians are so called upon; there is, I believe, the legitimate Christian vocation of the contemplative life). But the question is *how* we act in the world.

If we are liberated by faith, we act in the full knowledge of the precariousness and tragic unpredictability of all human projects. Most important: we act in this world, *not* to be saved, *not* to attain some perfect purity or justice (which goals are not attainable), but to be of specific and necessarily limited service to others. Again, Paul addresses himself to the Galatians on this issue, when he insists that the freedom of the Christian is to be used as an opportunity for service, in love of one's neighbour (Gal. 5.13–14). Let me put this in as *worldly* terms as I can: we get no moral brownie points for good intentions or noble goals. The moral measure of actions is their probable consequences for others. This is especially so in the case of political actions, because this is a category of actions with particularly unpredictable and potentially disastrous consequences. Precisely because of this, we are most likely to be effective politically (effective, that is, in being of service to our neighbours) if we ground ourselves in a realm beyond politics, thus becoming free to deal with political reality soberly and pragmatically; we cannot do this if we look on politics as the realm of redemption.

But let me return to the central point of these observations, which point is the Church as constituted by the gospel. This is a community liberated, in faith, from all the constraining contingencies of both nature and society: 'There is neither Jew nor Greek, there is neither slave nor free, there is neither male nor female' (Gal. 3.28, RSV). We know, of course, that in this world no Christian group has ever lived up to this promise, but commitment to it is an essential part of what the Church purports to be. For this reason, catholicity has been counted among the 'marks of the Church'. That catholicity is denied if a Christian community excludes people on such grounds as race, class or gender. It seems very clear that catholicity is also denied if people are excluded on the ground of political affiliation or allegiance.

This is the final ecclesial implication of the politicalization of the Church: *wherever a political agenda is seen as constitutive of the Church, all those who dissent from it are excluded from the Church. In that very instant, the Church is no longer catholic; indeed, it ceases to be the Church.*

If I am told from the pulpit, or by the language employed in the liturgy, or in public pronouncements of church authorities, that a particular political agenda is mandatory for Christians, this has ecclesial as well as moral implications. If I cannot in good conscience subscribe to this agenda, I am implicitly (perhaps, of course, even explicitly) excluded from the Christian community. To take another ironic example, if the liturgy is translated into so-called 'inclusive language' (which is, in fact, an ideological jargon), then this very language excludes anyone who cannot in good conscience subscribe to the feminist agenda which the language represents. Empirically, of course, this is exactly what this linguistic strategy does in our churches today. But, *mutatis mutandis*, the same exclusion occurs when *any* political or cultural agenda is elevated to the status of 'gospel', no matter whether this agenda is of the right, the left or the centre. And here is the ultimate irony: *all such politicalization is an act of implicit excommunication. But, in politicizing its message, the Church is in actuality excommunicating itself!*

Finally, with some reluctance, I have to make some comments about one troubling phrase in the passage that I read at the beginning of this lecture – the phrase applied to one who preaches a 'different gospel' – *'let him be accursed'* (Gk. *anathema estō*). (Actually, Paul uses the phrase *twice* in the passage; perhaps out of embarrassment, I have read it only once.) Such a phrase jars the ears of most of us, who do not reside on the wilder shores of Protestant fundamentalism (or possibly in the secret chambers of the Roman Curia). And let me quickly reassure you that I am not about to conclude here by hurling anathemas: I am in the business of hypotheses, not curses. However, even if none of us is prepared to claim the apostolic *exousia* by which Paul felt authorized to utter this terrible phrase, we may usefully reflect on why the preaching of 'different gospels' in the Church might merit a curse.

I can think of one very good reason indeed: *because this false preaching denies ministry to those who desperately need it.* Our congregations are full of individuals with a multitude of afflictions and sorrows, very few of which have anything to do with the allegedly great issues of history. These individuals come to receive the consolation and solace of the gospel, instead of which they get a lot of politics. I can think of no clearer case of one asking for bread and being given a stone. Some time ago a friend of mine went through a very difficult period when it was suspected that he might be suffering from cancer. It turned out later that this was not the case, but during this anxiety ridden period neither he nor his family were given any attention by the clergy and the active members of his congregation. This is a congregation famous for its social and political activism. No one was interested in what, compared with the allegedly great historic challenges of our age, was the trivial matter of one man's fear of pain and death. The people of this congregation had more important things to do – attacking the 'root causes' of hunger by lobbying in Washington, organizing to 'show solidarity' with Nicaragua, going on record ('making a moral stand') against apartheid. My friend says that, during this time, he felt like an invisible man in that congregation. Needless to say, this is a congregation that religiously employs 'inclusive language'. (Again, I can hear some mutterings: can one not lobby in Washington and *also* minister to the sick? Perhaps. In the event, the first activity precluded the second. And one may reflect that it is easier to love people in distant lands than people next door.)

And this case leads me on to a further reflection: perhaps no apostolic anathema is required to damn the gospels of works-righteousness. *The curse is built-in.* Put differently: *those who put their faith into these works in the end damn themselves.* And here, again, it seems to me that this process can be perceived empirically, even without faith; Paul describes the unredeemed condition as one of being 'slaves to the elemental spirits of the universe' (Gal. 4.3, RSV). Yes, I too have read Bultmann; I too am a modern man who uses electric razors and antibiotic medication, and I am not sure (though I am not prepared to exclude the possibility) whether I believe in the sinister beings that Paul evidently had in mind. But I do think that the processes of history and politics, which I don't have to believe in, because I know them all too well, may safely be included among the powers to whom we are enslaved in this world. The gospel promises us liberation from *all* these powers, be they historical or meta-historical, natural or supernatural. What a terrible thing it is to turn away from this promise to the vain pseudo-salvations of social existence! Here indeed is a curse, but it is a self-activating one. Paul tells us as much: 'whatever a man sows, that he will also reap. For he who sows to his own flesh will from the flesh reap corruption' (Gal. 6.7–8, RSV). That corruption too is 'empirically available': it is the harvest of unintended consequences, bitter disappointments and tormenting guilt that is reaped by those who seek justification by political acts.

There is a form of discourse much favoured by intellectuals such as myself that may be called 'crisis-speech'. It consists of portraying an awful crisis and then suggesting that this crisis is about to happen *unless* the author's recommendations are promptly adopted. I am tempted, but I cannot quite conform to this formula. Speaking sociologically, I don't really see any great crisis: American society is, overall, in fairly robust condition; its class conflicts are more likely to end in compromise than in conflagration; and the various religious groups will adapt or fail to adapt to change, and if some of them (especially the denominations of mainline Protestantism) end up as rather marginal sects, I, for one, would not see this as a major catastrophe. Speaking theologically, there is a crisis of ultimate seriousness – it is the crisis brought on by the gospel being proclaimed, or not proclaimed, in any moment of history – yet it is a crisis that has been with the Church from its beginning.

We are justified by faith. This means that nothing depends on us: our personal destiny and that of the entire world rests in God's hands. It also means that everything depends on us: we are called, to the best of our ability, to serve both Church and world. I have said very little in this lecture about serving the world; most of my professional work is devoted to worrying about this and, when I am active politically, to doing a few things in this department. Serving the Church today, I believe, must begin with an understanding of the specific forms of apostasy that confront us today, to recall the true meaning of gospel, Church and ministry, and then to put our ecclesial houses in better order. I see very little evidence of any of this happening in American Christianity today, but then, if we believe that the Holy Spirit is active in the Church, we must also believe that its actions cannot be predicted. If and when the Spirit revitalizes the Church, this has the surprising quality of a summer thunderstorm. I wish for all of us that, in our lifetimes, we may yet be so surprised.

9
THE THEOLOGY OF LIBERATION IN LATIN AMERICA

Alan J. Torrance

INTRODUCTION

All Paul's letters were written in the context of problems, and out of his concern to interpret Christ in those contexts – the problems of a divided church in Corinth, the legalism of the Judaizers at Galatia, the fears and misunderstandings of the Christians in Thessalonica. Indeed, his passionate concern for people with their problems helped him to see the meaning of the person and work of Christ, as he expounds it in his letters. So in his concern for the poor Christians in Judea, he writes to the Corinthian church, 'Consider the grace of our Lord Jesus Christ, who though he was rich, yet for our sakes became poor that we through his poverty might be made rich' (2 Cor. 8.9). In other words, 'If you know who Christ is, and what he has done for you, how then do you respond to the needs of your poor brothers and sisters in Judea?' And it soon becomes plain that, for Paul, thinking in the light of Christ should lead us to desire an equal sharing and distribution of wealth (2 Cor. 8.13–15).

Liberation theology arises out of a concern to interpret the gospel in the context of the sufferings of the poor, and their cry for justice and freedom, their cry for humanity and dignity. The task of the theologian is not only to listen to the word of God, but to listen to the cry of the poor, the powerless and oppressed and interpret the word in that context. He or she must therefore interpret both the social context of his or her prophetic proclamation and holy scripture, and thereby gain a better understanding of the relevance of the gospel, and of God's concern to give to all people their humanity in Christ.

What *is* liberation theology?

To understand liberation theology, we must grasp one basic claim: suffering and its quest for freedom is the fundamental reality of human experience as well as the location of God, Christ and the church in history. Liberation theology urges action, strategy, and freedom in Christian witness. Consequently, liberation theology is a new language of God, seeking, in the present historical situation, to be the voice of those who suffer. (Chopp 1986, 3)

This is how Rebecca Chopp, in her excellent analysis of liberation theology, expresses its main concerns as she seeks to interpret the 'paradigm shift' – the shift in thinking and perspective – which distinguishes liberation theology from other forms of modern theology. This paradigm shift involves nothing less than a radically new perception of the nature and character of theology, offering a revision of the methods, content and domain of the enterprise as it has been traditionally conceived. Justice and freedom become central themes, while social and political categories of analysis become essential tools of interpretation. This, it is argued, is demanded by the brutal reality of the large-scale suffering of the oppressed, impoverished and marginalized in Latin America. The fact of this suffering requires us to break with the more tradtional approaches to the theological task – because the reality of this suffering 'ruptures' our academic theological systems.

The theology of liberation seeks to ask, out of the context of poverty and the human degradation which accompanies it, (a) how we conceive of the liberating message of the gospel in relation to this situation, (b) where God is to be found in such contexts, (c) what the implications of the crucified Christ are for our perception of the oppressed and our relation to them, and (d) how we are to conceive of the New Testament message of *hope* in situations characterized by the passive despair of a people who are so oppressed to the extent that their attitude or mentality is conditioned into being dominated by those who would exploit their poverty for profit. The theology which emerges may be described as the faith of the Christian community of the oppressed of South America seeking understanding.

ITS BACKGROUND AND CONTEXT

Liberation theology is not an academic system of theology. It does not engage in the abstract ordering of theological concepts. Rather, it seeks to reflect a concrete form of Christian perception, the perception of faith. It is a practical, theological apperception or 'way of perceiving' the world and its suffering, grounded in what the Latin American Church has become in and through its engagement within

the context of South America. As José Míguez Bonino points out, it
emerges

> *after the fact*, as the reflection about facts and experiences which
> have already evoked a response from Christians. This response,
> undertaken as Christian obedience, is not the mere result of
> theological deduction, or of political theory. It is a total, synthetic
> act, often going far beyond what one can at the moment justify
> theologically. Then as one is called to explain, to understand the
> full meaning or to invite other Christians to follow the same path,
> a theology is slowly born. (Míguez Bonino 1975, 61)

Because this theology sees itself as irreducibly rooted in the concrete
existence of the poor in South America, we cannot expound or indeed
evaluate it without looking at it in its context – to seek to lift this
kind of theology out of its particular setting and then evaluate it in
abstraction from the cruel poverty and oppression which has given
rise to it would involve a radical distortion of what it itself perceives
to be its nature and function.

Latin America is characterized by desperate poverty on the one
hand and extremes of wealth on the other. A United Nations report
in the 1950s describes the situation out of which the theology of
liberation emerged as one where 'Two-thirds, if not more, of the
Latin American population are physically undernourished to the point
of starvation in some regions', 'Three-fourths of the population in
several of the Latin American countries are illiterate', 'One-half of
the Latin American population are suffering from infectious or
deficiency diseases', 'An overwhelming majority of the Latin
American agricultural population is landless. Two-thirds, if not more,
of the agricultural, forest, and livestock resources of Latin America
are owned or controlled by a handful of native landlords and foreign
corporations.'

José Míguez Bonino describes in the mid-1970s how scenes of
appalling poverty are almost universal, with children combing
garbage dumps around the cities and, in the rural areas, chewing
cocoa leaves and even mud to dull hunger pains. Unemployment is
high and wages are low, creating a context of widespread exploitation
by multinational corporations. Medical services are meagre and
disease rife. Governments are unstable, oppressive and undemocratic,
stifling protest movements and attempts to introduce reform.

The immediate historical context of Latin American liberation theology is the period since the early 1950s. This has been characterized by the 'First World' engaging, on the one hand, in the exploitation of Latin America through the medium of its multinational corporations while, on the other, operating various programmes of development in the optimistic belief that technological expertise and financial aid would soon produce 'developed' First World countries in Latin America. While the former interests flourished the latter failed, and the term 'developmentalism' is now used pejoratively, conjuring up images of feeble attempts by the First World to lessen the offence of its primary role as exploiter. In the 1960s, following ten years of development programmes, the gap between the rich and the poor was wider than ever and the political regimes of the countries in question more unstable than ever. Dictatorships emerged, and these were supported by the increasingly extensive (and sometimes undercover) involvement in South America by the government of the United States, motivated by the desire to protect American business interests and to oppose communism in all its forms in the name of freedom and democracy.

The failure of developmentalism, which was to become the symbol for liberation theology of all that was wrong with the First World (and its churches) in relation to the poor and the oppressed, was due to the fact that, as Gustavo Gutiérrez argues, 'the supporters of development did not attack the roots of the evil'. Consequently, they not only failed but they 'caused instead confusion and frustration'. He continues:

> Development must attack the root causes of the problems, and among them the deepest is the economic, social, political and cultural dependence of some countries upon others – an expression of the domination of some social classes over others . . . Only a radical break from the status quo, that is, a profound transformation of the private property system, access to power of the exploited class, and a social revolution that would break this dependence would allow for the change to a new society, a socialist society – or at least allow that such a society might be possible.

For this reason, he concludes, 'to speak about the process of *liberation* begins to appear more appropriate and richer in human content. Liberation in fact expresses the inescapable moment of radical change

which is foreign to the ordinary use of the term *development*'
(Gutiérrez 1973, 26–7).

It was the failure of developmentalism, therefore, in the midst of
appalling oppression, exploitation and suffering, which occasioned the
cry for liberation – a cry which reverberated throughout the Church
of Latin America and which was to question and, in many contexts,
to redefine its structures, its understanding of its role and function, its
socio-political world-view and its theology. And it was the vacuum
left by the failure of 'First World charity' which was to lead the
theologians of liberation to look to Marxism for what they hoped
would be more adequate answers.

THE CHURCH AND *AGGIORNAMENTO*

The failure of the developmentalist approach in addressing the
problems of a continent characterized by encroaching poverty and
oppression and the ever starker contrasts between the rich and poor
compelled the Church to break with the dualism between the spiritual
and the temporal realms which traditionally characterized its message
and restricted its utterances to expressing concern for the *spiritual* and
moral (rather than social) welfare of its people. Following the
attempts of Pope John XXIII through the Second Vatican Council 'to
open the windows of the Church to let in fresh air from the outside
world', a new awareness of the relevance of the Christian faith and
the obligations of the Church in situations of poverty emerged. By a
natural progression the concern in the Roman Catholic Church for
renewal ('*aggiornamento*') quickly became a call for the transformation of oppressive social and political structures.

Two documents proved to be of immense importance and significance here. *First*, there was the response of fifteen bishops speaking
on behalf of Third World nations to the encyclical *Populorum
progressio*. The encyclical had spoken unambiguously of 'building a
world where every man, no matter what his race, religion or
nationality, can live a fully human life, freed from servitude imposed
on him by other men or by natural forces over which he has no sufficient control' and denouncing elsewhere the 'international imperialism
of money', and the growing gap between rich and poor countries. The
open document which the fifteen bishops produced in response to this
went much further, affirming that the 'peoples of the Third World are
the proletariat of today's humanity' and that the Church had a duty

not to find itself 'attached to financial imperialisms'. The role of the Church was to identify with those who are exploited, in the attempt to help them recover their rights. This document played an important role in forming the conclusions deriving from the Second General Conference of Latin American bishops held in Medellín, Colombia, in 1968. *Second*, there were the documents that emerged from this which (together with the statement from the fifteen bishops) were to become the foundation documents of Latin American liberation theology and which were to lead to the formation and proliferation of grassroot 'basic Christian communities' which characterized the movement of liberation as it took place within the context of the solidarity of the oppressed.

In dealing with the themes of justice and peace, evangelization and spiritual growth, and the nature of ecclesiological structures, a dominant concern at the Medellín conference was to find ways of involving the masses in the decision-making processes as they affected their lives. Two concepts came to the fore here which were to denote central themes in liberation theology, namely *participation* and *conscientization*. '*Concientización*' was a word coined by Paulo Freire to denote the process of the 'making aware' of the people so that they might come to 'own' their own futures (Freire 1972). This meant liberating the oppressed from their 'dominated-conditioned attitudes', and involved, as Freire describes in his *Pedagogy of the Oppressed*, a movement on their part from 'naïve awareness' to an enlightened 'critical awareness' where they themselves actively begin to analyse their problems, replacing magical explanations with real causes, and boldly and freely come to engage in genuine dialogue with their circumstances. 'In this process . . . the oppressed person rejects the oppressive consciousness which dwells in him, becomes aware of his situation, and finds his own language' (Gutiérrez 1973, 91). *Participation*, on the other hand, denoted the need to identify with the oppressed and dispossessed, to engage in their struggle for liberation from the chains of their exploited circumstances, and to participate in their attempt to realize their humanity and dignity. It spoke, therefore, of loving the exploited 'concretely', that is, refusing to 'abstract' the exploited from their social setting in the act of loving them, and this meant in practice to stand in solidarity with the oppressed in their class struggle. 'To participate in class struggle not only is not opposed to universal love; this commitment is today the necessary and inescapable means of making this love concrete. For this participation is what leads to a classless society without owners and dispossessed, without oppressors and oppressed' (Gutiérrez 1973, 276).

Accordingly, the Church's concern for 'renewal' was to find expression in its working for the renewal of the humanity of the oppressed. *Aggiornamento* meant, in the context of Latin America, the renewal of society by following Christ and working in faith and *within history* for the new creation, for the kingdom and for the renewal of humankind. This required nothing less than the decisive action of the Church in faith, and the rupture of the traditional social structures as they sustained the status quo – a conclusion which could only savour strongly of Marxism.

LIBERATION THEOLOGY AND MARXISM

The influence of Marxism is explicit in the writings which characterize the development of liberation theology, and not least in the Medellín documents themselves. This influence led some church leaders and theologians to criticize the theology of liberation as a thinly veiled baptism of Marxism by an uncritical translation of it into theological categories. Even Jürgen Moltmann, a theologian profoundly sympathetic to their concerns, would later criticize the liberation theologians for their 'school-book Marxism'.

What was the appeal of Marxism, and is this criticism justified? The appeal lay not so much in the detail of its economic and social analysis, nor indeed in its claims as a philosophical system, but rather in its ability to provide, on the one hand, some form of analysis of the problems of Latin American society and, on the other, a new and dynamic conception of the human being in society and of his/her role in working for a future free from polarization and the vicious cycle of poverty and hopelessness. In other words, if the gospel was effectively and realistically to address the suffering of the vast majority of the people of Latin America it required specific tools of social analysis, new political options, and a new understanding of history and the role of the human being – and this was precisely what Marxism seemed to have to offer.

In his very useful book on liberation theology, Andrew Kirk outlines five areas of Marxist influence. First, it emphasized praxis as the epistemological reference for all theoretical thought. Second, it contributed socio-political tools of analysis to inform and structure the interpretation of 'the signs of the times'. Third, it offered an objective means of detecting and liberating false ideologies which underlay and gave support to systems of oppression. Fourth, it focused on the freedom of the human being as an agent in control of his/her future destiny in seeking to realize truly human community. And finally, it encouraged the interpretation of the Christian faith by the liberation theologians in essentially prophetic terms (Kirk 1979, 41).

Perhaps the most important general area of Marxist influence, however, is reflected in what has been described as the central theological 'base point' of liberation theology, namely its emphasis on history as the primary arena for God and human action, where 'history' denotes the social, political and economic realities of daily existence. As Gutiérrez himself admits, 'it is to a large extent due to Marxism's influence that theological thought . . . has begun to reflect on the meaning of the transformation of this world and the action of man in history' (Gutiérrez 1973, 9).

It is also in this area, however, that one realizes that the dialogue with Marxism was not an *uncritical* one. At the heart of Marx's analysis of the problems of society lies 'alienation'. This alienation concerns, on the one hand, the estrangement between human subjects and their products and, on the other, the related estrangement of human beings in their social relationships. These are the key factors which lead to the failure of human beings to fulfil their nature as social beings (what Marx called their 'species-being'). However, in terms of his deterministic view of history, he sees the movement of history as irreversibly progressing towards the manifestation of the new society where alienation will be no more and there will be manifest the social equivalent of the 'synthesis of opposites', of which Hegel spoke, in the form of the classless society. The liberation theologians, however, could have no such commitment to the natural outworking of any social principle, because they understood *sin* as an irreducible dimension of alienation. The fact of sin meant that the manifestation of 'Utopia' was ultimately contingent upon the redemption of society by divine engagement within history through the medium of the Church. The Christian conceptions of creation, sin and redemption significantly conditioned, therefore, the use of the Marxist conception of the nature of humanity and the out-workings of history. This is made clear when Gutiérrez outlines three levels of meaning in the notion of 'liberation': (a) political liberation,

(b) the liberation of man through history, and (c) liberation from sin and admission to communion with God. He writes, 'These three levels mutually effect each other, but they are not the same. One is not present without the others . . . they are all part of a single, all-encompassing salvific process.' This means, first, that the growth of the kingdom cannot be 'reduced to temporal progress'. Second, we discover through 'the Word accepted in faith' that it is sin which is 'the fundamental obstacle to the Kingdom' and 'the root of all misery and injustice'. And third, 'the ultimate precondition for a just society and a new man' is the growth of the kingdom into which we are introduced by Christ and by the gift of his Spirit (Gutiérrez 1973, 176).

In response to those who see the liberation theologians as uncritically echoing the theme tunes of a foreign ideology, one would also have to point out the extent to which the liberation theologians saw their theological perspective as being in a position to provide a constructive perception of issues and problems inherent in historical praxis, such as 'fellowship', 'death' and 'sacrifice', which Marxist ideologies 'ignored or refused to face' because, as Míguez Bonino argues, 'they lack categories to grapple with them' (1975, 73).

This brings us to the question: What were the distinctive themes and emphases in liberation theology which, although emerging in dialogue with Marxism, succeeded in distinguishing it from Marxism?

THREE BASIC THEMES IN LIBERATION THEOLOGY

Although there are a number of themes, categories and characteristics – biblical and otherwise – which occur and recur throughout the writings of the Latin American theologians of liberation, following Rebecca Chopp I shall focus on three of these which are of universal and elemental importance. These are: (a) the preferential option for the poor, (b) the conception of God as liberator, and (c) the need for the liberation of theology and for its grounding in praxis (Chopp 1986, 22–7).

THE PREFERENTIAL OPTION FOR THE POOR

The failure of the developmentalist approach to poverty in South America engraved on the minds of the theologians of liberation the fact that the Church's obligations towards the poor cannot take the form of charity, which is itself a feature of, as well as a consequence of, class division and the polarization between rich and poor. The Church is called to a bias towards the poor, to express a preferential option for the poor, to strive for their rights to speak, to eat, to work and to be engaged in the decision-making process as it affects their future. This 'bias' or 'preference' must seek therefore to redress the imbalance obtaining in contexts of opposing extremes of wealth and poverty which, in a sinful world, can lead to a vicious downward spiral of oppression and 'dispossession'. This preferential option does not simply derive from the influence of Marxism and the desire for the 'revolution' of the social order; it emerges clearly from the Bible when it is read with eyes which are not blinded by foreign 'Western' ideologies.

This perception is reflected clearly in Gutiérrez's analysis of the ambiguities in the meaning of the word 'poverty' in the Bible. In one sense of the term, poverty is seen as a scandalous condition and is expressed in the Old Testament with words which reflect the extent to which it degrades the human condition – '*indigent, weak, bent over, wretched* are terms which well express a degrading human situation', terms which in themselves 'insinuate a protest'. But this kind of poverty is not simply denounced, the Bible advocates 'positive and concrete measures to prevent it becoming established' with, in Deuteronomy and Leviticus, 'very detailed legislation designed to prevent the accumulation of wealth and the consequent exploitation' (Gutiérrez 1973, 292–3). But there is another use of the term, to denote 'spiritual childhood' where the poor person is the 'client of Yahweh', someone who has no other sustenance than the will of God.

In the person of Christ, however, in his act of voluntary impoverishment (2 Cor. 8.9) and *kenosis* – self-humbling or self-emptying (Phil. 2.6–11) – a synthesis of the two different forms of poverty is to be found. Poverty applies to him in both senses, and these are integrated in his mission of salvation. His physical poverty and self-emptying is not a taking on of humankind's condition in order to idealize it, but rather it is done in

> love for and solidarity with those who suffer in it. It is to redeem them from their sin and to enrich them with his poverty. It is to struggle against human selfishness and everything that divides men and enables there to be rich and poor, possessors and dispossessed,

oppressors and oppressed. Poverty is an act of love and liberation. It has a redemptive value . . .

The Christian commitment to poverty, therefore, serves to 'witness to the evil which has resulted from sin and is a breach of communion' (Gutiérrez 1973, 300).

The Christian act of becoming poor in solidarity with the oppressed and to participate with them in the struggle for justice is what the liberation theologians refer to as 'liberation praxis'. This is not the result of a romantic asceticism, but is an act which derives from faith in and communion with God as the One who is the liberator and the power of liberation within history.

GOD AS LIBERATOR

Liberating praxis is grounded in and flows from God as the liberating God. This is reflected in the continual reference to the Exodus, which becomes a recurring allegorical *motif*, symbolizing and signifying the redemptive engagement of God in the history of his people. The Exodus manifests a 'politics of God':

> Israel is not merely conscious of having liberated itself, but of having been liberated; a future which was objectively and subjectively closed (because of Egypt's oppressive power and its own 'slave consciousness') is broken by a God who reveals himself as free from history (namely, from the determinations of history) and for history . . . God as the future of freedom and freedom for the future makes the liberating project possible even in the most oppressive circumstances. (Míguez Bonino 1975, 77, expounding the thought of Rubem Alves)

The activity of God in the Exodus is paralleled in the redemptive work of his incarnate Son. Gutiérrez writes:

> In the Bible, Christ is presented as the one who brings us liberation. Christ the Saviour liberates man from sin, which is the ultimate root of all disruption of friendship and of all injustice and oppression. Christ makes man truly free, that is to say, he enables man to live in communion with him; and this is the basis for all human brotherhood. (Gutiérrez 1973, 37)

Elsewhere he writes: 'In Christ the all-comprehensiveness of the liberating process reaches its fullest sense . . . In him and through him salvation is present at the heart of man's history, and there is no human act which, in the last instance, is not defined in terms of it' (Gutiérrez 1973, 178).

God's liberating purposes are further 'incarnated' in the Church as the sacrament of God, the visible presentation of God's invisible liberating grace. Here the 'base-level Christian communities' are interpreted as liberating society by 'living the values of the Kingdom' (Gutiérrez), liberating the poor from the chains of poverty and the wealthy from the bondage of their wealth, such that all humanity can be liberated to receive the 'gratuitous gift of the Kingdom'.

The notion of God as liberator testifies, therefore, both to the unity of history and also to its open-ended character, in that it witnesses to the continuity between divine creation and redemption understood in terms of God's creative and liberating engagement in and through history.

THE NEED FOR THE LIBERATION OF THEOLOGY AND
FOR ITS GROUNDING IN PRAXIS

> The theology of liberation offers us not so much a new theme for reflection as a *new way* of making theology. Theology as critical reflection on historical praxis is thus a liberating theology, a theology of the liberating transformation of the history of mankind and, therefore, also of that portion of it – gathered as *ecclesia* – which openly confesses Christ. (Gutiérrez 1973, 15)

There has been strong criticism of this theology from some quarters for attaching too much weight (by way of insisting on the relevance of praxis and the sociological context for the task of theology) to *historical circumstances*, when the primary concern of theology should be 'the timeless and objective study of God'. Assmann (1976) has responded to this by arguing that attaching a determinative weight to historical circumstance is and has to be of the very essence of the task. Indeed, the very supposition that one can start from 'purely' abstract and objective sources could be seen as testimony itself to the compromised idealism of the 'rich world'. The West idealizes the detachment, the isolation and the abstraction of Christian truth – and its theology exemplifies this! Truth is interpreted in terms of transcendent formulations belonging to a remote (lit. removed) realm of ideas. God is defined as an abstract, transcendent being who is 'isolated' and 'above' historical reality. But those who advocate this fail to realize the extent to which they are projecting on to God their own individualistic self-understanding as beings who are self-contained, removed and detached from the real world. Underlying this conception of God, it is suggested, we find the self-understanding of the wealthy, those who are in a position to 'transcend' and isolate themselves from the reality of suffering in the world. And this they can do only by belonging to the world of the oppressor and self-possessed rather than that of the oppressed and dispossessed.

No theology, however, can be done in abstraction, and it is the convenient myth of the First World to think that it can be. The conviction that 'objective' theology is detached in this way is a presupposition which cannot be true to the God who refuses to be 'detached from the world'. Accordingly, for the liberation theologians, one of the central tasks of theology must be the unmasking of those subtle ideologies hidden in the pseudo-objective theologies of the past, so that we can begin from the standpoint of faith grounded in the concrete realities of history and not be seduced by elements and systems foreign to the historical reality of the kingdom.

Theology is 'in reality' act–ual in that it has its 'beginning from concreteness', from 'particular realities'. Accordingly, all theology conceived in abstract, metaphysical terms is ruptured by the reality of the historical person who is 'the way and the truth and the life', the incarnate Son, the crucified God. Christ determines that 'truth is at the level of history, not in the realm of ideas'. Christian truth cannot be 'truth', therefore, while being abstracted from reality. Torn from reality, it can only cease to be truth. The love of God as it is conceived in and through the truth of Christ, and him crucified, necessitates the fact that knowledge of God *in truth* can occur only in the context of union and communion with God as the one 'given' and engaged in history. Accordingly, 'just as the criteria for an effective love of God belong to the historical and human order of the neighbour' (Míguez Bonino 1975, 73; cf. Assmann 1976, 123), the context of historical solidarity and identification with one's neighbour is the only possible ground for the *knowledge* of God, since knowledge of God can only derive from communion with God, that is, by our being redeemed and reconciled into the kingdom of God

'real–ized' in space and time in the Church as the sacrament of God
and the *place* of theology (*locus theologicus*). This redemption is
actualized just as Christian truth is 'ver–ified' (lit. 'made true'), as
Gutiérrez argues, in praxis – that is, in active and engaged solidarity
with the oppressed and suffering. Accordingly, *orthopraxis* (right
practice), rather than *orthodoxy* (right belief), becomes the criterion
for theology. This is not, however, to deny the importance of true
belief, it is rather to see the place of Christian belief in proper
perspective: 'the goal is to balance and even to reject the primacy and
almost exclusiveness which doctrine has enjoyed in Christian life'
(Gutiérrez 1973, 10).

This has profound implications for our conception of the nature
and function of theological language and, concretely, for our choice
of terms in theology. Marx believed that philosophy should stop
explaining the world and start transforming it. For the liberation
theologians this applies to an even greater degree to theology, and has
profound consequences for our understanding of theological language.
We must leave behind the belief that words and meanings have access
to a theological reality outside history. We must, in the words of
one theologian, 'resign reference to a metaphysical realm, a world
of ideas in which theological categories have their referents'.
Consequently, 'the only possibility is to relate a language to forms of
conduct, to action, to a praxis'. Theological language as the language
of the Church should be seen to be 'performative', since the meaning
of the expressions used must be inseparable from what they actually
do. (An example of a 'performative utterance' would be, 'I baptize
this child, Mary Anne.' This sentence is meaningless independently of
the *act* of baptizing the child! When a minister makes this statement
he or she is not simply describing what he or she is doing but is
actually doing something in and through the uttering of these words.)
Theological expressions and statements, if they are to have meaning,
must actually transform the way things are rather than merely
describe abstract entities.

This Copernican revolution in theology, relating both to the
function of its terms and the nature of interpretation, means that
theology is no longer 'an effort to give a correct understanding of
God's attributes or actions, but an effort to articulate the action of
faith, the shape of praxis conceived and realised in obedience'
(Míguez Bonino 1975, 81). In the words of Gutiérrez, 'the
understanding of the faith appears as the understanding not of the

simple affirmation – almost memorisation – of truths, but of a commitment, an overall attitude, a particular posture toward life'
(Gutiérrez 1973, 7). And its function is therefore 'evangelical', that
is, it concerns the spread of this faith, this commitment.

In terms of this total transformation of the traditional conception of
the language and function of theology, there ceases to be any
'possibility of invoking or availing oneself of a norm outside praxis
itself'. 'This does not involve a rejection of the scriptural text or of
tradition, but the recognition of the simple fact that we always read a
text which is always incorporated in a praxis, whether our own or
somebody else's' (Míguez Bonino 1975, 81). Engagement with the
text is the engagement not of praxis with theory but of praxis with
praxis, and the correction of the one in the light of the other. This
includes the freeing of contemporary praxis from (Western) ideologies
which distort the form and therefore the content of Christian truth by
making it 'abstract'. Such abstracting (lit. 'dragging away') of the
faith from the real world leads to our 'spiritualizing', 'privatizing'
and 'individualizing' the Christian faith – and this process culminates
ultimately in the destruction of faith as we discover it in the Bible,
rooted as it is in the everyday life and practice of the people.

Theology, for the theologians of liberation, therefore,

> does not stop with reflecting on the world, but rather tries to be
> part of the process through which the world is transformed. It is a
> theology which is open – in the protest against trampled human
> dignity, in the struggle against the plunder of the vast majority of
> people, in liberating love, and in the building of a new, just and
> fraternal society – to the gift of the Kingdom of God. (Gutiérrez
> 1973, 15)

CRITICAL EVALUATION

We have sought to present liberation theology not as a new or
modernistic system of theology, but as a form or way of theology
which has grown up in response to the brutal realities of suffering in
Latin American society. For this reason we have chosen to present it
historically rather than *systematically*. In accordance with its own
claims, it should not be seen as 'another' theology in the traditional
mould, but as attempting to bring about in us a 'paradigm shift' –
a radical change in our whole approach and way of thinking – in
relation to the very nature of the theological enterprise. This is

something which one dare not forget when one engages in critical evaluation. Indeed, its exponents may argue that any criticism lodged at the purely intellectual or theoretical level has necessarily missed the mark!

However, it is precisely this 'paradigm shift', defined over and against traditional European theology, which points to an area of weakness arising from the negative side of liberation theology, where it can be seen as a reaction against certain tendencies in the 'First World'. This is best discussed if we look for a moment at the weakness of European theology and its disjunction between theory and practice – what is seen by the liberation theologians to be the abstraction of theology. This can be traced, at least in part, to the influence on European thought of the seventeenth-century French philosopher René Descartes, who can properly be described as one of the founders of modern thought.

For Descartes (1641) the self was defined as essentially a 'thinking thing' (res cogitans). The fact that 'I think' is the most fundamental and indubitable truth about my own being and, as such, must be seen as defining the very essence of the self. Due, however, to Descartes' failure to realize that thought is a form of physical activity, he established an absolute dualism between the *mind*, as the independent domain of thought, and the *body*. That is, he introduced a dichotomy between the spiritual or mental on the one hand and the physical or material on the other.

On the basis of this dichotomy he went on to assert the superiority of the realm of thought on the one hand and the secondary and derivative nature of mere activity or practice on the other. The effect of this on European thought, not least on theology, has been inestimable. Theology was interpreted as the product of the realm of thought or reason, such that the influence of any extraneous concerns, be they physical, emotional or practical, was deemed to undermine the intellectual purity of the discipline. Accordingly, there tended to be a divorce between, on the one hand, the task of theological investigation and, on the other, the realm of ethical or political concern and practice. The former was regarded as 'theoretical', whereas the latter was interpreted as belonging to the realm of 'applied' or 'practical' theology – where the 'outworkings' of theories which emerged in abstraction from the historical realm were simply *applied*. The direction of influence between the two sides of this split – between the doctrinal, theological realm on the one hand

and the ethical, political and practical realm of application on the other tended to run in one direction: from the higher realm of contemplation of the divine to the lower realm of pragmatic concern; from a realm of primary and inherent value to a lesser one of secondary and derivative 'application'. The effect of this was that the harsh realities of real life were effectively prohibited from calling in question or challenging both the content of the faith of the Christian Church and therefore its practice, since these were decided upon by academic theologians who, in order to do good theology, withdrew to live lives in isolation from the everyday world of ordinary people. In other words, the dialogue between the problems of the everyday life of the people and the content of the Christian faith which was so fundamental in Paul could not take place.

For the theologians of liberation, however, the brute fact of suffering ruptured this order. In the face of the human tragedy of suffering and exploitation we can no longer do theology or interpret the Christian faith in abstraction from the real world, from the realm of practice. Consequently, we witness in liberation theology a swerving to the opposite extreme, whereby it finds itself compelled to assert the primacy of the practical while giving theological belief a position of derivative and secondary importance. In this total reversal of the relationship, orthopraxis comes to take pride of place over orthodoxy – the 'I act' over the 'I think' of Descartes. The emphasis shifts from saving *belief* to saving *work*, and we find Miranda suggesting, 'The human disposition to do "good works" or not to do them . . . is the only criterion for who is to be saved and who is to be condemned that we find in the New Testament' (Miranda 1977, 192). Likewise the emphasis shifts from who God is to how God acts, where the tendency is to identify the action of God with *our* action to the extent that we *are* the Church, the sacrament of God. Simultaneously, there is a tendency to interpret the role of the Holy Spirit, who retreats in significance, simply in terms of our spirituality, the 'spirituality of liberation'. It is in Christology, however, that the most noticeable shift in emphasis takes place. The person of Christ tends to be displaced by an emphasis on the value of his salvific *work* – interpreted in terms of its *effect* in the world. Knowledge of the person of Christ is effectively reduced to a mere knowledge of his benefits. All this culminates in a subtle move away from the incarnation conceived as the once-and-for-all, gracious self-gift of God in Christ, to a reinterpretation of 'incarnation' in much more general (and less concrete?)

terms as the somewhat amorphous and impersonal presence and engagement of God in the world in the form of the Church as the sacrament of God. Paradoxically, this has tended to lead to a characteristically European weakness of 'translating' the message of the kingdom of God into a human programme and set of human ideals such that the kingdom of God stands in danger of being conceived of as a human ideological construct. In sum, the concern to emphasize the 'praxis' side of the theory-practice dualism (which has been characteristic of European theology since Descartes) has led to the fusion of, and confusion between, the act of God and human praxis.

A key contribution of the theologians of liberation has been their revelation of the extent to which the traditional dualism inherent in the Church's theology has led to the transformation of the gospel into something which is in many ways quite alien to the New Testament. However, the weakness in liberation theology has been to operate in terms of the same dualism by simply emphasizing the other side of the disjunction, focusing now too exclusively on praxis and on our work and action – and hence leading to the transformation of the gospel into *another* alien form. In this way liberation theologians have tended simply to import and impose on the Latin American people European categories (as are those of Marxism, as Jürgen Moltmann (1976; Anderson and Stransky 1979, 57–70) points out in his open letter to José Míguez Bonino) and, contained within them, European dichotomies and polarizations which serve only to undermine the express concern of the liberation theologians to do theology and interpret the Christian faith *with*, *for* and *from* the people of South America.

What was really demanded by the situation was that they seek to work for new and more adequate forms of understanding which did not condition the gospel, but allowed it to interpret itself in a manner true to itself (rather than to foreign philosophies and ideologies) in the Latin American context. In this way the person of Christ as the focus of the faith would be interpreted not in terms of prior categories which create a divorce between his person and his work, but as he gives himself to be known by reinterpreting and redeeming all our prior categories in an *act* of reconciling us to himself and transforming our *whole* being through bringing us into communion with his *person* in and through the Church. This would allow for a conception of the self – unpolluted by Western dualisms deriving from Descartes, and closer to that of the early Church – where the self is conceived neither simply as the 'thinking subject' nor as the 'agent of work' but in terms of another unitary and holistic category of 'personhood' where the essence of the person is conceived in inter-personal terms as constituted by communion. In this way a person would be defined as having his or her being in loving, where this love is reduced neither to a form of social praxis nor (by way of individu-alistic categories) to a form of private, subjective perception, but is rather conceived as a way of being which unites all our capacities and capabilities, our thought and our agency, as we are drawn to participate cognitively and actively in that communion which flows from the being of the triune God, made manifest uniquely in Christ and known in union and communion with him through the Spirit. This is a communion which at one and the same time transcends the world and history while at the same time sending us into the world in radical solidarity with those who are suffering, in manifestation, by the Holy Spirit, of the reality of Christian hope as it transforms this world and yet is neither confined to this world nor limited by it.

In these terms the kingdom of God is conceived as transcending and judging all our human, social and political systems in such a way that it can never be identified with any of these since it is defined in terms of communion with the God whose reign is conceived solely in terms of divine grace. This is not to 'spiritualize' or 'privatize' the kingdom, since it is 'humanized' by the active presence of the person of Christ in this world as the one who 'realizes' the kingdom in human history by the activity of the Holy Spirit. The kingdom, conceived in this way, is *neither* realized by being 'given up' to human history (that is, by being naïvely identified with some social or political programme, as some of the liberation theologians tend to do), *nor* by being 'evacuated from' human history into some spiritualized realm (as the First World has tended to do), but is realized rather by its being 'opened up' to human history in such a way that we can glimpse in space and time, in and through the body of the crucified Christ as it exists *in* and *for* the world, God's eternal purposes for this world defined in terms of total, personal communion and characterized by peace, justice and liberation of the most radical kind.

10
AGAINST RELIGIOUS PLURALISM

Gavin D'Costa

INTRODUCTION

There was a time when Eastern religions were accessible only to those who spoke Sanskrit or Pali and had travelled to distant continents. Today most public libraries will contain English translations of the Hindu *Bhagavad Gita* or the Buddhist collection of teachings *The Dhammapada*. To meet Hindus one need not travel to the banks of the sacred river Ganges – the Thames or the Mississippi will suffice. There was a time when Muslims were viewed as 'infidels' and 'religious wars' were waged against them by popes and barons. Today the pope visits Muslim countries as a friend and fellow worshipper of the transcendent God, and the barons have been replaced by terrorists on both sides! The twentieth century has inescapably witnessed the meeting of the major world religions. This meeting has produced racism, intolerance, bloodshed, co-operation, hope, love, and equal doses of sympathy and misunderstanding. Religious pluralism raises many practical questions, personally, socially and politically. It also raises profound theological questions for Christians.

In this essay I want to examine an increasingly popular response by some Christians to the questions posed by non-Christian religions. Very often these theologians are children of modernism and their whole approach is dictated by highly questionable assumptions. I want to draw out these assumptions and show that central Christian concerns have been slowly abandoned and covertly replaced by a post-Enlightenment rationalism, with an emphasis on experience and a historical relativization of truth claims. This position is often presented as the *only* viable and tolerant Christian approach to a pluralist society. I want to suggest an alternative. Here my purpose is twofold: to expose and criticize what I shall call 'Christian pluralists'; and to suggest an approach that I shall call 'Christian inclusivism'.

THEOLOGICAL PLURALISTS

What is the stance of 'Christian pluralists', and what are the claims
that they make for their approach? The most apt analogy to encapsu-
late their view is the Buddhist parable of the blind men and the
elephant. Pluralists often employ this story. Saxe's poem humorously
tells the parable:

> It was six men of Hindostan,
> To learning much inclined,
> Who went to see the Elephant,
> (Though all of them were blind):
> That each by observation
> Might satisfy his mind.
>
> The first approached the Elephant,
> And happening to fall
> Against his broad and sturdy side,
> At once began to bawl:
> 'Bless me, it seems the Elephant,
> Is very like a wall.'
>
> The second, feeling of his tusk,
> Cried, 'Ho! what have we here
> So very round and smooth and sharp?
> This wonder of an Elephant
> Is very like a spear.'
>
> The third approached the animal,
> And happening to take
> The squirming trunk within his hands,
> Then boldly up and spake:
> 'I see,' quoth he, 'the Elephant
> Is very like a snake.'
>
>   . . . . . .
>
> And so these men of Hindostan
> Disputed loud and long,
> Each in his own opinion
> Exceeding stiff and strong,
> Though each was partly in the right
> And all were in the wrong.

Pluralists argue that in relation to other religions Christianity has often acted like one of the blind men in the parable. A Christian claiming that Christ is the way to salvation and that other religions are not as adequate is like a blind man claiming that only his perception of the elephant is correct and all others false. Pluralists advocate that Christians should regard Christ as just one among many revelations of the infinite God. Each of the revelations and the religious tradition that has formed around· it may consequently be viewed as an alternative and equally valid path to one divine reality. Hence, Hindus will call this divine reality *Brahman*, mediated through the sacred scriptures; Buddhists, *Nirvana*, the path to which is taught by the Buddha; Muslims, *Allah*, whose final and authoritative messenger is Muhammad; Jews, *Yahweh*, whose will is definitively revealed in the Torah; Christians, *God*, who is revealed in Jesus Christ. This list can be extended of course to include Zoroastrianism, Sikhism, Jainism, and Chinese, Japanese and African religions – to name just a few.

This pluralist approach, according to its exponents, has the virtue of abandoning theological arrogance and fostering harmonious and fruitful relations between the religions of the world. Christians need not defend untenable claims that only in their religion is the single saving revelation found, nor need they defend the idea of 'mission to the heathens' which too often has been a covert form of Western imperialism. And pluralists insist that Christians need not abandon the belief that through the person of Jesus they have encountered the God who saves, heals and restores. But, they argue, while this is a perfectly reasonable claim, it should not be taken negatively and unreasonably to imply that only through Christ can God be savingly encountered.

One can appreciate the attraction of this position, but like the music of the sirens it also lures us into dangerous waters.

As a way of dismantling this approach and inspecting its various presuppositions, I will list below some of the basic tenets held by pluralists and then deal with each by turn. I have numbered each supposition for clarity and cross reference.

PLURALIST PRESUPPOSITIONS

1. The Christian God is a God of love and would not exclude non-Christians from salvation simply because they are non-Christians.

2. This means that Jesus cannot be seen as the special revelation of God, but is one among many equal revelations – all adequate for salvation.

Number two will usually be deduced from number one.

3. If we actually look at the religions around the world in their various forms it is difficult to deny that all religions seem to produce a history marked by both saintly and demonic behaviour. If 'by their fruits ye shall know them', then Christianity cannot win (or lose) when its history is compared.

Number three supports the contention of number two.

4. We can also see that for the majority of men and women throughout history the religion to which they belong is determined by birth – and for many this means that they would never have even heard of Christianity.

Number four is closely allied to number one.

5. Christians cannot ground their claims concerning the uniqueness of salvation brought by Christ on the basis of their experience. The golden rule is to grant to others what one deems reasonable for oneself. Hence, if Christians base their claims on their own experience, then equally the *experience* of people in other religions must be granted equal status. If the Hindu, Muslim or another claims to experience salvation through his or her own religion, then, as our claims are based on experience, so must his or her claims be respected.

Number five supports numbers two and three.

6. One difficulty for Christians is that their view of truth has been determined by an *either–or* model. Either *x* is true or *y* is true: either it is raining outside or it is not; either this table is square or it is round – either Christianity is true and other religions false or all religions are equally true. But when we deal with the infinite God then the logic of finites is not appropriate. With a finite object (tables, or rain outside my window) we can say that an either–or notion is appropriate. However, with the infinite God we need not adopt a view that if one revelation is true then all others are false. The logic of the infinite allows for the plurality of a *both–and* model of truth – 'Yes, both this revelation is true and so is that one. God cannot be captured and limited by a single revelation.'

Number six provides a theoretical framework to facilitate number two.

7. Christians with this pluralist approach can now be released from imperialist and sometimes racist attitudes towards adherents of other religions. This new-found respect will provide the environment in which interreligious co-operation can tackle the global problems of famine, wars, suffering and hatred. Otherwise, religions will always be locked in a combative embrace.

Number seven provides a practical benefit for the acceptance of number two.

8. Pluralism calls for a new form of 'mission'. Clearly traditional missions will be redundant, except perhaps to the atheist/secular world. Towards each other, the religions can now learn and grow through the mutual sharing of the riches of their respective traditions. Mission now concerns serving one's neighbour in an international sense: aid work, medical supplies and the fostering of human development in under-developed and deprived countries. Furthermore, without the dangerous justification of saving souls at all costs, many misdeeds of previous missionaries need not be repeated.

Number eight points towards future developments within this pluralist approach.

I should stress that individual pluralists may hold all or only some of the eight propositions above. Clearly they develop and express these points in a variety of ways and in different styles. All eight points are, however, based on pluralist writings, and I have carefully documented my sources elsewhere (D'Costa 1986a). As I have tried to indicate, all of the points are interrelated, so that the weakening of one may result in the weakening of others. (The domino theory is applicable to a certain extent.) What can we say in the face of such arguments?

THE PLURALIST CASE EXAMINED

The most important of the pluralist suppositions are contained in the first two points: 1. that a God of love would not allow the perdition of millions of people simply because they are not Christians; 2. that consequently Jesus must be seen as one among many equal salvific revelations if all religions are equal paths to the one God.

Point two is crucial, and represents the influence of post-Enlightenment rationalism, which leads increasingly to the utilization of humanistic criteria to judge and dictate religious truth and revelation. Christianity is dictated to by these alien criteria, rather than dictates the terms in which it conducts the debate on religious pluralism.

Let me develop these remarks in more detail.

If the first pluralist presupposition were true, then the force of the second could carry conviction; but we need to qualify it to a considerable extent if we are to be true to strands present in the Christian tradition. Christians from different denominations have tried to tackle this first point while remaining thoroughly Christocentric (Christ-centred), rather than jettison its central affirmation of God's love. If it can be shown that God does not simply abandon millions of people who have never had a chance to encounter Christ, then we will see that the pluralist programme has been set up incorrectly from the start. In this essay, however, I can point in only a limited number of directions rather than develop a systematic argument (see also D'Costa 1986b for fuller discussion).

From the very beginning of Christianity's history, Christians were troubled by the question of the just men and women in the Old Testament. As sons of Abraham, Isaac and Joseph, and so aware of their sacred heritage, they faced precisely the question faced by Christians today: What of those men and women who persistently followed the promptings of the Spirit in their heart before the time of Christ? Are they lost through no fault of their own? Clearly there are men and women in non-Christian religions who are in an analogous situation inasmuch as, historically and existentially, they have not been confronted with the gospel. The answer evident in some of the New Testament material and non-canonical literature explored the solution of the descent into hell by Christ to preach to the just souls and redeem them. While most of these early Christians considered only the Jewish saints of old, some, like Clement of Alexandria, also considered the just of the pagan world.

A number of modern Protestant and Roman Catholic theologies have developed this idea to allow for some sort of confrontation with Christ by the non-Christian either at the last judgement or immediately after death and before the general judgement. While there are a number of significant differences among theologians here, what they have in common (with each other and with the early Christians) is their insistence on the centrality of Christ for salvation.

It is this same insistence that has marked the work of some Roman Catholic theologians who argue that the saving grace of Christ can be present and effective even when a person has not been confronted by

Christ. In a sense, the God who revealed himself to Israel as a holy, merciful, just and jealous God – for all the imperfections of his people – was nevertheless the Father of Jesus, and hence a trinitarian God. Hebrews 11, among other New Testament passages, testifies to Christ's hidden presence before the incarnation, as does John's '*Logos*'/'Word' theology. A number of the early Fathers such as Justin, Clement and Irenaeus took up this idea of the Logos as fragmentarily and obscurely present throughout the world – and now finally revealed and unobscured through the incarnation. This view, too, demands that Christ is the mediator of all salvation – always and everywhere.

What is important to note about these different solutions is that they attempt to answer the question set up by pluralists in their first point. If God is not a despot who consigns people to perdition for no fault of their own, then this indicates that one need not necessarily follow the pluralist path in reflecting upon religious pluralism.

But, before proceeding, a few other points need to be noted. Pluralists are often in danger of trying to force salvation upon everyone! It is one thing to say with 1 Timothy 2.4 that a loving God *desires* the salvation of all men and women; it is another to insist that this amounts to universalism – that is, that all men and women *are* saved. If freedom is real freedom to accept or reject God, then it would surely be presumptuous to claim that all people will be saved. We may hope that this will be the case, but we also have a graphic and devastating picture of the extent and depth of human sinfulness – in the cross. The cross is a constant reminder of the painful inadequacy of human striving, and a warning against liberal humanistic optimism. However, the cross and resurrection must be balanced dialectically together: despite the resurrection, humanity has not collectively experienced the salvation won by Christ. The kingdom of God is a present and future reality.

One last point. It must be made clear that the above points do not sanction other religions as a way to God *per se* – but only inasmuch as the adherents from those religions have not been confronted by the gospel. If a person is truly confronted by and rejects the God revealed in Jesus, then this must amount to a sinful rejection of God. Whether the gospel is always confronted when historical Christianity is presented – given the sinfulness of Christians and their sometimes disgraceful methods of proselytizing – is an issue that must be left open.

'The Christian God is a God of love and would not exclude non-Christians from salvation simply because they are non-Christians.' Given the comments above, it is possible to subscribe to this point *without* being a pluralist. Clearly, point two does not logically follow – but it is to point two that I now turn to pursue my investigation further. It is at this juncture that the slippery slope of relativism is encountered.

Pluralists answer point one by (unnecessarily) suggesting that if it is true (which it is), it must mean that 'Jesus cannot be seen as the special revelation of God, but is one among many equal revelations – all adequate for salvation.' The most decisive difficulty in adopting this solution is that it is self-defeating! Why is this?

God is not an idea or theory. Our understanding of God is based on revelation and the gratuitous self-disclosure of God. The doctrines of the incarnation and Trinity provide the grammatical safeguards and regulative stipulation that when we speak of God – as Christians – we cannot but also speak of Christ and the Spirit, while at the same time saying they are distinct and in unity. Christianity from its earliest days has maintained this linking between Jesus and God. Not only are the pluralist suggestions in danger of severing this link (which they deny), but in asserting point two they actually cut the link while maintaining it! This is because the assertion of a 'God of love' who cares for all men and women (point one) requires grounding. If the Buddhist or humanist, for example, were (understandably) to question this notion of God, then the Christian could only point to Christ as the basis for such talk of God. And this is precisely why point two is self-defeating. The pluralist grants equal validity to different views, some of which by definition cut across the *raison d'être* of the pluralist case. For example, could a Christian pluralist justify his or her assertion that 'God is love' to a Buddhist, whose beliefs he or she claims are equally true, if that Buddhist does not believe in a God – and even thinks that the question about God is unnecessary for 'salvation'? ('Salvation' thereby has very different implications within these two traditions, a point to which I shall return later.)

There are many examples of the way in which point two leads to self-refutation. The above example concerns the basic theistic underpinning of the pluralist case being contradicted by non-theistic religions. The oddness of the pluralist case is that it legitimizes and defends such contradiction by granting equal validity to all religions. It is difficult to see how the pluralist case can get off the ground when

its basic point concerning an all-loving God cannot rationally be sub-
stantiated or defended as the revelatory event it depends on is
relativized.

If the above issue is a fundamental problem, there are many other
difficulties with the pluralist suggestion. Again, I will give only one
example. Muslims faithfully hold in accordance with the Qur'ān that
Jesus did *not* die on the cross, although the Qur'ān holds that Jesus
ascended into heaven and was born of a virgin. If the Qur'ān is to be
taken as an equally valid revelation as the New Testament revelation,
we are then confronted with a dilemma that can bear only an *either–
or* answer. Either Jesus did or did not die on the cross. Upon this fact
Christianity depends, and upon the opposite depends the authority of
the Qur'ān. A 'both–and' solution is inadmissible, particularly since
many Western theistic religions tend to place a strong emphasis on the
historical and particular. How can we decide or adjudicate? We have
seen that the pluralist option leads into a cul-de-sac. The one other
alternative, which some pluralists adopt (thereby implicitly acknowl-
edging their standing outside the Christian circle of discourse), is
that we have to judge the truth or falsity of the revelations by criteria
outside of any one revelation. That this option is adopted is indicative
that all Christologically centred thinking (and therefore Christian
thinking) seems to be abandoned. It leads to non-Christocentric
criteria such as Jungian notions of wholeness defining 'salvation', or
to equally problematic and sometimes vacuous criteria which would
often be more satisfying to humanists than to many adherents of the
world religions.

The pluralist refuge in non-Christological criteria indicates both its
'strength' and its weakness. (Depending on where one stands, they
are actually the same thing!) Its apparent 'strength' is that it produces
a non-controversial and watered-down version of Christianity: a
Christianity that does not gain its meaning, its challenge and its
promise from the person of Christ. It produces a Christianity that is
not a salt to the earth or a light to the Gentiles, but is rather a
Christianity that will accommodate all claims to truth – even when
they are contradictory. If this is the price of 'harmony', then it is a
'harmony' based on principles alien to the gospel. Such principles are
probably equally alien to many adherents of world religions – who
would also refuse to surrender their truth claims. If Christianity has
anything to offer a troubled world, then it is Christ – the source and

criterion (although it may appear folly to many) of true harmony, justice and peace.

The pluralists relinquish the central teaching of the Christian tradition that ultimately our only criterion for talk of God, goodness, grace, truth and light derives from Christ. Christ judges the entire world, and that includes the religions of the world, one of which is of course Christianity. It is by subjecting ourselves and all things to the judgement and mercy of God in Christ that Christians have something really significant to offer in a religiously pluralist world. Not in terms of a triumphalist self-glorification, but in accepting and pointing to the scandal of particularity that culminates in the cross. It is by the criterion of the crucified Christ that Christians can evaluate and provide the framework for assessing the truth claims made by the various religions. The scandal of particularity also implies that it is more likely that, rather than assuming multiple and equally valid revelations, God has chosen to reveal himself in a definitive and normative fashion once and for all – and irreversibly. This particularity does not deny that God has acted elsewhere in history (Israel is testimony to this), but it requires that God's action and nature can be discerned only through a primary focus that then allows all history to appear in its proper perspective. The Christian confronted by religious pluralism – as with any other question – must wear Christological spectacles, so to speak, or is in danger of losing sight and vision.

It is nearly time to develop these comments further in order to indicate a positive alternative to pluralism and its relativistic tendencies by working through the remaining points of the pluralist programme. But first, let me summarize my argument so far.

The pluralist introduces a false solution to a badly posed question! To relativize the salvific revelation of Christ so as to facilitate that non-Christians may possibly be saved is self-refuting (from a Christian standpoint) and theologically destructive and unnecessary. Through this manoeuvre, pluralists relinquish all normative criteria for talk of God, grace and salvation, and thereby cannot even properly assert that God acts in all religions. One may ask: On whose God and from which revelation are such claims based? They minimize historical, theological and philosophical truth claims, and by relativizing such claims eventually abandon the notion of religious truth. Their both–and model of truth, as opposed to an either–or model, has limited application. While Christians claim that Christ was *totus dei* (totally divine), they do not claim that he was the divinity in its totality. Hence, insights and wisdom from the world religions can often be incorporated within a Christological outlook, enriching and deepening the faith of the Christian. But this is a far cry from entertaining truth claims inimical to faith in Christ while at the same time confessing the Christian faith. It is a simple matter of rational coherence.

The pluralist case relies on its cumulative force. While I have tried to counter its main arguments, what of some of the remaining points?

Point three concerned the maxim 'by their fruit ye shall know them', and argued that the history of religions would fail to vindicate any one religion as being better than another. Hence, all religions could and should be viewed equally. There are two fundamental flaws in this argument, which again highlights the humanist-rationalist outlook of pluralists.

First, Christians do not claim that they themselves are superior or better than the next person. In fact, a venerable doctrine within the Christian tradition affirms that the Church is a Church of saints *and* sinners. However, Christians do proclaim the crucified and risen Christ. Therein lies the truth of Christianity, a truth which judges the Church and all religions and human life. To argue that Christianity bases its claims on having morally better adherents is absurd. Revelation is the issue at stake, not the history of religions.

Second, the pluralist view assumes a God-like vantage and a naïve causal equation: where good works operate, then there is God's grace. While this may certainly be the case, the genuine difficulty of seeing the deep and secret ways of the heart is neglected. Can we really tell by someone's outer actions alone where their heart is? Deception, jealousy, pride – these and many more factors operate in our motives, motives ultimately known only to us and God (and not always clearly at that for the former!). The saints will not always blaze the pages of history, and are often those who have silently and patiently accepted God's will in hope, faith and charity in their unglamorous and difficult lives.

There is a truth contained in this third point which should not be obscured. Where and when grace is responded to outside Christianity – and the history of Israel is evidence of this – this grace is always and everywhere the grace of the true God, disclosed in Christ and maintained through the Holy Spirit. There is no need to try and discredit or deny the existence of saintly figures in the world religions. Given the qualifications above, we can rejoice that the Spirit of

God groans in creation and blows where it will. As in the analogous case of Cyrus in the Old Testament or the Samaritan woman in the New, persons from outside 'our group' may often have much to show and tell us.

The fourth point concerned the fact that the majority of people have had their religion determined by their birth. There is an element of truth and falsity present in this claim. Taken strictly, the argument would amount to a form of determination denying any real freedom to the human agent. While many people are born into a religion, through the process of maturation and adulthood they can come radically to criticize, change, and even leave the religion into which they were born! This happens all the time. Conversion, in whatever direction, is an important phenomenon that also requires explanation. In fact, most of the founders of the various world religions were born into a religious environment which they challenged and changed. Muhammad, Guru Nanak, the Buddha and Jesus are all examples. To suggest that all religions are true because people are born into them and often have no alternative is analogous to suggesting all beliefs are true because people hold them! In a logical sense one cannot reduce truth to a function of birth without incurring a lot of odd implications. For example, if one was born and brought up a Nazi in Hitler's Germany, can we say that Nazi beliefs are thereby true? It is an extreme example, but it underscores the logical point I am making. We can of course have sympathy for the person born into such a situation, but in an analysis of freedom and morality we must clarify the theoretical issues. Truth is surely not a function of birth.

The positive aspect of this fourth point is in reminding Christians that many people have never encountered the gospel and have often lived their lives without the chance explicitly to confess Christ. We have seen how non-pluralist theologians have attempted to reflect on this issue, suggesting a post-mortem confrontation with Jesus Christ or suggesting that Christ may be implicitly followed through the promptings of and openness to grace. These inclusivist theologians do not believe that all non-Christians are inevitably lost, and therefore do not require that one adopt the suspect 'truth is a function of birth' argument. This point, then, should be an inspiration for mission. The gospel must be proclaimed to the ends of the earth, and until the missionary imperative is carried out sensitively and respectfully, the catholicity of the Church in its true sense – its universality – is only partial. This fourth point should also be a reminder to Christians that they should always be self-critical as to whether their own faith is based on mature and responsible free choice or simply on habit, upbringing and societal pressures. When Christianity becomes a matter of 'What I was born into' rather than 'What I am called to by the crucified and risen Christ', then Christians too are in danger of allowing birth – rather than revelation – to determine perceptions of truth.

The fifth point has similarities with the previous one: if Christians base *their* claims on *experience*, then equally other claims based on experience must be legitimate. Hence, other religious claims must also be considered true. But again, such a strategy is self-refuting and the basic assumption betrays post-Enlightenment humanist and rationalist influences. To take the latter issue first. Schleiermacher was instrumental – in the Kantian tradition – in putting experience rather than revelation centre-stage. Inevitably, such a move has exalted experience at the cost of the object of experience. Sociologists have been quick to point to the similarities of experience of the Nuremberg rallies and revivalist evangelical meetings. That this similarity tells us nothing of the motives, intentions and focal objects of such meetings is significant. We arrive at the same cul-de-sac in granting equal validity to claims based on experience. Contradictions abound. The self-refuting nature of the argument becomes clear. If the theist experiences a world infused with God's presence and the atheist does not, would it be appropriate to say both are correct? They may both base their claim on experience, but this tells us nothing of the truth or falsity of the object and interpretation of that experience.

Furthermore, this stress on experience removes attention from another vital issue. When a Buddhist or a Muslim or Hindu claims to *experience* 'liberation' or 'salvation', they may actually mean very different things. On one level we have the difficulty of making adequate and appropriate translations from Pali, Arabic or Sanskrit words into English terms. During the process of translation, echoes from one tradition (the host translator) may falsely colour the original terms (the translated tradition). If I literally translated 'It's raining cats and dogs' into Chinese, my Chinese friend may well think I've been drinking when she looks for evidence in the street! Similarly, translating the (Zen) Buddhist notion of *Satori* into 'salvation' may detract from the issue that the Zen Buddhist does not believe in a God or in individual souls; similarly for the Advaitin Hindu notion of *moksha*. Can 'salvation' in Christ be said to be similar to the experience of 'salvation' in another religion in which the soul, God and often the reality of the world is denied or viewed quite differently?

The point I am making is that if we strongly emphasize *experience* (and even make it an argument for religious equality), we inevitably get further away from the real issue: the object of revelation and the type of 'salvation' being spoken of. If we take other religions seriously, we must also take seriously their specific claims about the nature of reality and our relation to that reality – not just their claim that in *experiencing* this they have gained what may loosely be termed 'salvation'.

The sixth point concerning either–or/both–and models to deal with truth claims has already been treated above, so I shall pass on to the seventh: that Christian pluralists can be freed from racist and imperialist attitudes towards those of other religions; that global problems can finally be tackled constructively; and, furthermore, that without a theological pluralism religions will always be locked in a combative embrace. While the sincere attitude of pluralists cannot be questioned, their extraordinary theological and political naïvety can.

While Christians and Christian history cannot be immune to the charge of racism and imperialism, one may question whether these traits are intrinsic to the gospel. This is surely the point at issue. If Christ's message is taken seriously, then surely the critique of racism and imperialism is supplied by the gospel itself. To suffer with and care for the oppressed, outcast and lowly is central to the crucified founder of Christianity. And precisely to believe that the cross discloses the true face of God is also to believe that all forms of oppression are sinful. To hold to Christ, rather than relativize Christ, actually protects the values of human dignity so dear to pluralists. If Christ can be relativized, why not the ethical values that derive from the gospel? It can be argued that a Christian truly committed to Christ must also be committed to justice, peace and equality. To unpack these terms is a complex matter, but for my present purpose (and without being a pluralist) it would certainly mean that each person's dignity and freedom are paramount. There is to my knowledge no major Christian church that does not uphold the right to the freedom of religious belief (and that means *all* religions) within due limits, and also condemns coercion and other unlawful forms of proselytizing. It is somewhat facile to think that equal rights for different religious practices and beliefs automatically entail equal validity.

Hence, the second part of this point is also misleading. A non-pluralist theology can be firmly committed to attacking global problems of famine, suffering and hatred. Such a programme is hardly the prerogative of pluralists. In the light of Christ, the Christian must try and sow the seeds of peace and hope wherever she or he can. When this means co-operation with people of other faiths, there is no injunction from the gospel to desist. Clearly, in a pluralist society each person will bring the 'solutions' from their own perspective to bear upon common problems. In many cases there will be substantial room for agreement and joint action. History is complex and one cannot lay down absolute guidelines, except to say that in all decisions the Christian is accountable to his or her community, to his or her own conscience and to God. Instances of inter-religious co-operation are found throughout history and thankfully are increasing today – without the requirement that participants relinquish their central beliefs.

Finally, it may be said that in a troubled world the abandonment of the central tenets of Christian faith as a solution to the clash of world-views represents at best a liberal desire to please everyone (and consequently no one) and at worst a policy that enhances rather than relieves the crisis. If Christ is a light to the nations, then it is odd to hide this light under a bushel in embarrassment.

It is appropriate to finish this essay on the issue of mission. By now, it will I hope be clear that the pluralist version of mission amounts to a humanist version of social service! It is of course absolutely right that the welfare of the whole person be the centre of Christian concern. Poverty, disease and famine all endanger the glory and beauty of God's creation. But ultimately, if the salt is to keep its flavour, the source of these values and the source of eternal salvation must also be proclaimed. If the Christian truly wishes to share with and love the non-Christians then, as with a close friend, one's most treasured beliefs and commitment should also be shared. Proclaiming the risen Christ through one's deeds, thoughts and words is always, and has always been, the central challenge of the gospel.

However, it should be added that any real dialogue and friendship requires mutual trust and respect. In the same way that the Christian would expect his or her right to mission, he or she must equally be willing to listen to and be challenged by his or her partner's faith. This openness does not imply a lack of commitment, or a suspension

of one's beliefs (a phenomenological *epoché*), but a genuine respect
for the person as he or she is.

CONCLUSION

I began this essay by outlining our situation of religious pluralism in
the twentieth century. The title 'Against Religious Pluralism' is
directed at the pluralist theology that has arisen in the light of this
situation – and *not* as a comment against non-Christian religions!
Certainly, this new situation challenges us to rethink our faith. My
suggestion is that we do not rethink it along the lines of theological
pluralism, as this avenue seems more of an abandonment than a
rethinking.

Elsewhere I have developed what I have called 'Christian
inclusivism', that is, a critical appreciation of the worth and limitation
of non-Christian religions (D'Costa 1986b; D'Costa 1987). In this
essay I have tried to show that Christian theology can be faithful to its
central claims and beliefs about Christ without thereby implying the
condemnation of most of non-Christian humanity. I have also tried to
argue that for Christians a true evaluation and appreciation of non-
Christian religions can arise only from a Christ-centred theology
rather than a humanist-rationalist one. If this essay acts as a signpost
towards new avenues in need of further exploration and as a warning
against other paths of exploration, its purpose will be achieved.

11
A FOX HUNTER'S GUIDE TO CREATION SPIRITUALITY

Lawrence Osborn

THE FOX PHENOMENON

In the past decade the Dominican priest Matthew Fox has achieved a remarkable degree of popularity or, at least, notoriety. He has been variously described as 'one of the best-loved Catholic theologians in the United States' (Newman 1992, 5), dismissed as 'an entertainer, not a serious theologian' (Goodall and Reader 1992, 105), and accused of providing 'an ideological preparation for . . . a potential new Holocaust' (Brearley 1989, 48).

The reason for this controversy is his advocacy of what he calls creation spirituality. In order to promote his ideas he has founded an Institute in Culture and Creation Spirituality and co-founded a publishing company, Bear and Company (which publishes several of Fox's books, various anthologies of creation mystics and books by several New Age authors).

This new spirituality came under investigation by the Vatican following complaints from conservative Roman Catholics. At first Fox's superiors resisted demands that he be disciplined. However, he was finally silenced for a year in 1989 (Peters 1989). Predictably, this had the effect of making Fox more popular than ever.

Since then the Dominican Order's tolerance of Fox has apparently worn thin. He is currently under threat of expulsion for refusing to obey a ruling that he should return to the Midwest Province.

WHAT IS CREATION SPIRITUALITY?

Creation spirituality possesses an immediate attraction for many who are unhappy with the way in which the Christian churches have accommodated themselves to modern Western culture. Fox is outspoken in his opposition to the forces driving the environmental crisis. But he sees this as just one symptom of a much more widespread spiritual malaise. Other symptoms include the death of mysticism and creativity, the reduction of wisdom to information, the destruction of native cultures by the homogenizing forces of modernity, and the rise of various kinds of fundamentalism.

Creation spirituality is Fox's attempt to articulate a constructive response to these destructive powers. In a series of books published in the 1970s Fox gradually developed the various elements which are now recognizable as creation spirituality (Fox 1972, 1976, 1979). These elements finally emerged in their mature form with the publication of Fox's edition of Meister Eckhart's sermons (Fox 1980). He gave this interpretation of Eckhart a fourfold structure: creation; letting go and letting be; breakthrough and giving birth to self and God; the new creation – compassion and social justice. This same structure later became the framework for *Original Blessing* (Fox 1983).

The first path, the *via positiva*, is the path of befriending creation. In contrast to what he argues is the dominant Christian emphasis on sin and redemption, Fox calls for us to focus on God's first act: creation. The material world was intended to be a blessing, not a curse. It is God's good gift to us and to all creatures, to be enjoyed responsibly; not a prison which separates the soul from God. Thus he defines mysticism as ecstasy and suggests that its goal is to get high. Among the strategies he advocates for achieving this state are 'chants, . . . fasting, abstinence, drugs, drink, celibacy, Yoga and Zen exercises, TM, biofeedback' (Fox 1981, 55).

The second path, the *via negativa*, is the path of befriending darkness. This involves letting go of our images and words to find God in silence and the luminous darkness of Christian mysticism. In it, Fox recalls us to the true function of asceticism: not a denial of the world and the body, but a purification of the senses.

With the third path, the *via creativa*, we move into a more active mode. This is the path of befriending creativity. Like many Western Christians, Fox identifies the human capacity for creativity with the divine image. Thus he is also able to call it 'befriending our divinity'. This path stresses the value of artistic activity as a form of meditation. But Fox does not limit creativity to what is conventionally understood as art. This would be to introduce a divisive elitism into spirituality. On the contrary, Fox presents the whole of life as a work of art to be undertaken creatively for the glorifying of God and the beautifying of God's good creation.

The fourth path, the *via transformativa*, brings us back to Fox's original emphasis on a prophetic concern for social justice. This is the path of 'befriending new creation', the path of compassion. It calls us to look outwards to the world around us, marred as it is by the fruits of false ideologies. It calls upon us to work out our Christian faith in the very practical activity of seeking personal, social and ecological justice.

These four paths must be taken together. They are not four alternative modes of spirituality. Nor are they four steps in an ascent to God. Fox's preferred metaphor is that of a spiral in which each of the paths enriches and is enriched by the others.

A RELIGIOUS PARADIGM SHIFT

Why have Fox's four paths generated such opposition? Is it just that he makes unfortunate use of outrageous metaphors in his efforts to shake us out of our complacency? Is it simply that his style grates on the ears of the more sober members of the Christian community? Or is that his opponents have sensed that he is engaged in something far more radical than a reform of contemporary Catholic spirituality?

Fox himself is quite open about this. Speaking of modern Roman Catholic worship, he asserts that 'Liturgy in its present context is not redeemable' (Fox 1988, 216). In fact, what he wants is nothing less than a paradigm shift: 'Augustine has failed to solve the problems of religion for the West, and thus, it is time to give a less sexist, less dualistic, less anthropocentric religious paradigm its chance. This paradigm can be found in a creation-centered mysticism' (Fox 1988, 80).

The popularity of this concept of paradigm shifts owes a great deal to the work of Thomas Kuhn, an American historian of science. Kuhn argues that science proceeds by revolutions (or changes of paradigm) rather than by reform. He defines a paradigm as 'the entire constellation of beliefs, values, techniques, and so on shared by the members of a given community' (Kuhn 1970, 175). Thus paradigm change is nothing less than a change in world-view. Competing paradigms are simply incommensurable (Kuhn 1970, 94). This incompatibility even extends to data, concepts and terms which appear to be unchanged: familiar concepts take on unfamiliar meanings (Kuhn 1970, 135).

This suggests that when Fox speaks of a new religious paradigm he is signalling that nothing can be taken for granted. We cannot simply

assume that we know what he means when he uses terms like God,
Jesus Christ or Holy Spirit! The terminology may be familiar while
the content it is given is entirely novel.

FROM FALL/REDEMPTION TO CREATION

According to Fox, the problems confronting Western culture and
religion are rooted in a faulty perception of the cosmos.

ORIGINAL SIN AS DUALISM

Fox rejects the Augustinian conception of original sin. He denies that
human nature is inherently disordered. Instead, we enter sinless into a
broken world. It is our assimilation to that world which imposes upon
us an 'original sin mentality' (Fox 1988, 29).

According to Fox, the cause of that brokenness is the sin behind
sin, namely, dualism (Fox 1983, 214). Thus he identifies all forms of
dualism as original sin (Fox 1984, 88).

As is well known, dualism opposes the rational subject to the
material object. Fox accuses it of encouraging rationalism, individualism, anthropocentrism, reductionism and determinism. A dualistic
perspective also suppresses creativity. Furthermore, it results in
master–slave relationships; relationships characterized by 'power-
over' rather than 'power-from-within'.

Fox's language is extravagant and, at times, hard to take seriously.
Is it really true, as he seems to suggest, that all the evils of the
modern world may be traced to the faulty theology of Augustine?
Even if we trace the roots of Augustine's 'errors' back to Plato or as
far back as the emergence of patriarchy, it seems inherently unlikely
that prior to such a time the human race enjoyed a paradisaical
existence. To suggest, with Fox, that dualism is the root of all evil
seems to credit human ideas with far too much power.

SALVATION AS HOLISM

If our 'fall' can be identified with the emergence of a faulty perception of the world, it follows that an idea can save us: 'Creation-
centered spirituality names dualism as original sin and offers . . . a
wonderful alternative. For it defines salvation as holism, as making
whole, making one, and therefore making healthy, holy, and happy'
(Fox 1984, 88).

By looking away from ourselves to creation as a whole we become aware of the biological reality of interconnectedness. Taken as a metaphysical principle, this concept provides Fox with the necessary corrective to dualism and separation.

Everything is related to everything else. Awareness of the inter-relatedness of all reality encourages us to delight in creation, unblocks the wellsprings of creativity and enables communal healing to take place.

Because of this emphasis Fox is sometimes wrongly accused of advocating monism (e.g., Brow 1989). However, Fox insists on a dialectical approach to reality. Faced with deciding which is prior, the one or the many, Fox would want to say 'both': 'All things are one, yet each is separate, individual, unique' (Starhawk 1979, 25).

While it may be possible to reconcile a dialectical view of reality with orthodox Christian theology, the suggestion that salvation is merely a matter of adopting a different perspective is problematic. This is, strictly speaking, a gnostic view of salvation. When the theologians of the early Church (including Fox's arch-enemy, Augustine) rejected gnosticism, it was not just because of its dualism. Equally important was the Christian insistence that sin and evil go deeper than our understanding and perceptions. Knowledge of the good does not ensure that I will choose to do the good.

FROM THEISM TO PANENTHEISM

Corresponding to Fox's shift from fall/redemption to creation is an equally radical change in the Western understanding of God: a shift from theism to panentheism.

REJECTION OF THEISM

Theism is the dominant understanding of God within Judaism, Christianity and Islam. It is a blanket term which is capable of covering a wide range of interpretations, from the detached watchmaker of the deists, through an interventionist deity (the most popular interpretation in those cultures most affected by the Enlightenment), to a God who is intimately involved in every aspect of creation. However, there are certain features common to all forms of theism, namely, the transcendence of God and the notion that creation is a voluntary divine act. Together, these imply that, if such a God is related in any way to creation, it must be a personal relationship.

According to Fox, such a view is incorrigibly dualistic. It opposes creatures here to a God 'out there': 'The idea that god is "out there" is probably the ultimate dualism . . . All theism sets up a model or paradigm of people here and God "out there." All theisms are about subject/object relationships to God' (Fox 1983, 89).

In rejecting this view, Fox appears to be denying the possibility of any personal relationship with God. Elsewhere he writes: 'in a panentheistic world view there is no other. God is not other . . .' (Fox 1984, 100).

PANENTHEISM

Fox feels that to settle for a voluntary personal relationship between God and the world is inadequate. The metaphysical principle of interconnectedness must govern this relationship as well as the relationships between creatures. Thus he presents panentheism as the only adequate way to ensure an intimate relationship between God and the world (Fox 1988, 134).

One leading process theologian defines it as 'the doctrine that all is in God. It is distinguished from pantheism, which identifies God with the totality or as the unity of the totality, for it holds that God's inclusion of the world does not exhaust the reality of God' (Richardson and Bowden 1983, 423).

In panentheism God is the ultimate environment of creation: the matrix of the world. As Fox points out, such a concept of God lends itself to maternal imagery (Fox 1983, 223); for example, he speaks of the environment as a divine womb (Fox 1984, 84).

The relationship between God and creation which results from this conception of God may be described in dynamic terms as a process of flow and return. Beginning from its enclosure in the divine, creation flows out into multiplicity and returns to unity. This is traditionally known as emanationism, and Fox takes over traditional emanationist imagery from the medieval mystic Hildegard of Bingen: 'every ray of God is God (though not all of God). Thus, every creature is a ray of God, a radiance of God, a divine expression of God' (Fox 1988, 111). However, he is reluctant to admit this since emanationism is characteristic of the Neoplatonism he finds so distasteful in Augustine. Alternatively, the God–world relationship envisaged by

panentheism may be presented by means of an analogy with the
relationship between mind and body (Fox 1991, 63–5). However,
there are difficulties with this analogy. It may seem attractive to say
God is related to the world as mind is to body. But how *is* mind
related to body? This is one of the most intractable problems of
Western philosophy. In using this analogy, Fox is simply transposing
that problem into theology.

CREATIVITY AND COMPASSION

Fox's tendency to emanationism is also clear from his account of
creativity and compassion. These are polar aspects of Fox's God: the
twin forces which drive cosmogenesis.

Fox frequently refers to *dabhar*, a Hebrew word which is usually
translated as 'word' but which Fox prefers to interpret as the creative
energy of God (Fox 1983, 37–8). For Fox, this divine creativity is
revealed primarily in creation itself (Fox 1983, 38). Thus the universe
becomes the primal mystery into which the mystic must enter (Fox
1988, 40).

This primordial revelation in nature takes priority over any written
revelations. Thus theology must be built upon a view of nature (Fox
and Swimme 1982, 30–1). In saying this, Fox is simply following in
the footsteps of Roman Catholic tradition since Aquinas. However, as
Barth pointed out, the danger with such an approach is that is vulner-
able to distortion: that which is self-evidently obvious to a culture is
regarded as natural, and through natural theology may be projected on
to God.

By rejecting the association of *dabhar* with 'word', Fox detaches
it from its association with morality and order. It becomes the
unqualified amoral creative self-outpouring of God: the force that
drives the outward movement of divine emanation. Small wonder
that the imagery of giving birth should seem so appropriate.

The self-outpouring of divine creativity is balanced by compassion.
Fox rejects both the popular understanding of compassion as 'feeling
sorry for others' and the conventional theological understanding of it
as 'entirely free and gracious, bestowing rather than recognizing and
desiring goodness and lovableness' (Richardson and Bowden 1983,
341). Instead, he sees compassion as 'an awareness of the interconnectedness of all things' which entails 'the struggle for justice or
for seeing the balance to things restored when it is lost' (Fox 1984,

100). Compassion is the force that overcomes dualism, the force that unites the many.

Elsewhere Fox describes this force as Mother Love (e.g., Fox 1983, 225). He also uses the concept as the basis of a redefinition of grace (Fox 1984, 99). It ceases to be God's free gift of himself, and becomes instead deity's awareness of its need for the creature, and the related activity is to ensure a harmonious balance between deity and creature.

These twin forces of compassion and creativity come together in another concept which emerges in Fox's thought, namely, *eros* or 'love of life' (Fox 1983, 9, 55). It is explicitly related to *dabhar*, creativity. But he also relates it to the desire or lust that unites creation when he speaks of cosmic unity as 'the union of love' (Fox 1988, 50) or relates human erotic love to desire for the Cosmic Christ (Fox 1988, 165). In summary, Fox's *eros* is the power of fertility (Fox 1983, 53) in both its outpouring, ejaculative, aspect and its unitive, copulative, aspect.

Eros is a recurring feature of Graeco-Roman spirituality. In any world-view which sees the cosmos as an organism rather than a mechanism, sexual reproduction is a natural metaphor for cosmogenesis. Plato and his successors extended the concept so that it became the force which unites this world of multiplicity with the divine One (Armstrong 1986, 86).

Nor was this the exclusive preserve of pagan philosophers. *Eros* entered Christian theology primarily through the work of two theologians, Augustine and Pseudo-Dionysius (Beierwaltes 1986). So powerful was their influence that the historian of ideas, Arthur Lovejoy, could comment 'God's "love" . . . in medieval writers consists primarily rather in the creative or generative than in the redemptive or providential office of deity' (Lovejoy 1936, 67). Fox would repudiate any connection with Augustine. However, he does admit that two of the theologians whom he most admires (Aquinas and Eckhart) were influenced by Pseudo-Dionysius.

FOX'S COSMIC CHRIST

This is another good example of Fox's efforts to redefine traditional Christian terminology. Contrary to some of the over-reactions against Fox's spirituality, there is a clear Cosmic Christ tradition within the New Testament as well as in various Christian traditions. However, where this motif occurs, the Cosmic Christ is always clearly identified with the historical Jesus.

For Fox, the Cosmic Christ is first and foremost a symbol or archetype which 'encourages us to reverence our origins' and also 'our divinity and our responsibility as co-creators' (Fox 1988, 1). It is an expression of the divinity of all creation, since all creation is marked with the image of God (Fox 1988, 140, 241). More especially, it is an expression of our divinity. At one point he asks, 'Is the Cosmic Christ not an archetype about how we are all in some way anointed kings, queens, priests, and messiahs?' (Fox 1988, 242). We are all Cosmic Christs (Fox 1988, 137, 235).

But how does this concept express the divinity of ourselves and the cosmos? In seeking to name the Cosmic Christ more clearly, Fox highlights a number of familiar features: coherence (Fox 1988, 135), interconnectedness (Fox 1988, 141), (sexual) union (Fox 1988, 164ff.) and creativity (Fox 1988, 148, 202). He effectively identifies the Cosmic Christ with the divine *eros*: it is symbolic of the divine power of fertility which permeates the universe and drives its evolution.

Fox insists that the Cosmic Christ and the historical Jesus are interdependent (Fox 1988, 141). However, it appears that they are interdependent only in the same sense that Christ and all creation are interdependent, since he is equally insistent that Christ is immanent in all creatures (Fox 1988, 2). Jesus was *an* incarnation of the Cosmic Christ. Thus Fox asks, 'Does the fact that the Christ became incarnate in Jesus exclude the Christ's becoming incarnate in others – Lao-Tzu or Buddha or Moses or Sarah or Sojourner Truth or Gandhi or me or you?' and gives the answer, 'Just the opposite is the case' (Fox 1988, 235).

In spite of his attempts to maintain that there is something special about the relationship between Jesus and the Christ (e.g., Fox 1988, 154), Fox cannot hide the fact that Jesus was only one agent or vehicle of the Cosmic Christ (Fox 1988, 152). His view of Jesus and the Christ is reminiscent of the classical Christological heresy of adoptionism as well as of New Age discussions of the Christ (Osborn 1992, 143–52).

DIVINIZATION OF THE COSMOS

Fox's emanationism means that there is a continuity of being (or substance or essence) between God and the world: the cosmos is essentially divine. It may not exhaust what is meant by 'God', but when we speak of the cosmos we are, according to this view, speaking of an *aspect* of God.

Fox expresses this continuity in a variety of ways, but one of the most interesting (given contemporary developments in Western culture and religion) is the metaphor of 'Mother Earth'. For Fox, she is a unique example of the divinity of all creatures (Fox 1988, 147). He presents her as a conscious agent, suffering at the hands of an exploitative human race but capable of defending herself and executing judgement upon us in her own time (Fox 1988, 18).

Fox compares the sufferings of Mother Earth with those of Jesus upon the cross. Both the crucifixion and ecocide are examples of the same crime: matricide. This identification of Mother Earth with Jesus leads Fox to a grotesque reinterpretation of the eucharist. He suggests that we should see it as a celebration of the dying and rising of Mother Earth (Fox 1988, 149ff.): it is the 'sacrament of the wounded earth' (Fox 1988, 214).

Fox can make this identification of Mother Earth with Jesus because he has already identified her with the Cosmic Christ (Fox 1988, 145). She is the source of creativity and life. In other words, she is another symbol of the divine *eros*.

FOX'S NEW HUMANITY

THE IMAGE OF GOD

For Fox, all of creation images forth God. However, human beings are, in a unique sense, the images of God because we are the point at which creativity becomes self-conscious.

This identification of the image of God in humankind with our capacity for creativity is, like other aspects of Fox's theology, by no means new. In spite of his sexual imagery, Fox locates creativity firmly in the human psyche. Thus it may be seen as a development of the Augustinian view of the image of God. Fox merely shifts the emphasis from the structure of rationality to our creativity and imagination.

However, if we say that the image of God in humankind consists in our creativity, we imply that God is essentially creative. Fox would apparently agree, since he asserts that 'divinity means creativity' (Fox 1983, 184). But this view was firmly rejected by the early Church since it implies that God needs creation, that God and creation are co-eternal and, hence, that creation is itself divine.

HUMAN CREATIVITY AND COMPASSION

As images of the divine, we possess the divine power of creativity. As was the case with Fox's understanding of God's creativity, human creativity is not qualified in any way. It is raw creative power that will flow forth from us whether or not we acknowledge it: 'Creativity, the divine power of Dabhar, is so powerful and so overwhelming in us that we simply cannot deny it, cannot keep it down. If we are not consciously bent on employing it for life's sake, it will emerge on its own for the sake of destruction' (Fox 1983, 182). For Fox, modern consumerism is just such a destructive expression of our creativity.

Human creativity is to be celebrated in diversity, since 'Behind all creativity there lies not just a tolerance of diversity but a reverence for it, a passionate need for it' (Fox 1988, 204). This is especially true of sexual diversity. Thus 'The Cosmic Christ celebrates sexual diversity . . . The Cosmic Christ can be both female and male, heterosexual and homosexual. This is the way nature made the human species, and nothing that is natural to the cosmos is foreign to the Cosmic Christ' (Fox 1988, 164).

At the same time we possess the divine power of compassion. We express our compassion through unitive love (Fox 1988, 50) and the struggle for justice understood as harmony or balance (Fox 1988, 62-3).

If we are images of God, we are also microcosms of the universe (Fox 1988, 202). We image forth all aspects of deity. Interestingly, it is the human psyche that is the microcosm of the universe. This again recalls the Augustinian emphasis on psychological analogies for the Trinity, in spite of Fox's dislike for what he regards as Augustine's unhealthy introspection.

It follows from this understanding of the image of God as conscious possession of the divine powers of creativity and compassion that human beings are co-creators with God. Again Fox gives a modern interpretation to a traditional term. We are co-creators not in the sense that our creativity is ordained by God. Rather, we take an equal divine share in the creation of the universe. We share in the process of cosmic evolution (Fox 1983, 214). Furthermore, we

possess the ability to create our own realities: 'we live in the world
we create for ourselves. If we deserve better than what we have, we
must birth it from our souls' (Fox 1988, 206).

THE GLOBAL IMPLICATIONS OF OUR DIVINITY

This capacity to create our own future is the basis for Fox's faith in
the emergence of a global civilization. But, because it derives from
our divinity it is imbued with eschatological significance. It is a
process initiated by the divine spirit within us and, hence, a process
involving rebirth and conversion (Fox 1988, 160–1). Elsewhere, Fox
presents it in terms reminiscent of Teilhard de Chardin's vision of the
Omega Point as the emergence of a planetary soul (Fox 1979, 257–
66).

Such a process will depend upon the establishment of a deep
ecumenism. In contrast to the shallow ecumenism of the World
Council of Churches, this will involve an ecumenical council of all
religions (Fox 1988, 7). But this will not be so much the cause of
deep ecumenism as an expression of what is for Fox the truth about
religions.

Fox asserts that, at heart, all religions interpenetrate since they
have a common basis in mystical experience (Fox 1988, 65, 229ff.).
The particularities which mark one religion off from another are no
more than an ideological husk. All religious traditions, in their own
way, bear witness to the Cosmic Christ (Fox 1988, 228).

FOX'S ABUSE OF SCRIPTURE AND TRADITION

Fox has vigorously mined the Christian traditions for historical
precedents. This has led him to classify Christianity into two quite
distinct streams: the creation-centred tradition and the fall/redemption
tradition.

THE CREATION-CENTRED TRADITION

Fox identifies this stream with the Judaeo-Christian Scriptures (particularly the Jewish Wisdom traditions and the Christian Gospels),
Eastern Orthodoxy, Celtic Christianity (which, he believes has been
influenced by Hinduism, e.g., Fox 1988, 230), Thomas Aquinas (but
emphatically not Thomism), St Francis and the Franciscan Dante,
and, above all, the Rhineland mystics (Meister Eckhart, Hildegard of

Bingen and Mechthild of Magdeburg) and Julian of Norwich. Fox unites this apparent diversity of voices by subjecting them to a creation-centred hermeneutic consisting of the four paths of his own spirituality (e.g., Fox 1980, 1987, 1992). This raises the question whether his authorities are being allowed to speak for themselves. On closer examination, it appears that they are, in fact, being subjected to a bed of Procrustes. That mythological character used to measure travellers against his bed – if they fell short, they were stretched to fit; if they were overlong, amputation was the order of the day.

Amputation certainly seems to be the operative word when one examines Bear and Company's edition of Hildegard's *Scivias*. The preface acknowledges that passages which were regarded as 'irrelevant or difficult to comprehend today' have been omitted. Hildegard scholar Barbara Newman points out that these omissions amount to about half the original work and include 'lengthy passages promoting orthodox sexual ethics, commending virginity, expounding the theology of baptism and Eucharist, condemning heresy, upholding priestly ordination and celibacy, defending the feudal privilege of nobles, and exhorting the obedience of subjects'. She concludes that 'Hildegard is welcome to Fox's mystical pantheon so long as she refrains from being a twelfth-century Catholic' (Newman 1992, 7).

But the authors in question have also been subjected to the rack of eisegesis. Fox's fellow Dominican and Eckhart scholar, Simon Tugwell, complains of Fox's treatment of Eckhart: 'It is difficult to avoid the feeling that the mistranslation is deliberate, intended to minimise anything that would interfere with the alleged "creation-centredness" of Eckhart's spirituality' (Tugwell 1984, 197).

Fox also seems to insert novelties into the tradition without textual support. For example, he asserts that the Noachic covenant of Genesis 9 is a covenant between humankind and creation, rather than between God and creation (including humankind) (Fox 1988, 151)! Similarly, he asserts that the Holy Spirit is the fount of the Trinity in Eastern Orthodoxy (Fox 1991, 64–5). This is simply untrue: the Greek Fathers are united in their insistence on the priority of the Father within the Trinity.

The feminist theologian Rosemary Ruether, who is by no means unsympathetic to Fox's programme, comments that

> The good guys and girls all come out sounding exactly like Matthew Fox. They share entirely his same agenda, whether they be Jesus Christ, Meister Eckhart, Hildegard of Bingen, Sufis,

Hasidic Masters, Buddhists or Native Americans. Fox lacks the
basic requirement of historical scholarship, and critical distance
from his own agenda. (Ruether 1990, 172)

THE FALL/REDEMPTION TRADITION

Fox contrasts the creation-centred tradition with the dominant
fall/redemption tradition which he associates particularly with
Augustine. It would be no exaggeration to say that the latter is Fox's
bête noir. Augustine is the subject of vitriolic attacks which, taken in
combination, create the impression that his theology is the source of
all that is wrong with Western Christianity (and, by extension,
Western culture).

Significantly, Fox fails to substantiate his accusations. He
occasionally cites authorities who are critical of Augustine, but he
never offers a systematic critique of Augustine's thought. In reality,
Augustine is far more complex than Fox is prepared to admit. It has
been argued that Augustine was, in fact, the creation theologian
par excellence (Santmire 1985, 55–73). The truth probably lies
somewhere between these extremes (Osborn 1993).

THE LEGITIMATION OF FOX'S SPIRITUALITY

A recent British critique demonstrates that Fox uses a variety of
strategies which have ideological potential (Goodall and Reader
1992). For example, his classification of various Christian traditions
may be seen as involving both *unification* (the artificial suppression
of diversity to create a tradition) and *fragmentation* (the artificial
separation of voices which, taken together, might call into question
his position). Similarly, his extensive redefinition of Christian
terminology may be interpreted as *dissimulation* (the process by
which language is manipulated to conceal relations of domination). In
short, Fox systematically distorts the traditions he discusses in order
to lend support to his own spirituality.

CREATION SPIRITUALITY AS A RETURN TO PAGANISM

COSMOGENESIS AS A SEXUAL PROCESS

Fox's divinization of the world is a clear pagan theme: divinity is not
conferred upon us by the gracious action of a transcendent God, but is

ours simply by virtue of our creaturehood. Related to this is his stress on cosmogenesis as a sexual process. There are clear parallels between Fox's account of *eros* and contemporary pagan thought; for example, his colleague Starhawk describes cosmogenesis in the following terms:

> The Goddess falls in love with Herself, drawing forth her own emanation, which takes on a life of its own. Love of self for self is the creative force of the universe. Desire is the primal energy, and that energy is erotic: the attraction of lover to beloved, of planet to star, the lust of electron for proton. Love is the glue that holds the world together. (Starhawk 1979, 25)

In keeping with this understanding, Fox presents sexual activity as religious celebration and encourages men to celebrate the sacred phallus through native ritual (Fox 1988, 177)! Thus Christianity is transformed into a fertility cult in direct contradiction of clear elements within the Judaeo-Christian Scriptures.

THE CONQUEST OF TIME

Another disturbing feature of Fox's theology is his tendency to suppress the temporal and historical. Fox would deny this accusation, claiming that we need to maintain both space and time in dialectical tension. However, he consistently allows space to dominate time.

To begin with, his divinization of the world effectively converts nature into a sacred space – a point he acknowledges when he speaks of Mother Earth as a temple (Fox 1988, 146). Furthermore, he argues that Western theology has been guilty of an idolatry of time (Fox 1988, 141, 143).

Perhaps the clearest indication of his preference comes in his discussion of time and space in relation to the death and resurrection of Jesus. The death of *Jesus* pertains to time; the resurrection of *Christ* pertains to space (Fox 1988, 143): 'The resurrection is nothing if not a conquest of time and place (death on Golgotha) by space – that is by an empty (space-filled) tomb where sadness and death no longer are granted place' (Fox 1988, 141). Time is associated with death and decay. But could it not be argued that time is more properly associated with life? Thus the resurrection is the victory of time (and life) over space (death; the tomb). Clearly, for Fox, it is space that is the dominant reality.

Another indicator of his bias towards space is his form of realized eschatology. For Fox, the fulfilment of all things is located in the present rather than the future – it is the depth of the present. However:

> The invitation to explore the depths of the Now time is also an invitation to let go of all time. For an entry into the divine power of the present constitutes an entry into that divine space where all time stands still, where timeless play is operative, where time is at last suspended, forgotten, shed, so that God may be 'all in all'. (Fox 1983, 106–7)

Finally, his bias against time is seen in his inability to take history seriously. This inability is witnessed in his essentially a-historical treatment of the Christian (and other) traditions touched on in the previous section. It is visible in his mythologization of the Christian Scriptures in his efforts to find evidence of his mythological Cosmic Christ to supplant a historical Jesus. And it is clear in his rejection of the historical particularity of religions in favour of a mythical and mystical common spirituality.

This tendency is disturbing precisely because the predominance of space over time is characteristic of paganism. According to Paul Tillich, 'Paganism can be defined as the elevation of a special space to ultimate value and dignity' (Tillich 1964, 31). By contrast, Christianity begins with God's self-revelation in historical terms:

> The God of the gospel is the Hope at the beginning of all things, in which we and all things are open to our fulfillment; he is the love which will be that Fulfillment; and he is the Faithfulness of Jesus the Israelite, which within time's sequences reconciles this Beginning and this End. (Jenson 1982, 25)

In other words, Christianity is trinitarian and, as such, inescapably rooted in history.

Whereas Christianity can look forward to the fulfilment of all things, existence under the dominance of space is ultimately tragic: all existence is governed by the inexorable cycle of genesis and decay, birth and death, outpouring and return – precisely the powers celebrated by Fox in his theology. Thus, instead of prophetic promise, the characteristic form of religion under the dominance of space is a time-denying form of mysticism (Tillich 1964, 34), often accompanied by a stress on myth and ritual re-enactment. Fox desires that he be seen as a prophetic figure, but the dominant impression left by his writings is precisely this combination of mythology and mysticism.

Fox's emphasis on space at the expense of time is corrosive not just of trinitarian Christianity but also of human relationships. This is because relationships exist in time. The abolition of time effectively walls the mystic off from contingent human existence and, hence, from personal relationships with others (including God). As Carl Raschke points out: 'In the endeavor to stop time, man runs the risk of undercutting his relations with others; indeed, he threatens to stab to death his very humanity' (Raschke 1980, 22). In a similar vein, Tillich accuses paganism, with its emphasis on space, of being inherently unjust (Tillich 1964, 38). A tragic cosmos leaves no room for Christian concepts of justice and love. Instead there is only will to power.

It seems that Fox has achieved Aldous Huxley's vision of a spiritualized Christianity:

> From the writings of Eckhart, Tauler and Ruysbroeck, of Boehme, William Law and the Quakers, it would be possible to extract a spiritualised and universalised Christianity, whose narratives should refer, not to history as it was . . . but to 'processes forever unfolded in the heart of man.' But unfortunately . . . Christianity has remained a religion in which the pure Perennial Philosophy has been overlaid, now more, now less, by an idolatrous preoccupation with events and things in time. (Huxley 1958, 63–4)

FOX'S SHADOW

But whence has come this paganism? What are the roots of Fox's new paradigm? Many critics look, with some justification, to the New Age movement. A number of themes in the foregoing analysis certainly point to affinities with the New Age – and these affinities are strong enough for Fox to have been invited to speak at Findhorn (one of the foremost British New Age communities). Similarly, one may draw parallels between Fox's work and that of his colleague Starhawk, a leading radical feminist neo-pagan.

However, affinities and parallels are not the same as roots. There can be little doubt that Fox's roots are firmly bedded in the soil of Roman Catholic Christianity. As I have hinted at various points in this essay, Fox's writings show a clear indebtedness to the very theologian he goes to pains to repudiate, namely, Augustine. Earlier I described Augustine as Fox's *bête noir*; I might have said, drawing on Jung, that Augustine is Fox's shadow.

I have already indicated several points at which this indebtedness to Augustine (and Neoplatonism) is particularly striking: the role of *eros*, the tendency to emanationism, the psychological locus for the image of God. Another point of similarity is their shared suspicion of time.

Finally, on the rare occasions that Fox discusses the Trinity, he adopts a characteristically Augustinian form of the doctrine. He insists that the *filioque* (the procession of the Holy Spirit from Father *and* Son) is 'the' traditional form of the doctrine (Fox 1983, 214). Indeed he even suggests that this Augustinian innovation is the most important feature of trinitarian thought (Fox 1988, 191). As might be expected, there is a corresponding suppression of the personhood of the Spirit which is variously identified with love, compassion, divine *eros* (e.g., Fox 1984, 100; Fox 1988, 145).

CONCLUSION

Far from turning his back on Augustine, Fox has unwittingly perpetuated some of the key Neoplatonic themes of Augustine's theology. It is the inattentive acceptance of these themes which is integral to Fox's return to paganism.

This may strike readers as a hostile critique. However, if there is hostility in it, it is because I share many of Fox's concerns about contemporary culture and Western Christianity. Fox is entirely right to want to shake Western Christianity out of its Babylonian captivity to Enlightenment liberalism. He has also pointed to some valuable resources to aid us in that task (specifically the Scriptures themselves; the Eastern Orthodox tradition which, at its best, achieved a transformation of classical culture that might be described as cultural conversion; and Celtic Christianity, a less intellectual but nevertheless highly successful example of enculturation).

However, I believe the attempt to mythologize (or paganize) the tradition is fundamentally mistaken. Such a process can never revive 'a religion of time aiming at the sanctification of time' (Heschel 1966, 7). It cannot restore *shalom*: a concept which might well be summarized as 'justice, peace and the integrity of creation'. If Fox is serious about such issues, he would do better to start with trinitarianism.

12
KNOWING GOD PERSONALLY: REFLECTIONS ON THE FEMINIST CONCEPT OF PATRIARCHY

Andrew Walker

INTRODUCTION

One of the many slave-spirituals that have survived the American Civil War begins, 'When I get to heaven I am going to argue with the Father, and chatter with the Son.' There is something deeply moving about these few words. Written in the ante-bellum period of American history when African Americans, like the slaves in Plato's *Republic*, were outside the protection of the law, they are a declaration of hope and joyful anticipation.

Of course, we moderns might say that such spirituals are also anthropomorphic projections into an idealized future state. No doubt this is true; but if this is so, such projections reveal something of the context in which African Americans found themselves. Slaves on the farms and plantations of the American South were denied the full status of human beings, for by definition slave-masters were owners of property and chattels, not people. While on the one hand slaves were asked, like people, to 'obey their masters' as a Christian duty, on the other hand they were denied, as sub-humans, the rights of ordinary citizens.

The endemic problem of the one-parent family among African Americans in today's inner cities is rooted in slavery, where no family was safe from the absolute power of the slave-owner: both women and men were raped, beaten, and killed. Children were sold to other farmers and households, women were separated from their husbands, and life was literally 'nasty, brutish, and short'.

Even the apparent kindness of Christian slave-owners flattered to deceive. One of Harriet Beecher Stowe's most scathing attacks in *Uncle Tom's Cabin* is reserved for Mr Shelby, the Christian gentleman who literally sells Tom down the river (the Mississippi). Although Shelby is depicted as decent and genuinely fond of Tom, when it comes to a time of hardship the economies of scale dominate his morality and he demonstrates that at depth for him Tom is essentially a commodity of capitalism.

For many slaves, family life was either a fantasy or a fleeting reality; the family was characterized by impermanence and more often than not a missing or forgotten father. An overriding problem, then, for slave-mothers and children was not patriarchy, but its absence. American slaves were, we ought to remind ourselves, African, with their cultural roots in tribalism. Patriarchy within such a social structure could perform much the same oppressive role as secular feminists believe it plays in contemporary Western societies. But there was also a positive side to it.

A few years ago a Nigerian reminded the British Council of Churches, who were debating the merits of artificial insemination, that for most Africans the significance of fatherhood is not a question of sexual politics, but of self-identification. Not to know your father is to lose your identity within the complex web of kinship that constitutes the African tribe. (This would not be so for all Africans, for some tribes are matriarchal, where personal identity and communal acceptance is handed down from the mother.)

In what Levine (1977, Part One) has called 'the sacred world of the slaves', ante-bellum African Americans, cut off from their traditional families and tribal eldership, came to identify themselves symbolically with the children of Israel:

> When Israel was in Egypt's land,
> Let my people go.

The politics of oppression for the slaves was not black patriarchy, but what Kenneth Stamp (1956) has called 'the peculiar institution' of slavery. The slave-owner was the enemy, like the Pharaoh of old, but his comeuppance was sure:

> O Mary don't you weep,
> Pharaoh's armies got drowned.

The symbolic transformation of slaves into the chosen people fuelled both a genuine theology of redemptive suffering and the demand of an oppressed people for liberation and justice. The chief helpers in slave-salvation were 'brother Jesus' and 'brother Moses'.

Significantly, neither Moses nor Jesus were the sentimental figures of later black gospel music: they were warrior kings, deliverers, messiahs. Jesus in particular was identified as no less than the emancipator of Israel: 'I am the Lord your God, who brought you out of Egypt, out of the land of slavery' (Deut. 5.6).

Slave-spirituals were coded so that white Christian masters could not fully understand the abolitionist message of 'Roll Jordan, roll' and 'Canaan's land'. Even the apparently pious and apolitical 'Steal away to Jesus' was a militant call by slave-leaders to defy the authorities who in the name of a white Protestant hegemony forbade Christian slave-religion. To steal away was to leave the slave-quarters at night and go to the secret 'hush harbours' where, surrounded by firs soaked in water to deaden the sounds of liturgy, slaves would dance the sacred dances and sing the songs of freedom (Raboteau 1978).

In the light of this secret yet defiant religion, perhaps the fragment quoted at the beginning of this essay begins to look not merely moving, but somehow right. Admittedly, no mother-figure appears in the glimpse of heaven – mother is always with us, unlike father who is absent – but the text tells us nothing about the gender of the song-writer. The author of the spiritual may have been a woman. If she was, there would be something particularly satisfying about the family portrait of life in heaven. (Imagine the scene as one where a daughter is arguing with her father and chatting with her brother.) We have in this picture a tableau of perfect equality, for this is an image not of deference, but of robust personal relationship.

Of course, such an imagining is probably too far fetched: theologians might think that the slave's glimpse of heaven reflects a binitarian view of God, where the argumentative Father and the chattering Son drown out the still small voice of the Spirit who will have no face 'until we have faces'. However, coming from a Western tradition that finds it difficult to conceptualize God as Trinity and which tends to conceive of God as two male buddies from a Hemingway novel or as a Father and Son who are so locked into each other in mutual admiration that they exclude all others, such a dismissive view of slave-spirituality is uncalled for. The true signific-ance of the slave-spiritual lies not in whether it measures up to Augustinian (or Cappadocian) orthodoxy, but in what it tells us about knowing God. And what this fragment tells us is that the slave has found a Father whom she knows and trusts well enough to argue with, just as Job (as Jung so insightfully saw) was mature enough to answer God back. Jane Williams captures the importance of growing up to face God as he is, and ourselves as we are, when she says of those who unquestioningly accept the fatherhood of God: 'How can they hear the gospel of the crucified Christ, if they have their thumb in their mouth and their head on the bosom of the Father?' (Williams 1991, 91).

But before we move on, let us take one more glance at our slave-spiritual, for we find that in heaven not only is the liberated slave confident enough to argue with the Father, but that there is no evidence from the text that the Father will forbid such argumentative discourse: arguing is impolite on formal occasions, but it is normative among friends and family. It is this lack of formality that is so delightful in the spiritual: in heaven we argue with the one and we chatter with the other. You can only chatter when you are at ease with someone, say with friends round a table, or at home. Chatting is light-hearted talk with someone of equal standing. To chatter with a slave-owner would be an impossibility. Even smalltalk with a king could not be properly described as 'chatting', for you have to be given permission to join in the conversation. But talking with 'brother Jesus' is as natural as talking to a comrade-in-arms or a fellow sufferer in a refuge for battered wives. We chatter with him because he is one of us, or because we are one with him.

The eschatological vision of the slave is the fulfilment of creation, where the barriers are down between God and humankind: rapport is established, broken relationships are mended, and yet each member of this eternal conversation is free to be themself. It is perhaps too much to suggest that the *sensucht* (the brief thrill of joy) of the slave is nothing less than the beatific vision where the redeemed are caught up in the coinherence of the divine Trinity, but we are nevertheless offered a glimpse of freedom and fellowship, sisterhood and brotherhood, distinctness but togetherness. In this glimpse we may also imagine that the scene of gossip and reminiscence, of argument and self-assertion, takes place around a table laden with food. Being in heaven is, after all, nothing less than the divine banquet of the kingdom where there is neither slave nor freeman, male nor female, lord nor subject. The image is not so much one of equality – certainly not of uniformity – but of communion.

FEMINISM, PATRIARCHY, AND CHRISTIANITY

Over a hundred years ago Marx and Engels (1975) saw an analogy between slavery and the inferior position of women in society. Today, with some justice, feminists argue that men still treat women as chattels, drudges, sex objects, virtual slaves. The polemic against men is not so much in individualistic or moralistic terms (not all men are sexist), but rather in institutional, linguistic and symbolical ones. The gloss feminists usually put on this cultural dominance of women by men is 'patriarchy'. Patriarchy, then, is not used anthropologically as an index, say, of tribal leadership, nor is it a synonym for dominant fatherhood (though such dominance would be an example of patriarchy). To talk of patriarchy is to highlight the relentless oppression and marginalization of women by men. In this respect slavery in the American South was also, in feminist eyes, a brutal example of patriarchy.

Since the 1960s feminists scholars utilizing hermeneutical, historical and philosophical studies have been at pains to spell out meticulously the reality of patriarchy from the political arena to the novel. Even the icons of liberal permissiveness have not escaped. It is doubtful, for example, whether readers will ever feel the same again about the writings of D. H. Lawrence, Henry Miller or Norman Mailer when they see how in her *Sexual Politics* (1969) Kate Millett exposes their contempt for women.

Feminism, however, is not all of a piece. Not only has there been for the last twenty-five years a distinction between the socialists and other radicals, but the non-socialist radicals are themselves divided into opposing camps. There are anarchists and revisionists, separatists and integrationists. These in turn can be distinguished from liberal feminists and even post-feminists. Within the radical and liberal camps there are also philosophical and ideological distinctions ranging from existentialism to process philosophy to deconstructionism.

These many divisions, and others too, are reflected in religious feminism. Those who hold to a Christian orthodoxy should bear this in mind. It is misleading, if not wicked, to classify (as some conservatives tend to) the majority of religious feminists as lesbians or gnostics, members of Wicca, or followers of the New Age. Nor should traditionalists insist that there is any logical connection between the ordination of women (regardless of whether we are for it or against it) and a radical reconstruction of Christian theology along feminist lines.

This is so because religious feminism is a plurality within which we can find writings that are compatible with Christian orthodoxy. So, for example, Janet Martin Soskice's work (1985) has a postmodernist thrust to it, but she is a very conservative Catholic compared to the more liberationist Rosemary Radford Ruether (1984). And even she has fiercely maintained her Catholic allegiance, and is deeply critical of Daphne Hampson (1990), who has left Christianity behind for a post-Christian theism.

There are, of course, other feminists who have felt compelled to abandon Christianity – one thinks of the still influential Mary Daly (1985) and of the avowed paganism of Judith Plaskow (Christ and Plaskow 1979). Yet many who have stayed loyal to Christianity are quite modest and reformist in their aims. The conservative feminism of Elaine Storkey (1988) and of Alwyn Marriage (1989) comes to mind; and the radical orthodoxy of Sarah Coakley (1990; 1992) and of Sally McFague (1987) has a great deal to offer classical theology, and cannot simply be dismissed as modernist or fashionable. In short, to reiterate an earlier point, feminism *per se* is not a threat to Christian orthodoxy: it is a matter of isolating those feminist strains that are inimical to the gospel and of welcoming those which are at the heart of it.

Some feminists insist, however, that patriarchy is not an epiphenomenon of Christianity, but of its essence – the Christian gospel is itself, so the argument goes, irredeemably sexist. Daphne Hampson, for example, eventually decided to leave Christianity because she became convinced that no amount of social reconstruction could rescue it from patriarchy. Against Dr Hampson, Christian orthodoxy maintains that the heart of the gospel is not patriarchy, but the personal love of God for the world. Following St Paul, we assert that 'God was reconciling the world to himself in Christ' (2 Cor. 5.19). This reconciliation allows us to respond to the love of God so that we, like the slave in the spiritual, can come to know him personally.

But such an assertion, though it may be an insistence that love is the *bona fides* of the gospel, is not a refutation of the claim that patriarchal thinking and practice permeate Christianity. On the contrary, to read Hampson, Ruether and Daly, and then to go on to read Elizabeth Clark's (1983) and Peter Brown's (1990) work on the early Church is to recognize that there is genuine evidence for the feminist claim that Christianity is patriarchal. Christianity does not get off that lightly, for there is a genuine case to be answered.

However, there are two things that need to be clarified.

First, that a great many of the theological opinions of the Fathers of the early Church were themselves influenced by the patriarchy of their own cultures, so that they inadvertently imported sexist presuppositions into Christian theology. Second, that much of the language used of God in the Bible – and hence in dogmatic orthodoxy – is indeed *male*; but, as we shall see, it is debatable whether this is truly patriarchal.

In so far as we have inherited many of the Fathers' presuppositions about women, the first problem can be dealt with only by repentance, for here we are talking about sin – we may be able to excuse the Fathers and our ancestors for ignorance, but not ourselves. The second issue is more complicated, for it is probably impossible to translate the original linguistic context of the gospel into language acceptable to many radical feminists. Furthermore, were such a successful translation possible, it would win only a token victory for feminism, but at the cost of losing much of the content of the gospel. Ironically, it is trinitarian orthodoxy itself that offers a solution, as we shall see.

THE RISE OF OPPOSING ARCHETYPES OF WOMEN IN CHRISTIAN TRADITION

A brief look at the theological anthropology of the early Church will demonstrate clearly what we have isolated as the first problem, the overt sexism of the Fathers of the early Church.

Ambrosiaster, writing in the fourth century, said: 'For how can it be said of woman that she is in the image of God when she is demonstrably subject to male dominion and has no authority? For she can neither teach nor be a witness in a court nor take an oath nor be a judge' (Elwes 1992, 19).

We might think this a very odd way to do theology, but in fact the usual way of explaining women's intrinsic inferiority to men was, following St Paul, to insist that women are not made in the image of God: 'A man ought not to cover his head, since he is the image and glory of God; but the woman is the glory of man' (1 Cor. 11.7).

Actually, the Fathers conceived the superior image of men in different ways. St Augustine, for example, in a way typical of his thinking, saw the divine image as a property which the man possessed but the woman did not. This rather physicalist sense of spiritual inheritance is analogous to his belief that original sin is a property of all human beings since the fall.

St John Chrysostom, on the other hand, understood the *imago dei* more in terms of authority than property: 'Then why is the man said to be in the "image of God" and the woman not? Because "image" has rather to do with authority, and this only the man has; the woman has it no longer' (Clark 1983, 35). Chrysostom may here be echoing that Neoplatonic view more fully expressed by St Gregory of Nyssa, who unlike Augustine saw man and woman as both made in the image of God in a sort of humanoid or androgynous state; but then there was a second creation, as it were, where human materiality was manifested in the forms of male and female nature. Subsequent to the fall into humanity (or the coming to be in fallen humanity), the woman became a helper to the man and submitted to his authority (Coakley 1990, 349-50).

Even where the Fathers were positive about the equality of women and men in terms of the *imago dei* (Gen. 1.27), two factors combined to keep women in a position of inferiority:

1. The Fathers understood the begetting of the Logos in eternity to denote not an event, but to highlight the one nature and being of the Father and Son. However, when they came to Eve's begottenness in space and time, they tended to say (to parody Arius): 'There was a time when she was not.' To continue our Arian parallel, we could say that they saw the subsequent creation of woman as secondary to or less than the fullness of the male prototype. (It is probably unjust to accuse the Cappadocians of this view – Harrison 1990.)

2. In the Genesis narrative Eve is the first to sin, and this is taken to mean she is therefore more culpable than Adam. The perfidiousness of Eve is then projected on to all womankind. Tertullian's hounding of the second sex is well illustrated by his infamous and oft-quoted remarks: '. . . you are the Devil's gateway; you are the unsealer of the tree; you are the one who persuaded him whom the Devil was not brave enough to approach; you so lightly crushed the image of God, the man Adam; because of your punishment, that is death, even the Son of God had to die' (Clark 1983, 39).

Women as the second and therefore secondary sex were doubly cursed, then, because the second sex sinned first. Women were often viewed in terms of this doubly dimmed divine image, so that an antinomy was created between the male as rational and therefore more like God's image, and the female as carnal, lower, bodily, subordinate, dependent, and therefore less like God's image. Bodily materials, superabundant in women, were potentially dangerous if not treacherous. In later scholasticism, for example in Aquinas, the woman was seen as an illegitimate or 'misbegotten male' (Hayter 1987, 84).

The view of women as lacking authority, carnal, unreliable, and potentially treacherous, developed at its worst into an archetype of Eve the temptress or the pagan sorceress Morgan le Fay. This is a type popular with misogynists. Sometimes she is made even more horrifying by being endowed not only with cunning, but also with power. Rider Haggard's *She* comes to mind, or the Lady Janis in C. S. Lewis' *The Magician's Nephew*. As with Sax Rohmer's evil Fu Manchu, women, like the Chinese, can be seen to be far more threatening if they are diabolical.

More usually, however, the carnal, bodily woman has been characterized as passive rather than powerful. She is responsive to men rather than an initiator, fecund rather than truly passionate; she is not so much Mother Courage as Mother Earth.

In the early Church, women could become more spiritual, and hence more like men, if they overcame their bodies in ascetic endeavour. This became an increasingly acceptable form of spiritual and social advancement for women in the early middle ages (though even as early as the third century there were Syriac women ascetics whose heads were shorn to show their at-one-ment with men).

Gregory of Nyssa, under the influence of his saintly sister Macrina, clearly found the base and lewd archetype demeaning to women. Following his lead, over time a more positive archetype of women developed which militated against the misbegotten/diabolical/doubly-dimmed model. This was made possible by emphasizing the positive spiritual virtues of the woman as the helper, supporter, altruist, intuitionist.

From the early middle ages, in both East and West, the cult of Mary as the *theotokos* (literally the God-bearer) gave bodily and human expression to the 'high' view of female spirituality where purity, virginity and self-abnegation - 'Be it unto me according to thy will' - reinforced the virtues of altruism. In medieval icons the Madonna presents her child as an offering to the world, while her eyes do not look at us demanding recognition, but are turned inwards in mystic contemplation of the Word of God whom she has also mysteriously brought to life.

It is surely a curious fact that today this more positive but one-sided view of women, reinforced by Jungian archetypes, finds support from both traditionalists and some feminists. The extreme representative of this view is Leonardo Boff, who attempts to link the Holy Spirit, women, and the *theotokos* ontologically (Boff 1979). Alwyn Marriage, who falls into the category of what Ruether has called 'conservative romanticism', finds herself in broad agreement with the Orthodox priest Thomas Hopko, for they both see a direct relationship between womankind and the Holy Spirit, whom they consider feminine in character (Marriage 1989; Hopko 1982).

However, for many feminists today both archetypes – women as unspiritual and women as super-spiritual – are caricatures of reality. The one condemns them to a permanent status of moral and intellectual inferiority – appendages to men, like the created Eve who was made from Adam's 'spare' rib – and the other spiritualizes them to the point of powerlessness and sexlessness: where are the positive aspects of passion and authority to be found?

In the era of date rapes, battered wives, and household skivvies, the suffering-servant model of spirituality is on the one hand a truism for many women, and on the other hand unfortunately only too true. As the suffering servant, Christ was neither a masochist who revelled in a cult of suffering nor was he forced to suffer against his will: he voluntarily went to the cross. In the Christian tradition, suffering is made redemptive because of grace and the power of God in weakness, not because there is anything intrinsically good in it or because it is the peculiar charism of women. Even such an unlikely source as Walt Disney's *Beauty and the Beast* gets this right. Belle, a modern girl of independent mind and spirit, voluntarily submits to the beast for a higher purpose, and in the end comes to love him.

On the surface it might seem sensible, as Marriage does, to identify the Spirit as feminine so that women can feel personally identified with the godhead. This might seem less radically feminist than renaming the Father 'mother', or refusing to call God Father at all. If we were to feminize the Spirit, would not this be in concert with a distant and rare strain of the Fathers, and thus the Christian tradition? Would it not mean that women could come to know God as personally and as naturally as the slave came to argue with the Father and chatter with the Son?

The short answer to both questions is 'no'. There are a number of problems here. To begin with, Boff, Marriage and Hopko suffer from the problem of convincing us of the legitimacy of the spiritual feminine archetype just as much as we have difficulty in accepting women as intrinsically perfidious. Most neurological investigations of men and women recognize only minor differences in intelligence and aptitude. Cross-cultural studies demonstrate that the givenness of biological distinction between the sexes does not match gender roles in any isomorphic way (Arthur and Lloyd 1982).

From an anthropological point of view, it is clear that to talk of feminine and masculine traits is to talk of a cluster of archetypical attributes which are scattered throughout the human population, both male and female. No doubt the debate on the intrinsic differences between men and women is still open, but experience suggests that good and bad, spiritual and unspiritual, initiation and response, rational and intuitive, domination and submission cut across gender categories rather than reinforce them. Even the much disputed meaning of the Greek word *kephalē* in St Paul (Eph. 5.23; cf. Col. 1:18) appears to refer to a principle of covenanted headship, not a list of male and female attributes.

Typically, however, counter-evidence does not seem to cut much ice with archetypal thinking, whether Neoplatonic or Jungian. Empirical and experiential evidence is put down as distortion, atypicality, perversion, or merely surface evidence. Jungian archetypes, we need to remember, are truly a priori: we take them on faith in Jung, not from revelation or through analytical reasoning. May it not be that Jungian archetypes, like all feminine and masculine archetypes, are social constructions and culturally determined ideas rather than objective realities?

To doubt the reality of archetypes is to engage in a philosophical argument that is as old as Plato and the Stoics, but there are two more things to say. First, from a feminist perspective, we find that the idea of a feminization of God in the person of the Spirit does not militate against patriarchy: it reinforces it. The Spirit as the *vinculum amoris* (literally the bond of love) is self-effacing between the Father and the Son. She is discreet, like a veiled handmaiden, or cramped and fleeting, like an eternal Cinderella. Projecting femininity into the Trinity in this way does not balance the seemingly male dominance of the Father and Son. On the contrary, it introduces a dangerous form of subordinationism in which the Trinity is depicted, in descending order, as a father, his dutiful son, and a submissive daughter who also defers to her brother.

Such feminist objections shade into orthodox theological ones. To depict the Holy Spirit solely as altruistic and self-abnegating is to achieve for the Spirit what the *filioque* did for the Western tradition. Go-between gods, or handmaidens, have a habit, like good servant-girls, of remaining so much in the background that no one can remember their names. In Barth's theology, for example, angels are ontologically weak because they are, as messengers from God, only messages of God. Similarly the Spirit's ontological status as the feminine loving-bond is uncertain in a godhead where a new note of subservience seems to have been introduced. The Son may be said to be subordinate to the Father as a matter of will but not of nature, but if the Spirit ceases to be 'the Lord and giver of life', as the Nicene creed insists, what is the hypostatic status (personal reality) of this Spirit?

Attempting to raise the status of women by aligning them with the third person of the Trinity may be a valiant attempt to ameliorate the worst aspects of patriarchy, but it has the unfortunate effect of reducing both the Spirit and women to second-class citizens. In short, this seemingly reformist move neither satisfies radical feminism nor orthodox Christianity, for patriarchy is reinforced and the Holy Spirit is lowered to the status of a servant-girl.

GENDER AND PERSONS

One does not usually find radical feminism and Christian orthodoxy agreeing in this way. However, there is surely no room for agreement on the question of whether we should call God 'Father' or replace him with some other notation (or even another god)? On this issue, some feminist reconstructions of the fatherhood of God are undeniably inimical to orthodoxy, but orthodoxy itself needs to be reminded of its own history.

For example, it may be in order to assert that God is Father ontologically as long as God as *pater* is understood, in the words of Maximus the Confessor, to be the *pege theotētos* ('divine fount') of the Trinity. It is illegitimate to imply, however, that God as Father is masculine in any way (cf. Oddie 1984). The overwhelming view of the patristic age is that gender is an inappropriate label to attach to the godhead. Strictly speaking, the only legitimate sense in which we can talk of gender and God is to mention the incarnate Son. We cannot say that Jesus was male from all eternity, for God is Spirit and gender is a biological, creaturely attribute. *Ipso facto* we cannot say that God as Father is male or the Spirit is female.

The Arians were guilty of literalizing the fatherhood of God by insisting that Jesus was the consequence (or product) of the Father's begetting. Indeed, part of St Athanasius' attack on Arianism was directed against its inability to recognize metaphorical language. The thrust of John 3.16 and the language of begetting suggest not maleness, but divine origin or unity of being with the Father. This is why, in the West, the Council of Toledo in AD 625 felt it perfectly in order to refer to the Son as from the father's womb (*de utero Patris*).

We might want to assert, as many traditionalists do, that the ascension means that there is now a man at the heart of the Trinity. However, this can be misleading, for it might be taken to mean that the assumption of our Lord into heaven has grafted only maleness into the godhead, and St Gregory Nazianzen's aphorism, 'That which he could not assume he could not restore,' might then be wrongly used to say that Jesus did not recapitulate all human nature in his own person, and that women are therefore excluded from salvation. It is clear, however, that this was not what St Irenaeus meant when he spoke of the incarnation as a *recapitulatio* (*Adv. Haer.*, 11.20.3). Surely the paradoxical message of the gospel's 'scandalous particularity' is that, in the person of Jesus of Nazareth, God is reconciling *all* the world to himself, whether free or bond, male or female, Jew or Gentile.

On a more controversial note, Gregory Nazianzen's friend Gregory of Nyssa believed that the risen and ascended Lord did not remain a mere man: he, like the divine Trinity, is also beyond gender.

It is difficult for us to appreciate this androgynous view of personhood, for as creatures we cannot, for the most part, understand ourselves apart from the fact that we are sexual beings (even many feminist groups think in terms of 'sisterhood' rather than asexuality or unisexuality). Gregory of Nyssa was of course influenced in his view by Platonism, but he also drew on the New Testament, with Jesus' insistence that 'at the resurrection' men and women would not marry, but would be like the angels (Matt. 22.30).

Nyssa's argument can best be appreciated if we realize that for him human personhood is not a function of gender, but the trace or stamp of God's own personal life in creation. Gender is made necessary because of the exigency of procreation, but personhood is beyond necessity and is not bound to nature. For him, the concept of person is a theological not a biological category. We are persons because we share, albeit brokenly, in the personal life of God. This sharing occurs through the *imago dei*. But because of Christ's passion we can now be adopted by the Spirit into the very life (or body) of Christ, where we begin to grow to maturity. We are still limited by our creatureliness, however: we can only see God 'in a glass darkly' – as sons, daughters, friends. At the final judgement we shall see God as he is, for we will have obtained true personal stature ourselves. Human nature will not be obliterated, but it will be transfigured into new life, no longer differentiated by gender.

But to return to ourselves, living in a gender-soaked world as we do, outside of direct mystical experience it is not possible to envisage or image a personal God beyond gender. That is why we have so much difficulty with the hidden personality of the Holy Spirit. And that is also why personal knowledge of God has to be mediated through a human understanding and experience of personhood. God, after all, mediated his divinity to us through the humanity and particularity of his incarnate Son.

But do we have to image God *exclusively* as male? To be as blunt as it is possible to be: to conceive of God as male is idolatry, and therefore blasphemy: It is true that in the Old Testament the language used of God is overwhelmingly masculine – no doubt reflecting a patriarchal culture and reacting against immoral fertility cults. However, the name of God – the name that is above every name – is beyond imaging. This God, this Yahweh – in being the 'I Am That I Am' – is truly (in the literal Greek sense of agnostic) unknown by us. Although the names 'mother' (once) and 'father' (eleven times) are used to describe the God of Abraham and Isaac (here we see the positive understanding of patriarchy that we noticed in our slave-story), on the whole Yahweh is the God who will be what he will be: 'Thou shalt make no graven image . . .'

When we turn to the New Testament, an initial reading of it might suggest that God has been cut down to size – domesticated as it were – by becoming simply 'father' (mentioned 170 times). Is this not a loss of otherness, a diminishing, through imaging, of God?

We could take it to be that, but in fact there are two movements towards God in the New Testament. First there is the humanized and immanent God that we see portrayed in the relationship between Jesus and his heavenly Father. It is not so much that Yahweh is denied, but that like the Russification of the Byzantine icons of Christ we move from the stern to the tender, from the wholly other to the known. The shocking and yet touching use by Jesus of 'Abba' may not be quite 'daddy', but it is certainly the personalized 'thou'. (Jesus, of course, could not call God 'mother', for she, like the slave's mother, was present with him.)

And yet the New Testament also struggles against the cosy and domestic warmth of Father/Son language. The epistle to the Ephesians, for example, begins with an unmistakable trinitarian movement that moves beyond the more usual Christocentric language of Paul. We are reminded in the first chapter of Ephesians, as the Fathers would later make explicit, that God remains transcendent, all-powerful, and unknown. The developing *apophatic* tradition in the Orthodox East was a recognition that God is always more than we can say, imagine, or image. The self-revelation of God in Christ was also, for the Fathers, an invitation by Christ through the Spirit into the heart of a personal life that shattered the meagre, though reassuring, icons of domesticity or the self-absorbed bonding of Father and Son.

FATHERHOOD, PARRICIDE, AND THE TRINITARIAN PROMISE

Let us look briefly at God as Father and as Trinity, and ask ourselves whether such traditional God-talk amounts to patriarchal language.

We might start by saying that the faith once delivered to the saints is contingent on the culture and history of its time. It might seem unreasonable to insist that the language of this culture is binding on us. But if it is true to say that the gospel needs to be inculturated into each new historical epoch and national culture this is not the same thing as saying that it can be adapted willy-nilly to new cultural forms without loss of content.

Can we differentiate the gospel from its linguistic context? Bultmann thought that we could, but it can be argued that his existential search for the kernel of truth left him with nothing but the husk of his own philosophical system. We remember Tyrrell's comment that the nineteenth-century quest for the historical Jesus resulted in the German theologians finding nothing but their own reflections in the well of history. Since Feuerbach and Freud, we have become accustomed to a patriarchal God who is nothing more than our projections. This argument grew out of an acceptance of the idea that the Kantian noumenal world was a closed system that reflected back human desires and ideologies.

The Christian use of 'Father', however, is not due to an insistence on the intrinsic maleness of the Godhead that somehow shines through from the beyond, nor is it even because the Father notation for God is sanctioned in liturgy and by tradition. We call God Father because Jesus did. God is Father for us, if you will, because together with our Lord we are the *totus Christus*.

We need not be afraid to be simply biblical about it. Father language, as St Athanasius recognized, is the language of the New Testament, and we have no right to cut and paste the sacred text as we please (though, of course, that is precisely what some critical New Testament scholarship does). Yet if we are attentive to the gospels we cannot fail to see that God the Father as Jesus experiences him is beyond gender and stereotype, for he is motherly and protective as well as strong and holy; he is certainly not domineering and patriarchal.

And this brings us all, men and women, to a serious difficulty – calling God a father at all. The problem is a psychological and a pastoral one: how can we love God as our heavenly Father when our own fathers are often so emotionally crippling, dismissive and cruel? This problem has a corollary: could we call God mother (leaving aside for the moment the fact that there is no sanction for it in the biblical texts), if our experience of mothers is one of domination, cloying smother-love, or manipulation? If these descriptions sound as if we are falling back into sexist archetypes, let us be more provoca-tive: can an anorexic bring herself to call God mother? It is of course unfair to suggest that all women who suffer from anorexia are alienated from their mothers, but many are. Furthermore, many of us who do not suffer from eating disorders have other sad stories to tell of our failed relationships with our mothers.

In Western culture, perhaps the most significant function fathers can play for their daughters is to affirm them in their independence – 'When I get to heaven I am going to argue with the Father . . .' Grown-up girls no longer give their hearts to daddy, but to their partners; or, like Mary after the birth of our Lord, they ponder things in their own hearts. Good fathers relinquish their authority over their daughters and yet confirm them in their right to be themselves – maybe such fathers are more important for growth and mature human relationships than we imagine. It is difficult to think of such fatherhood as patriarchy.

Metropolitan Anthony, of the Russian Orthodox Church, has often spoken of the barrier that bruised relationships can impose when approaching God personally. He is convinced that we start with God

where we can, for he will meet us where we are. Starting from where
we are may lead us, in time, to be able to accept God as our Father.
But first we may need to be able to forgive him for being our Father,
or at least, in accepting him, to forgive our own fathers on earth 'who
have trespassed against us'. If we can do that we will discover that
God is also lover and healer, joy unspeakable, beyond God the
Father. This is not a question of a bitter pill for women to swallow in
the hope that the medicine may do them good – millions of men fear
and loathe their fathers; they too have been betrayed, bullied, abused,
abandoned, and savaged by other men. Did the crucified Son, who
had already suffered the anguish of anticipated death in the garden,
suffer a greater anguish in actual death because he was forsaken by
his father?

A radical orthodoxy for our day needs to begin to dissociate the
language of patriarchy (as feminists define it) from the New Testament language of fatherhood. This necessitates *complementary* – not
substitute – symbols and metaphors for God: the erotic language of
Christian mystics, the agape intimacy of friendship, the 'language' of
silent wonder. We need also to learn again that Jesus is 'Lord', not in
the sense of 'liege' or master, but as the liberator who brings freedom
to the oppressed (cf. Smail 1992). Such a proactive approach is
necessitated by (a) the clumsy nature of the English language, which
does not contain the nuances and feminine-sensitive pronouns that we
find in, say, Greek, French and Russian, and (b) because it is an
imperative of the gospel. It is not enough for men to shrug their
shoulders and say to women, 'The language of the Bible is male; it's
tough but that's the way it is; take it or leave it.' Unless Christian
men are prepared actively to show that they really do cherish women,
as Christ does the Church, many will leave it.

How many of our priests and theological educators take the trouble
to explain to laypeople that Christian orthodoxy denies the ontological
gender of the godhead? Do they imaginatively and creatively
demonstrate that God as Father is Mother too, and yet, against
Feuerbach, is the prototype of true personal relations, of which our
flesh-and-blood mothers and fathers are, at best, dimmed icons? It
may very well be that the feminist indictment against the Church
should not be directed at its male language and fatherly symbols but
at its failure to explicate these in the light of trinitarian tradition.

The holy Trinity by its very personal yet triadic nature constantly
militates against the overriding binitarianism of the Father/Son model·

God as Trinity bursts asunder preconceptions of God. It is not the manly erotic father, like Zeus on one of his many excursions of seduction, who lays with the maiden of Israel: she is overshadowed by the Spirit. Jesus wants to gather the inhabitants of Jerusalem like a mother hen gathers her chicks under her wings and yet he cracks the whip in the temple and overturns the money-tables. The Father is as proud as a mother at a bar mitzvah as he affirms his Son on the banks of the Jordan, 'You are my Son, . . . with you I am well pleased' (Mark 1.11).

These days, it is not fashionable to distinguish the so-called economic Trinity (God as he is revealed to the world) from the immanent Trinity (the hidden life of God's eternal being). Yet if, like the Greek Fathers, we were not so coy, we would find that the immanent God is not a monadic narcissistic being who is in love with himself, not two selfish, exclusive and adoring men, nor indeed a tritheistic committee of super-powers deciding the fate of the world from some empyrean Elysian fields. To look at the immanent Trinity would be to see in theological terms what the slave saw in vision and hope: God is personal love outpoured from the Father to the Spirit through the Son. The Spirit does indeed defer to the Son, but so do all the persons of the Trinity defer to each other in mutual reciprocity. God is love outspoken in perfect freedom and personal communion. This is no sop to modern feminism: it is the classical faith that, as a child of the Enlightenment, Daphne Hampson had already abandoned long before she insisted that the Trinity was itself irredeemably sexist (Hampson 1990, 154). True, many men and women are sexist, but ignorance, stupidity, sin or the lust for power are responsible for this, not the fatherhood of God and the life of the blessed Trinity.

It is time, however, to put the fatherhood of God back where it belongs: inside the Trinity, not over and against it. If God as Father is allowed out alone – as he tended to be by second-generation Calvinists – he soon comes to resemble at best John Robinson's bearded old man in the sky (Robinson 1963), or at worst he degenerates not into the lawgiver, but into a tyrant like the depraved slave-owner Simon Legree in *Uncle Tom's Cabin*.

In so far that he is still around, this despot, this 'father', this rogue patriarch, he needs to be killed. If this amounts to an Oedipus complex for women, then they need not be dismayed: killing him is justifiable homicide, for this is not God the Father but his distorted shadow, slouching to phenomenal existence through the open wounds in the noumenal world.

CONCLUSION

One could argue that patriarchy in Christianity is not essentially bound up with the male language of the godhead. Eradicating such language will certainly not eliminate patriarchy. Buddhism and Hinduism, despite their immanentist theology and imaginative use of gender names for God, are deeply patriarchal. Increasingly, many radical feminists are realizing this; replacing God the Father with Mother God, for example, is not a solution to patriarchy, merely a semantic substitution.

The more radical tack is to transcend gender concepts completely, and with them personal categories also. The seminal work here is Mary Daly's *Beyond God the Father*, where we are presented with a God of Power, Justice, and Love (Daly 1985, 127). Indeed, Daly's predilection for substituting non-personal nouns for personal ones is compounded by her preference for substituting verbs for nouns. Janet Morley's trinitarian blessing exemplifies a full-blown Dalyesque:

> May the God who dances in creation,
> who embraces us with human love,
> who shakes our lives like thunder,
> bless us and drive us out with power
> to fill the world with her justice.

This type of approach poses a far greater threat to Christian orthodoxy than Daphne Hampson ever will, or Wicca witches for that matter (for they can only beckon to us from the outside). Partly because it seems merely a minor matter of adjustment, but also because it panders to political correctness, we are witnessing a widespread and increasing use of functional and modalistic language which is replacing an ontological and a personal one. It is, for example, becoming a commonplace in many of our seminaries and churches to replace Father, Son and Holy Spirit with the functional substitutes, Creator, Redeemer and Sustainer. It seems innocent enough, yet such a schema is a disaster, for although it might score a surface victory against sexism, or at least 'cock a snook' at patriarchy, it has in fact sold the gospel, like Uncle Tom, down the river.

It fails on two accounts. First, it fails on a basic level of biblical adequacy. To say, for example, that the Spirit is the Sustainer is hardly a comprehensive description of the Spirit's attributes and economic functions. Is not the Spirit 'the Lord and giver of life', the mover upon the waters, the one who overshadowed the Virgin Mary, endowed Jesus with power, raised him from the dead, and baptized the Church with fire? Is Jesus not the Creator too, and the Father the Redeemer and Sustainer?

Traditional language is indeed inadequate to express the fullness of God, and no doubt lazy and harmful 'male talk' winds its way out of non-reflective usage and comfortable ways. But old language cannot be changed by ideological fiat or by the policing of political caucuses: there has to be a community change of consciousness over a considerable period of time before new concepts become the coin of common usage. Furthermore, it is sometimes necessary to resist such change if what we are offered is politically correct but theologically wrong. The Christian name for God is the holy Trinity. God as Trinity is revealed to us as Father, Son and Holy Spirit. These names need to be imaginatively and sensitively explicated – even buttressed by complementary names – but they are not open to negotiation or substitution. Patriarchy cannot be destroyed by abandoning 'Father' as a name for God, but orthodoxy can be. The difference between the apostolic faith and apostasy, as happened over the Arian dispute at Nicea, can hang on a single word.

This leads to the second problem with the non-sexist, functionalist schema: it is no longer sufficiently Christian to allow us to know God personally. Western modalism since Augustine has faced this problem, but at least Augustine, over and against Sabellius, was orthodox. But the triadic Creator–Redeemer–Sustainer is void of revealed personhood and empty of true personal content. Our slave would know this instantly. You cannot argue with the Creator as you can with your heavenly Father, for, as Job discovered, he will put you in your place. And how would you chat to the Redeemer if you could not also relate to him as your brother? Would you dare address him, let alone have a chat?

If the slave-spiritual did include a Sustainer, it would probably be a mother, the only rock against which slavery consistently broke. To say this, however, is to admit that we have gone as far as we can with the hermeneutic of the spiritual through which we have approached this essay. (Moreover, the Sustainer as mother would endear herself as little to feminists as St Paul's talk of being 'Christ's slave' (1 Cor. 7.22) would be helpful to real slaves.)

We do not need to be romantic and pretend that for the slave being in heaven was anything other than an anthropomorphic longing to 'move up a little higher'. But neither should we assume that that is all there was to it: such human yearning is not the betrayal of faith, but its essence. By grace we are called not to click smoothly into place with the clockwork saviour, the watchmaker, and the repair girl (or whatever other functional equivalent we can find for God). We are called, women and men, in Martin Luther King's words, to be 'free at last': free *from* fear and free *to* know God personally.

13
WOMEN'S PROBLEMS
Janet Martin Soskice

GOD LOVES WOMEN

Sometimes I wish I had never heard of 'women', much less discovered that I was one. 'Feminist' seems destined to be a term of opprobrium. In the last century 'feminists' were people who thought women should be allowed to take university degrees. In the early part of this one they were people who thought women should have the vote. Now we call people who think women should be able to go to university and be able to vote 'sensible people'. Success in the feminist field means that the changes campaigned for in the face of a sometimes violent opposition become accepted as 'just common sense', while the nomenclature 'feminist' is moved on to describe some other unspeakably radical group of activists in the female cause.

If you are a woman, and even if you are not, you have probably heard someone begin a comment with, 'I'm certainly no feminist, but . . .' We shrink from the label 'feminist', yet many Christian women, and Christian men too, realize that women around the world are cruelly disadvantaged and abused – to the point of death – in virtue of their sex. What term shall we use for our concern?

These essays speak from the perspective of committed Christianity to the challenges, in thought and deed, which we all face in the world today. It is because of my conviction of the truth of the Christian faith, and not despite it, that contemporary 'women's problems' (which can't, of course, be dissociated from those of men) seem so important to me. It would be easy to criticize some works of feminist theology, but equally it would be pointless to do so. This field is by now simply too broad to caricature – there are radical and post-Christian feminists, Catholic feminists, and reformed ones, liberal Christian feminists and evangelical Christian feminists. It is a burgeoning and lively area of theology, and as with all such lively areas there are a lot of tares among the wheat. But there is wheat – a rich harvest, and one the churches can disdain only at their peril.

Shortly after the publication of my first very tentative attempt at writing something on women's problems for a Christian magazine, I received a phone call from an elderly priest in a nearby village. Could he come and meet me? I awaited him with mixed feelings, but when he arrived he wanted no more than to sink into an armchair and say how delighted he was to be alive at this time when, it seemed to him, the Holy Spirit was animating the Church to new truths about the dignity and grace of women. Sooner or later every Christian woman, unless she lives a very sheltered life, will meet someone – often another woman – who will say, 'But how can you be a Christian when the history of Christianity with regard to women is . . . ?' If you reply to these questions with anything but silence, you are likely to be doing feminist theology.

This brings us to the interesting question of whether a man can be a feminist. The best argument in the negative which I have heard is that men cannot be feminists because men, except in very exceptional circumstances, do not have the experiences of a woman. The adequacy of this simple criterion was brought home to me recently as I stood in my college office at the photocopier, the secretarial staff busily employed about me. A student came to the 'hatch' and called me from the copier to answer a question. It was clear he thought I was a secretary, and why should he not? I was of an age with the rest of the women, dressed the same, and so on. I simply gave him his answer and off he went. I am quite used to being taken for a secretary. But on this occasion I realized that what was relatively commonplace for me, being taken for my secretary, would *never* happen to my male colleagues. Now the point of this anecdote is *not* that it is an ignominious tale, nor yet that it's a horrible thing to be taken for a secretary when one isn't one – it's not. Nor yet is one saying no one but women have such experiences. The point is this: as a female one is 'read' as a woman, and with your society's expectations of what 'women' do. If you are live to it, you will see it happening around you all the time.

Yet, I suppose, there was a time when I had not heard of 'women', or, at least, when I did not realize I was one. Let me explain by continuing in my somewhat anecdotal mode.

I have not always been interested in the topic of 'Women in the Church'. Throughout my postgraduate student days, splendidly isolated as a student of philosophy of religion at Oxford University, I was more interested in the place of the laity in the Church. I would

not have said, as I have heard some people say, that I had never
experienced disadvantage through being female. This was clearly and
empirically not the case. When I had applied to universities in the
United States a number of the best did not take women; and when
I came to Oxford, again, women were unable to apply to the
wealthiest, the most central colleges, the ones with housing and
scholarships. Women postgraduates in theology could not be members
of a college which had a Professor of Theology, and to which most of
the other (male) theology students belonged, and so on. But this, and
much else, one accepted as 'the way the cookie crumbled' – an
unfortunate and unjust aspect of the system, but no one's fault. The
exclusivity of the men's colleges was represented by the liberal dons
as an unfortunate but binding archaism which could not now be
altered. Much was the surprise of many, then, to see that when the
men's colleges discovered it was to their academic advantage to take
women, they managed to do so very quickly.

I became more aware of the difficulties of women in the Church
(or churches) when teaching at a theological college. The experiences
of my women students, as well as my own, gave me pause for
thought. We were all living, working and studying within a context
formed by men and for men, but in which, at many times, women's
lives (whether they be student, staff, or spouse) fitted oddly and
women's achievements were undervalued. A candidate who had spent
a couple of years working for a bank would be held to come with
'good life experience', whereas of someone who had raised a large
family it was said, 'But she hasn't *done* anything.' A young
unmarried man going into a curacy would have the ladies of the
parish round (sometimes whether the curate liked it or not) offering to
cook and even clean for him, whereas a woman curate not only was
not cooked and cleaned for, but was expected to entertain the
parishioners, and so on. This stream of little points of stress was
constant, and cumulative.

Debates within the Anglican communion at that time about the
ordination of women made it inevitable that we would be interested in
the history of theological discussion of the topic 'woman'. Historical
theology is, unsurprisingly, rife with accounts of women's mental and
moral limitations, their 'natural' subordination, weakness of will and
even (in the case of Richard Hooker) their 'imbecility' (Sykes 1990).
Literary, political and legal texts from the same historical periods
would no doubt give the same unfortunate picture, but none the less

one couldn't help wishing theology had been a bit more generous than
the other branches of human wisdom.

It made me aware of the exclusively 'male's-eye view' I was
getting, and to some extent was giving to my own students. For
instance, I was at that time teaching an Oxford postgraduate degree in
Christian Sexual Ethics. As I recall, none of the books on the reading
list, for aspects both ancient and modern, was written by a woman,
and the topics of the papers very much reflected the interests of the
male authors of the books. There was, for instance, a great deal on
homosexuality and divorce, but nothing on abuse within marriage, or
pornography, or the sex trade. Women, if they appeared in the texts,
appeared as 'bodies with problems' – unspecified moral agents who
might or might not take the pill, or have abortions, and so on. It was
even evident that some of the classical texts – for instance Augustine's
account in *The City of God* of what sexual relations might be had man
(*sic*) not fallen – depended for their analysis of sexual morality rather
heavily on male sexual and bodily experience. One could not help
wondering what a woman would have said. So enters the so-called
'hermeneutics of suspicion'. What might women have written? It
is not simply that women and men might (or might not) have
different opinions about the *same* issues – women and men might see
different things as issues in the first place.

On one occasion my students had a short placement at a chocolate-
bar factory. Most of the assembly-line workers were Asian women.
The managers explained they had trouble with these workers,
because if their children were ill they didn't come in to work. No
reference was made to the possibility of work-place crèches. My own
experience as a working mother with small children made me aware
of the child-care difficulties many women faced. Television and
'women's page' newspaper articles had recently exposed the atrocious
'patch-up' solutions to which many poorer women (and, shouldn't
we say, men?) had resort – ten children with an elderly auntie, and
only a television for stimulation, and so on. The social cost of this
early neglect of children can of course be dreadful.

About the same time, I met a bouncy young woman who was
employed by a Christian institute founded in the last century to
improve the workers' conditions. She explained that in the past they
had largely campaigned for canteens and lavatories, but now that
most work places had such amenities, they were concentrating on
trade union/management relations. 'What about work-place crèches?',

I asked, being full of all this worrying data on child-care. 'Oh,' she said brightly, 'our boss thinks that's just a women's problem.'

The enormity of this answer did not strike me for some time. What a multitude of things shelter under the phrase 'just a women's problem'. Is the neglect attendant on inadequate and unimaginative child-care facilities just a women's problem? More deeply, is the fact that so many mothers of young children in our society are obliged to work because the fathers are absent or irresponsible just a women's problem? Poverty, and especially child poverty in our country and world-wide, is in one sense 'a women's problem' because it is women who are, quite literally, left holding the babies. But are 'women's problems' not ones that need to be resolved by all of us? They certainly are problems from which we all, in the long run, will suffer.

It was at this stage that I began to understand what was meant by 'patriarchy' (a term I still regard as ugly and unfortunate, but maybe that has to do with what it signifies). It does not mean that some men are nasty to women. It is not about 'men versus women'. It is about structures that have been created, over hundreds of years, in which men were the main determinants – structures that do not take women's lives into consideration. It is about structures under which not only women, but children and men suffer. Furthermore, it is not just men who are 'sexist' in this sense. It is perfectly possible for women to be blind – even wilfully blind – to all these issues, particularly if their own circumstances shield them.

As one worked and lived in the theological college, a college which was trying its utmost to be kind to women, one couldn't help, as a woman, being aware of working with texts, traditions and structures created by men with a male population in mind. A feeling somehow grew that, in the texts of theology, my women students and I did not exist. Something important about us and our lives had not gone into forming this rich doctrinal, liturgical and pastoral mixture. Although there was much that one could learn and should learn from the great texts and tradition, somehow women's voices had not been heard, and we were all the losers for that.

I remember thinking on one particularly grim day, 'It doesn't matter, because God loves women!' – and somehow, and to my surprise, this recognition made me weep with relief. Of course, I had never, consciously, doubted that God loved women. I had never doubted that God loved everyone. But somehow the barrage of ancient opinion, the structures into which one was perceived to fit oddly, the little niggling but perduring negativities which one felt in a place which fit the young male candidates like a glove, all conspired to make one feel that women were not really quite as good as men, that God didn't care about women *quite* as much as men, that women's sufferings (so many of them not even figuring on the ethics or pastoral courses) didn't matter *quite* as much as those of men, that what happened to women in the home didn't matter *quite* as much as what happened to men in the work-place. In short, that somehow women didn't figure except as sources of gynaecological problems in Christian ethics, or people to make the tea.

There are so many variables to do with women in the churches, but I can say one thing with absolute certainty – God loves women. And I think I can make another claim with a high degree of confidence, and it is this: whether in theology or social theory, philosophy or politics, women's experiences have been left out, and we are all the worse for it.

HAS THE CHURCH OPPRESSED WOMEN?

I was once asked to give a talk on the title 'Has the Church oppressed women?' Stumped by so global a topic, I did something I tell my students never to do, and turned to the *Oxford English Dictionary*. I was not disappointed. There are four dense columns in the large O.E.D. on 'oppress' and its cognates, of which some highlights:

> to press injuriously upon or against; to subject to pressure with hurtful or overpowering effect; to press down by force; to crush, trample down, smother, crowd

> 1382 Wyclif *Mark iii* 9 Jesus seith to his disciplis, that the litil boot shulde seue hym, for the cumpanye of peple, lest thei oppressiden hym . . .

and later, chronicling some seventeenth-century architectural disaster,

> 1642 R. Carpenter, The upper part of a Church fell, and, the women sitting in the body of the Church, many of them were oppressed.

Proof positive that the Church has oppressed women!

But through all this talk of smothering, crushing and squashing, we might discern another term, 'to silence'. It could be said that women have been silenced in the churches – not just in the churches, but historically there as well as in other places; and in modern times, there more than most other places. Silenced not in the simplistic sense of there being no women priests or few women theologians. Nor yet in the sense that women don't speak out. There is a deeper kind of silencing which is sometimes referred to by its effect – 'voicelessness'. Cultural anthropologists speak of 'muted groups'; groups who do not speak in the dominant mode, where only the dominant mode of a group will be 'heard' or 'listened to'. The theory of mutedness does not require that the muted groups be physically silent – they may speak a great deal – but they do not have access to the decision-making, to the public domain. They are people from whose lives insights and decisions are not meant to come.

The French philosopher Michele Le Doeuff cites this passage from an anthropological account by Levi-Strauss: 'The next day, all the villagers sailed away aboard some thirty canoes, leaving us behind, alone with the women and children in the abandoned houses' (Le Doeuff 1987). As Le Doeuff notes, the women and children did not go away, yet for Levi-Strauss, 'le village entier' (the entire community) had left. A small omission you might think, but here we have a major practitioner of a social science speaking as though half the race didn't exist. What are we to make of the 'scientific' status of his account?

Language and power are closely linked. Not just who speaks and who is heard, but how we speak betrays balances of power. One of my students pointed out that the commonplace example, 'Columbus was the man who discovered America' is scarcely obvious to someone who is descended from the Aztec Indians. It's not even true. But by the time young English or American children have learned the 'correct' answer to the question 'Who discovered America?' they have learned to read world history from a particular perspective. 'Ours.' But who is 'we'?

What might a woman's voice do in theology? In 1960, much in advance of interest in feminist theology, Valerie Saiving Goldstein wrote an article entitled 'The human situation – a feminine view' (Goldstein 1960). Her suggestion was that one's soteriology (doctrine of salvation) was dependent on one's anthropology (doctrine of 'man'), and that the analysis of '*the* human condition' given by modern male theologians was very much from a man's point of view. She pointed out that Protestant theologians like Reinhold Niebuhr and Anders Nygren saw sin in terms of self-assertion, self-centredness and pride. But these, she said, are not necessarily the temptations of women. The sins of many women might better be suggested by terms like triviality and diffuseness, dependence on others for one's own self-definition, and so on – what she calls an 'underdevelopment or negation of self'. What is interesting about theology written by women, whether feminist or not, is precisely this hearing of another voice.

TWO WAYS TO IGNORE WOMEN

Although in our society we are all very practised at this, it might be helpful to point out two ways to ignore women. First, we can fail to see them; and second, we can see them as 'women'.

For the first, tragic examples can be found in the accounts of agricultural aid to African countries where aid packages, negotiated by male politicians and leaders, took little cognizance of the fact that the vast majority of Africa's agriculturalists are women, frequently with disastrous results.

For the second, we can again return to the chocolate-bar factory. Identify problems specific to women as 'women's problems', and eliminate them from consideration. Speak of 'women' or even 'Christian women' or even 'good Christian mothers', and ignore the diversity of tasks, gifts and obligations concealed here. Assert, contrary to all evidence, that since most 'women' don't work, we don't need to consider provision for working women. Pretend that all women are 'someone's wife', and that being 'just a housewife' is a rather mindless and idle occupation. No wonder Michelle Le Doeuff says:

> we do not think that feminism is an operation by which 'woman' wants to be like 'man', we insist on the fact that here are *women*, quite different from each, and there are *men* as well. 'Woman' is a mythical figure, a smoke-screen which prevents people from seeing the actual situations of real women. (le Doeuff 1987, 49)

Thus it is possible both to ignore women, and to say that, because certain matters are 'women's problems', they are somehow beyond our ethical consideration, or perhaps beneath it.

The philosopher Mary Midgley offers an explanation of why a woman's viewpoint could not matter:

> From the ancient hierarchical point of view (unchanged from Aristotle to Kant and beyond) it could not matter because women themselves did not really matter. They were in effect an inferior kind of man, with no distinctive character of their own. They thus shared in the human condition to the extent that inferior men did, and needed no special comment. (Midgley 1988)

This remark has a particular pertinence to the 'equal but different' line of thought which is now the official preferred line in some churches. The phrase 'equal but different' allows of this unfortunate reading: women are *equal* to men in so far as they do not have different insights or visions to bring to the Church, or spiritual needs to be met; but they are *different* in ways that make them unable to contribute fully to the Church's ministerial, theological and evangelical life. And thus continues the double-think about women. The only resolution to all these interesting questions will come when women's voices are heard and their experience is reflected in the whole of the Church's life. I imagine we are all suffering, in different degrees, from a blindness (to shift sensory metaphors) to the gifts and needs of women.

Amartya Sen, a distinguished Indian economist now at Harvard, wrote this in an article in the *New York Review of Books*:

> It is often said that women make up a majority of the world's population. They do not. This mistaken belief is based on generalizing from the contemporary situation in Europe and North America, where the ratio of women to men is typically around 1.05 or 1.06, or higher. In South Asia, West Asia, and China, the ratio of women to men can be as low as 0.94, or even lower, and it varies widely elsewhere is Asia, in Africa, and in Latin America. (Sen 1990, 61)

Death in childbirth and female infanticide are not the important features here; rather, he says, it is the persistent failure to give girl children and women medical care similar to that of the men, comparable food and equal access to medical and social provisions. When there are scarce resources, male children and men get them. Female children and women die in their hundreds of thousands. The title of Sen's article is 'More than 100 Million Women are Missing', because that is the minimum figure by which, if we projected from male/female ratios in the privileged world, we find a short-fall of women. We are one hundred million women short. Sexism does not simply hurt women's feelings, it kills millions and millions of them. If these morbidity figures were attached to a group discriminated against on the basis of race or religion, the churches would be up in arms. Why then have we been so slow to condemn sexism as a outrage?

It is still sometimes suggested that in a world that is full of suffering, women's issues should be a low priority. But who are the people who are suffering? In our own country, families falling into poverty are disproportionately those single-parent families headed by women. The average wages for women are significantly less than those for men, and the child-care and domestic responsibilities greater. In many poorer countries women are disproportionately underfed and overworked, at times (still) even sold into slavery, both sexual and domestic. The Western influence on these countries has not obviously improved the circumstances of women. In some parts of South-east Asia the largest 'cash crop' is the sexual services of women. Pornography is booming, and it is not, by the way, an ancient trade that has always been with us. The sinister modern pornography industry has grown exponentially since the 1960s into the world-wide and multi-billion dollar industry it is today. This issue deserves concerted Christian action, yet it is not one with which the churches are particularly associated. Why not?

And yet as Christians we must say, 'God loves women.' One reason why as an academic theologian I feel a certain obligation to write, among other things, on women's problems, is that one day I feel God might ask of me, 'You were there. You saw it. What have you done for these ones that I love, these women made in my own image?'

What we must also ask ourselves as Christians, women as well as men, is: Has our Church made things any better, or have we colluded in silencing the already half-voiced, and in making the problems of women, 'just women's problems'? Bodies are being broken day after day on linked wheels of poverty, prostitution, sexual abuse and domestic violence. How can we map these sufferings on the broken and risen body of Christ?

14
AT THE END OF THE WORLD: POSTMODERNISM AND THEOLOGY

Gerard Loughlin

Gerard Loughlin

THE TENOR OF THE TIMES

Human beings are calendrical animals. They are always noting changes, marking time. As they grow and mature, age and decay, so they mark bodily transitions from infancy through childhood to adolescence, from youth to middle and then old age. These changes are noted with all manner of festivities, with rituals and ceremonies, with tests and sacrifices; with routines, repetitions and returns. By means of the calendar, differences and changes are rendered significant and safe, or as safe as they can be. The day still passes into night, the summer into winter, the child into youth, innocence into experience: the human animal still has to leave the safety of the garden. But they know what is coming, they know what repeats and returns, and what doesn't. They can prepare.

But calendars come to an end and have to be remade. Seven days to the week, twelve months to the year, ten years to the decade, ten decades to the century, ten centuries to the millennium; and then some more? Each time human beings pass from one calendar to another, from the long days of summer and childhood to the ever shorter days of adulthood and winter, from one year to the next, they become anxious and fretful. Is there a day after tomorrow? The time just before the calendar ends is one of anticipation and sometimes dread, for at that time, time itself trembles: on the threshold it begins to fall apart. Humans are safe again only when the calendar has been remade and time has been re-established.

The endings of years, centuries and millennia are such times. For perhaps this time the calendar will not be remade, or remade so differently that it will mark not the return of time, but the beginning of something else altogether, a new sort of time – beyond time. At the end of an age certainties collapse and differences abound. It is as if time stops and there is no more sequence and progress, only multiplicity without procession or order.

The close of our century is potent with the sense of ending. The grand stories human beings used to tell themselves – about how tomorrow would not only follow today but be better than anything that had gone before – have become incredible. The idea of human progress has suffered one set-back too many. It is as if history has used up time and we are now counting the days on the world's last calendar. In a sense the eschaton has already arrived, it has already been realized: and this realization, a *delighted* realization, is postmodernism.

POSTMODERNISM

The above is an attempt to sketch the cultural space of post-modernism. In likening it to millennial fears, to the terror of unmarked time when all is permitted, I want to suggest not so much a new period in world history, as history's cessation. For post-modernism does not seem to be a new epoch. Older forms of social, political and economic organization still persist, along with the cultural ideals and values of earlier ages. The world is still dominated by capitalism, even if now entered upon a third phase, coming after 'home' and 'imperial' economies: the phase of multinational marketing (Mandel 1978). Equally there is still a place for so-called traditional and Victorian values, even if only as pastiche of their former selves (as in Thatcherism). Postmodernism is not the dawning of a new age, but of a day without a tomorrow, a time without a future.

Postmodernism is the idea that the once hoped for future of the human race has arrived. It is not a new age, because the ages have come to an end, and now everything that once was is to be recuperated and used – how we like – in our fashioning. There is a vast proliferation in all areas of life, but without direction, for without a future there can be no direction or point to our endeavours. We are not governed but managed, and efficiency is our watchword. But we no longer know why or care. For some this is wonderful; for others it is more terrible than anything imagined by the Seer of Patmos.

Postmodernism is a complex cultural phenomenon arising in capitalist societies of the late twentieth century. It takes many forms. One of the most noticeable is the postmodern style of building; indeed postmodernism was early announced by Charles Jencks in

206 Different Gospels

The Language of Post-Modern Architecture (1977). In buildings it is a
sort of eclecticism, the marriage of earlier idioms with modern techniques: pilasters and architraves upon steel frame constructions. (It can
be distinguished from deconstructive architecture, which seeks to
destabilize its form, inhabitants and environment.) Postmodernism
is the economics of the consumer market applied to all areas of
human life. There is nothing that cannot be bought and sold:
health, education, ideas, blood, bodies, babies. Postmodernism is a
fashioning of commodities – of films, food and clothes, and of people
(who no longer have characters but lifestyles). Postmodernism is also
a sensibility (camp), a philosophy (nihilism) and a theology.

How postmodernism is theology is the question of this essay.
Below I shall consider two possible answers. One embraces postmodernism as described above. The other redeems postmodernism by
finding in it, not the end of time, but the reappearing of what may be
called the 'future now'. Before proceeding to these answers, however,
we may better understand postmodernism by considering what comes
before.

MODERNISM

As its name suggests, postmodernism comes after the modern and its
cult: moder*nism*. But what is/was that? Accounts of modernism are as
various as those of postmodernism. For some the modern world
arrives with the industrial revolution in the eighteenth century, while
for others it begins in the seventeenth century with the scientific
revolution occasioned by Copernicus, Kepler, Galileo and Newton.
Some trace it further back, to the sixteenth century and the Protestant
Reformation, to the religious revolution which, according to Max
Weber, inaugurated the capitalist ethic. If we think of the modern as
not so much a period as a mode within cultural sensibility, we can,
with Erich Auerbach (1968), trace its emergence back as far as
Augustine and his *Confessions*. Here I have space to offer only one
brief description, from a postmodern vantage point.

The modern is the idea that humanity is the maker of its own
destiny, of progress towards technological and social utopia. Newton
produced the idea of constructing clear and powerful models of the
world's working. He provided a paradigm for scientific precision
and success. Everyone who came after him wanted to be the Newton
of their chosen field. He modelled the stars; Darwin modelled the

species. Marx modelled society; Freud modelled the mind. Others followed. Ferdinand de Saussure modelled language and Claude Lévi-Strauss modelled myth. Above all, there is Hegel and his story of the world as the self-realization of Spirit. In the modern moment, in the mind of the European philosopher, Spirit achieves consummation in a moment of perfect modelling or story-telling – telling it as it truly is. The modern is thus imbued with a great sense of its own importance, of its ability to comprehend the world and make it new. In this it is spurred on by its ability to transform the material environment through technology, and, through commerce, the matrix of society.

Here are some twentieth-century examples of the modern spirit. In the late 1920s a group of like-minded mathematicians and philosophers formed themselves into the Vienna Circle and published a manifesto, *The Scientific Conception of the World* (1929; Neurath 1973). The Circle was zealous for new ways of thought and living, for a scientific future and a socialist utopia. Wherever people turned to science and empiricism, there the spirit of the scientific world-conception was at home:

> We witness the spirit of the scientific world-conception penetrating in growing measure the forms of personal and public life, in education, upbringing, architecture, and the shaping of economic and social life according to rational principle. *The scientific world-conception serves life, and life receives it.* (Neurath 1973, 317–18)

They preached emancipation through science.

The architect Le Corbusier also wrote a manifesto, *Towards a New Architecture* (1927). It declared that the question of modern architecture was a question of morality. The question was one of architecture or revolution, and Le Corbusier believed that revolution could be avoided. Europe needed a new scientific architecture suited to the factory animal, endowed with the engineer's aesthetic. 'The Engineer, inspired by the law of Economy and governed by mathematical calculation, puts us in accord with universal law. He achieves harmony' (Le Corbusier 1927, 7). The design of liners, aeroplanes and automobiles showed the way; the modern architect would design machines for living in, houses that would be as 'healthy' and 'moral' as the 'big-business' that had transformed society (Le Corbusier 1927, 264).

Science, engineering, architecture, health and morality; these were
the weapons of the social revolutionary. With these, as the young poet
W. H. Auden declared, they would harrow the houses of the dead and
bring about a new world – 'New styles of architecture, a change of
heart.'

MODERN AND POSTMODERN STORIES

One way of understanding the modern is as the telling of a master
story with scientific rigour. A master story or grand narrative is a tale
which comprehends everything, telling us not only how things are,
but how they were and how they will be, and our place among them.
Such stories tell us who we are. Religious stories are often said to be
like this. The Christian story of creation, fall and redemption places
the individual soul within a divine drama of human possibility, of
salvation or damnation. The modern is not the end of such stories,
only their transformation. Marxism places us within the unfolding
dialectic of history; Darwinism puts us into the narrative of evolution;
Freud locates us in the theatre of the psyche. Cosmology wants to tell
us how the world began and how it will end.

When modern master stories are political, they are decidedly
utopian; they tell us that society will be better under their narration.
Such stories are always true because they make the world fit the
narrative. We can be characters within them because we can be
mastered by them. And it would seem that most of us want to be
within such a story; we want to be mastered or written into a narrative that is larger, longer, and stronger than our own. This is because
stories are secure places. We know how they begin and how they end:
'Once upon a time . . . happily ever after.' But what happens when
these stories begin to break down; when their narrators lose confidence and forget what comes next?

The French philosopher Jean-François Lyotard tells us that postmodernism is what happens when master stories lose their appeal
and become incredible (Lyotard 1984, xxiv). When the grand narratives of religion began to lose their credibility, the modern world
invented itself by retelling the old stories in a new way. It didn't
tell stories about God, but about history, evolution, the psyche, about
stars and scientific progress, about genetic manipulation and a
master race: about human emancipation through enlightenment and
'techno-science'. These stories, however, are now also incredible,

undesirable, horrible. And it seems that now there are no master stories left. We have to make up our own individual, little stories. We have to be our own story-tellers, our own little masters. And this is something good, something to be happy about; or so the story goes.

Here we are as postmoderns! We are our own little story-tellers, living among the ruins of our former grand narratives. We tell stories purely for pleasure. Today we tell one story, and tomorrow we will tell another. Stories are fashionable; we change them with the seasons, as we change our clothes. Perhaps because this is a new game, we make our stories out of the rubble of the old narratives we find lying around (Jameson 1991, 96). We mix and match, liking the fun of spotting where the bits have come from. Our novels and films are full of quotes and allusions; our buildings are a little classical, a little rococo, a little gothic, and even, sometimes, a little modernist. Our values and morals are equally various, equally changeable, commodities like everything else (MacIntyre 1985).

So there it is: the story of modernism as the attempt to build a better tomorrow without the aid of the divine, and of how the master stories of yesterday lost their appeal, turned sour, fell apart. Now there are only little stories. But as you will have noticed, this history is also a story, and a rather grand one. Postmodernism cannot escape the master narrative. If it is to understand itself, it has to understand everything; it has to establish its place in the world (Lyotard 1992, 40–1).

POSTMODERN THEOLOGY

Christian theology has responded to postmodernism in several ways. Some theologians are hostile, others curious, and others extremely enthusiastic, declaring themselves to be postmodern theologians. A few have done so because it is fashionable, but most because they believe that theology must become postmodern if the Church is not to be permanently eclipsed by modernity. Here I am concerned with only enthusiastic theologians, and of the three groups I discern among them – the fashionable but still liberal, the textualist but finally nihilist, and the fictionalist but really orthodox – I am concerned with the second and third. Mark C. Taylor and Don Cupitt are representative of textualist theologians (though I shall mostly discuss Cupitt), while fictionalist theology is well represented in the work of George A. Lindbeck and John Milbank.

NIHILIST POSTMODERN THEOLOGY

Mark C. Taylor is perhaps America's best-known postmodernist theologian. Noted for his work on Søren Kierkegaard, he came to prominence with his book *Erring: A Postmodern A/Theology* (1984). He had already published *Deconstructing Theology* (1982), and has since published *Altarity* (1987). *Erring* is an accomplished celebration of deferral, of the way in which meaning is always one step ahead of the signs in which we try to entrap it. For Taylor, language is like a vast and endless maze, in which we are forever running, turning this way and that, but never finding a centre or an exit. We never find God, Self or Meaning, for they are dispersed throughout the labyrinth, noticeable by their absence.

Don Cupitt, who announced that he was *Taking Leave of God* in 1980, has gone on to provide a brilliant if at times hasty manifesto for nihilist postmodern theology. Like Taylor, he believes that the old certainties have been dispersed across the surface of language. There are no longer any heights or depths, only a cultural skin of endlessly proliferating signs on which we must tread lightly, like *The Long-Legged Fly* (1987). In such a situation, religious values, like all values, have to be created out of nothing through the telling of stories, through make-believe. These themes are rumbustiously celebrated in Cupitt's most recent trilogy: *Creation Out of Nothing* (1990), *What is a Story?* (1991) and *The Time Being* (1992).

For both Taylor and Cupitt, postmodernity is welcome and irreversible, and for both it has to do with the radical textuality of reality. Both of them are deeply influenced by twentieth-century philosophies of language: by structuralism, poststructuralism and deconstructionism, and by the people who invented, developed or promoted these 'isms': Ferdinand de Saussure, Claude Lévi-Strauss, Roland Barthes, Jacques Derrida. Both Taylor and Cupitt believe that Christian faith and practice must adopt the new postmodern understanding of the human condition. Cupitt, especially, champions a new sort of Christianity: 'We want a new religion that makes liberation and bliss out of the way the world now is . . . for a beliefless world that is *rightly* beliefless, we'll need a beliefless religion' (Cupitt 1992, 117). What is this new religion of liberation?

Textualism is the idea that finally there is only language, understood as a vast and proliferating system of signs. Cupitt calls it 'culturalism' – the flowing together of language and world as a sea of signs in which we float and swim and have our being (Cupitt 1992,

64). Meaning is produced as the difference between signs. It is not
something other than signs, to which signs are somehow stuck, so that
I know what the sign 'cat' means because it has been stuck on to cats,
or what 'idea' means because it has been stuck on to ideas. I know
what 'cat' means because it is different from 'hat and 'mat' and from
other words of the lexicon, and because it is different from other
words in the sentence in which I find it, located in a certain order of
signs. These strings of signs have meaning because I know how to use
them to do things within my language community. I can tell someone
to get the cat off the mat.

The basic idea of textualism can be grasped by looking up the
meaning of a word in a dictionary. You want to know what the word
means, but all you find are other words, other signs. The meanings of
words can only ever be other words. Meaning is not outside, but
wholly inside language. This does not have to mean that there is
nothing except language in the world. When I hit my foot against a
stone it is not a word that causes my pain. But 'foot', 'stone' and
'pain' are all signs. If the world is to have meaning for me, it must
come into language, into meaningful being. It must be placed under a
description, categorized and indexed. Without language I would hit
my foot against a stone and feel pain, but I would not *know* that I was
feeling 'pain', that my 'foot' had struck a 'stone'. The event would
be painful but without meaning, for I would be without language.
'When I seem to see red', Cupitt writes, 'I am already interpreting
what I see, for I am classifying it. I am seeing it through a word. And
unless I see through words I don't see at all' (Cupitt 1992, 56).

The meaning of a word is always another word or words, and the
meaning of those words yet other words. Meaning is always one word
away; it is always different and deferred. In language we can never
have the thing itself; we can never stop the endless drift of meaning
from one sign to the next, from one sign-string to another. This, of
course, is why language is so wonderful. As we move the signs
around, putting them in new orders, producing new sign-strings – as
in the shifts of metaphor, the sign-strings of poetry – we provide
new routes for the ceaseless drift of meaning, and thus create new
meanings and understandings: new patterns of difference. But it is
also why language is so frustrating, why sometimes it is so difficult to
say what we want to say or stop what we have said from meaning
something else. Meaning is always one word away: we are never
fully in control.

Control, however, is one of our dearest desires, for when we are
in control we are safe. Thus is born one of our dearest myths: escape
from language to a place where meaning is self-present, where the
truth is not different and deferred from the sign, where the sign is the
truth. Here, then, is a route for escape: back from the written sign to
the spoken word; from the spoken to the silent word of inner speech;
from the silent word to the pure thought. If we can retrace the route
by which thought came to language, we can arrive at the truth itself.
This – so textualism teaches – is the great myth of language. It is a
myth because there is no escape from language. Pure thought, truth
present to itself – these are nothing more than ideas generated by the
differences between signs. Meaning does not stop when it comes to
these signs, but moves on through them, one step ahead, because
they also have meaning only because they too are different from
other signs, different from other sign-strings. They would not mean
anything at all if they were not so related, if they were not part of a
sign system which allows them to have meaning.

Story and narrative are fashionable topoi for theology, and Cupitt
takes to them with relish (Cupitt 1991). Everything is a story, for
stories produce every significant thing. Stories produce desire.
They manipulate and channel our emotions, directing them towards
objects we might otherwise find unexciting. Stories produce reality,
establishing certain orders and relations between things and people
and other people. They establish the significance of ages and genders,
of skin colours, classes and accents: of all the things that matter
and that could be otherwise, if told in a different story. Narratives
produce time, the positioning of things before and after, the placing
of the present at the complex intersection of individual and communal
time-narratives. And stories produce us, our sense of selfhood, of
being an 'I' with a past and a future, a narrative trajectory.

Religion, needless to say, is also a product of narrative; it is only a
story. But it is an important one, for religious stories provide our
lives with significance; they inspire moral endeavour and conquer the
Void (Cupitt 1991, 80). In the past we thought that God wrote the
story, but now we know that we ourselves have written God. Now the
religious task is to keep up the fiction, and not with a heavy, but with
a light touch. We must be 'cheerfully fictionalist' (Cupitt 1991, 96).
For the heavy hand produces a master story that weighs upon the
soul. Instead, we must be 'continually improvising, retelling,
embroidering, making it up as we go along' (Cupitt 1991, 154).

For the textualist theologian, such as Taylor or Cupitt, God is also a sign; one which, like any other, depends for its meaning on all the rest. God is not outside language, in a place where meaning and truth are self-present, for language has no outside. God is wholly inside language, make-believe like everything else; God is language. God is the play of signs upon the Void.

> The Void is just movement, change. Semiosis, signification, is a temporal moving process . . . Just reading a sentence, we should be able to feel on our pulses the way life and meaning continually come out of the Void and return into it. *That's* the new religious object. *That's* what we have to learn to say yes to . . . life's urgent transience.

> The sign is our only metaphysics, our little bit of transcendence. (Cupitt 1992, 61, 95)

The textualist's vision is a dark one. As Taylor's image of language as a maze suggests, we are forever enclosed, wandering in the labyrinth. No matter how long our piece of thread, there is no way out and nowhere to go. Cupitt, in a telling moment, imagines a reversed Platonic myth in which there is no way out of the cave. All we can do is to make it bigger. But no matter how much we dynamite or tunnel, we are still surrounded by rock, as dark as night. Cupitt complements this story with that of a house with no exterior doors or windows. We never go outside, and nothing ever enters. We never see a dawn or feel a breeze (Cupitt 1992, 33). Cupitt insists that he is not imagining a prison. But he is imagining a space without light; and without light human beings cannot long survive.

Cupitt's anti-Platonic stories answer to the postmodern condition of consumerist society. His windowless house and interminable cave could be descriptions of the modern shopping mall, which is already of indefinite extension, without windows and almost entirely hermetic. Fredric Jameson describes such places as 'postmodern hyperspace', a space which has 'finally succeeded in transcending the capacities of the individual human body to locate itself, to organise its immediate surroundings perceptually, and cognitively to map its position in a mappable external world' (Jameson 1991, 44). He gives the example of the Westin Bonaventure Hotel in Los Angeles and its lobby space, which 'takes on those who still seek to walk through it' (Jameson 1991, 43). Jameson suggests that such spaces are analogues of 'that even sharper dilemma which is the incapacity of our minds, at least at present, to map the great global multinational and decentered communicational network in which we find ourselves caught as individual subjects' (Jameson 1991, 44). But postmodern nihilism delights in precisely this network of disorientation.

PROBLEMS

The chief problem with textualist theology is that it is not textualist enough. It tells us that there are only stories, but it tends to obscure the fact that textualism is also only a story; and it tends to obscure the fact that it is a nihilist and not a Christian story. Here it is: 'The world remains fictional, as it must . . . Outside our stories there is still nothing but formlessness' (Cupitt 1991, 80). For textualism it is the story of 'formlessness' that goes all the way down. For textualist theology we tell stories *against the Void*. There is nothing beyond our stories except white noise (Cupitt 1991, 93). This is the master narrative, as Cupitt calls it: that there is, finally, only nothing. This radically differs from the Christian story, which teaches that really there is nothing whatsoever beyond God's story. It is the love of God that goes all the way down, really.

For someone like Cupitt, religious stories are tales told to keep the darkness at bay, until the night comes. However, one can ask: Are there no better stories we can tell, stories less complacent about contemporary society, less pessimistic about the human condition, more hopeful of change? There is some reason to think that the old ecclesial story of God's self-gift in Christ and Church is such a tale, since in the telling it looks for the coming of the dawn.

ORTHODOX POSTMODERN THEOLOGY

The Church's old story is maintained by those theologians I am calling fictionalists, of whom George A. Lindbeck and John Milbank are representative. They are fictionalists because, like the textualists, they accept the ubiquity of language. They believe that our sense of the world is formed by the socially constructed discourses in which we find ourselves, and to which we contribute. We are embedded in language, as is language in us. There is a reciprocal relation between story and story-teller. As I recount my life-story, my story produces the 'I' which recounts it. I tell the story by which I am told. And since I am part of a larger community – one in which others tell stories about me, just as I tell stories about them – I am the product of many interrelated narratives, as is everyone else.

Fictionalists also believe that stories go all the way down. Finally, our deepest convictions about the world and ourselves are constituted in stories alone. As such, stories are human constructions, socially enacted. When the stories that society tells about itself change, so does society. The world changes when we tell different stories about it:

> What is taken to be reality is in large part socially constructed and consequently alters in the course of time. The universe of the ancient Near East was very different from that of Greek philosophy, and both are dissimilar from the modern cosmos . . . In one world, for example, the origin of things is pictured in terms of a Babylonian myth; in another, in terms of Plato's Timaeus tale; and in a third, in terms of a scientific account of cosmic evolution. (Lindbeck 1984, 82)

However, fictionalists, unlike textualists, believe that what matters most in story-telling is not the telling itself – narrativity or textuality – but the stories told, the particular narratives unfolded. They are concerned not so much with the fictionality of the world, as with the particular world fictioned. Thus Lindbeck and Milbank are both orthodox theologians because they believe that the Christian narrative of Christ and his Church is preferable to all others. It is a story to live by.

In 1984 George Lindbeck published a short, powerful and provocative study on *The Nature of Doctrine*. In it he sought to outline an ecumenical theory of doctrine as the neutral 'grammar' of varied Christian discourses. Doctrines are understood not as propositions, but as regulations for our talk of divine matters, of God and Christ and Church. They are second-order rules for first-order talk. The creeds of the Church are regulative in that they tell us how to speak about Father, Son and Holy Spirit, and about Jesus Christ; or rather, they tell us how not to speak of them. Whatever we say of the Father, Son or Spirit we must say of the other two, but we must not suggest that one is the same as another. Whatever we say of Jesus Christ, we must not suggest that he was only a man or only God, nor that he was some sort of hybrid God-Man (Lindbeck 1984, 94).

Doctrines are rules for the imagining of God and world, in our story-telling, pray-acting and in our common-living. 'Doctrines regulate truth claims by excluding some and permitting others, but the logic of their communally authoritative use hinders or prevents them from specifying positively what is to be affirmed' (Lindbeck 1984, 19). Therefore, in addition to the rules of Christian imagining, we need a vocabulary of imagined stories for them to rule; stories which are also human lives, individual and communal.

The vocabulary of 'symbols, concepts, rites, injunctions and stories' for a doctrinally ruled Christian imagining comes largely from the Bible (Lindbeck 1984, 81). The canonical scriptures provide the basic narratives for how the Church imagines the world and itself in the world. The Church imagines itself within the narrative-world of the Bible, a written-world into which people can be 'inscribed'. Rather than understanding the Bible in worldly terms, the Christian understands the world in biblical ones; the Christian takes the biblical narrative, above all the narrative of Christ, as the fundamental story by which all others are to be understood, including his or her own story. 'The cross is not to be viewed as a figurative representation of suffering nor the messianic kingdom viewed as a symbol for hope in the future; rather, suffering should be cruciform, and hopes for the future messianic' (Lindbeck 1984, 118). The biblically formed narrative of Christ and his Church becomes the story which literally makes the world; it goes all the way down. (Here, one may be reminded of Karl Barth, whose theology is properly postmodern – Lindbeck 1984, 135.)

One can develop Lindbeck's idea by saying that when a person enters the scriptural story they do so by entering the Church's performance of that story: they are baptized into a biblical and ecclesial drama. It is not so much about being written into a book, as taking part in a play, a play that has to be improvised on the spot. As Rowan Williams puts it, people are 'invited to "create" themselves in finding a place within this drama – an improvisation in the theater workshop, but one that purports to be about a comprehensive truth affecting one's identity and future' (Williams 1989, 97).

On Lindbeck's postliberal view, language and story come first, world and experience second. We only recognize the world as *world* because we can say 'world'. Experience occurs within language. All that we have has been given in *words* (see further, Loughlin 1988). This is much the same as textualism. But where fictionalism differs is in its master story. Whereas for textualist nihilism it is the movement of signs upon the surface of the Void, for Lindbeck it is the story of Christ and his Church. One could say that the difference between these stories is the difference between Nothing and Everything, between ultimate darkness and hoped for dawn, between violence and harmony. This last way of stating the difference is after John Milbank, who has made the difference between malign and benign postmodernism a theme of his magisterial study, *Theology and Social Theory* (1990).

Milbank argues that all stories stage themselves; that is, they imagine a context for their telling, they imagine how the world must be for the story to make sense. As we have seen, Cupitt's story of shifting signs makes sense upon the stage of the Void. Milbank, however, argues that nihilism imagines not just an impassive Void but an incessant contest between powers. For where there are only differences, and no common ground, each difference is set against all the rest.

Nihilism condemns us to endless violence, as alone appropriate to its story. The Christian narrative, on the other hand, imagines the possibility of harmonious difference and peace as the inner dynamic of the triune God. The Church imagines people remaining in their 'many different cities, languages and cultures, yet still belonging to one eternal city ruled by Christ', in whom all humanity is fulfilled (Milbank 1991, 227). It is the idea of difference as music:

> For Christianity, true community means the freedom of people and groups to be different, not just to be functions of a fixed consensus . . . but a consensus that is only in and through the inter-relations of community itself, and a consensus that moves and 'changes': *a consentus musicus.* (Milbank 1991, 228)

Christianity is postmodern because it is not founded on anything other than the performance of its story. It cannot be established against nihilism by reason, but only presented as a radical alternative, as something else altogether (Milbank 1990, 389). It is also postmodern because its story – God's story – imagines a world 'out of nothing', a world of becoming, in which people are not fixed essences but life-narratives with a future. The story of Jesus Christ gives us the pattern of peaceful existence. It is an 'atoning' peace of mutual forgiveness and the bearing of one another's burdens. This peace is sought in the nomadic city of the Church, an open-ended

tradition of charity, of 'differences in a continuous harmony'
(Milbank 1990, 417).

DIFFICULTIES

From the point of view of Christian theology, fictionalist orthodoxy is
preferable to textualist nihilism, but postmodern fictionalism has its
difficulties (see further, Loughlin 1992). First, is it possible to affirm
the reality of God while allowing that such an affirmation can take
place only within a story, albeit a master story which is said to go all
the way down, without remainder?

Cupitt believes that any talk of transcendent realities, of things
beyond or outside language, is rendered 'silly' by the fact that it is
talk, and thus wholly within language (Cupitt 1992, 90). If God
appears in a story – as he does in the Bible – he must appear as a
human-like, gendered and speaking character, with ideas and
assumptions appropriate to his time, with feelings and intentions,
'behaving in general like an extra-powerful and demanding king'
(Cupitt 1991, 114). He will be all too human. And won't it be odd
that people can write about him, as if from God's point of view?
(Cupitt 1991, 118–19). Who was around when God made the heavens
and the earth, to tell us about it?

Jacques Derrida famously said that there is nothing outside the
text. But he did not mean that there is only text. He meant,
among other things, that whatever we know, we know in and through
language. But one of the things that we know *in* language is that there
are things *outside* language. Though words are used to talk about
things, we can use them to talk about things other than words. Cupitt,
it seems, forgets this, confusing words with the things we use words
to talk about. No one should pretend that talk of God is easy, but nor
should they think it impossible. Of course God is a human-like
character in the biblical narrative. But this does not mean that God is
a human being. Of course the first story of Genesis is narrated from
an impossible standpoint, it is a work of imagination after all. But this
does not mean that it is not an 'inspired', profound and true depiction
of the world as creation.

Truth is said to be another problem for fictionalism. How can there
be true stories when it is said that there are only stories? For it is
supposed that a true story is one that matches up to reality, to the way
things are. But if the way things are can never be known, because all

we can ever know are stories of one sort or another, we can never match stories against reality, but only against one another. Thus it is said that science is not so much the matching of scientific theories against reality, as the matching of theories against experimental data, observation statements and so forth, which are always already theory-laden. Science matches theory-stories against observation-narratives.

Whatever the case with science, Christian truth has never been a matter of matching stories against reality. It has always been a matter of matching reality-stories against the truth: Jesus Christ. For the Christian Church it has always been a life-story that comes first, against which all other things are to be matched. This life-story is what 'truth' means in Christianity. Nor is this a matter of making up the truth, because it is the truth that makes up the story. The story is imagined for us before it is re-imagined by us: the story is *given* to us. That, at any rate, is the Church's story.

It is said that fictionalism renders the Church sectarian. For fictionalism denies that reason provides an autonomous language in which everything can be discussed; rather it supposes a multiplicity of self-sustaining language-communities. There is no common language the Church can use to express itself to an unbelieving world. Post-modern theology rejects the idea that Christian discourse can be translated into alien tongues without ceasing to be Christian. But then it seems that Christian discourse is the in-language of an in-group, cut off from a larger commonwealth. But this is to forget that people can learn to speak more than one language without recourse to some 'common' tongue. Moreover, it is to forget 'that the history called Christ is the encompassing history *within* which all things live and move and have their being' (Jenson 1992, 293).

Finally, it is said that despite all the talk about 'harmony' and 'peace', fictionalist theology is itself violent in thinking the Christian story a master narrative that positions all other stories. It is the violence of having the last word. It must be remembered, however, that the Christian story is always provisional because not yet ended. It is performed in the hope that the one of whom it speaks will return again to say it. The last word is yet to be said; and when it is, the Church too will find itself positioned. Thus the Christian story resists mastery by being the prayerful tale of one who came in the form of a servant and who will return as a friend.

FUTURE NOW

In nihilist postmodernism we find the curious conjunction of paganism and modernity. It is pagan because it sets the world against the Void: a play of signs upon the surface of nothingness. But it is modern because instead of finding this a reason for despair or resignation, it finds it an occasion for delight and joy. The realization of the Void is the moment of human emancipation:

> The world is only an endlessly shifting purely contingent order of signs in motion, a Sea of Meanings . . . And just the ability to see this and say it is precisely what gives us our new and joyful freedom . . . Your God is only your faith in him, your values are only your commitment to them. That is liberation. You're free. (Cupitt 1992, 66)

Whether in the expanse of the open market, epitomized in the spaces of the shopping mall, or in the mazes and caverns of textualism, pagan modernity announces that the end of the story has arrived, human freedom and emancipation achieved. Ironically, it is the triumph of Hegelianism, the myth of perfect self-realization, the conjunction of sign and signified. Meaning no longer slips away, one word ahead, because now the meaning is the sign: the medium is the message. This is why nihilist postmodernism is a realized eschatology. We are at the end of the story; the end of the world.

However, such postmodernism is really only paganized modernity. Its exponents, including its theologians, have not superseded modernism. They still believe in the story of human emancipation humanly achieved, and because they understand the narrative as one of emancipation rather than of formation, they conceive its conclusion only negatively, as freedom from rather than freedom for. But the fictionalist theologians hold out the possibility of a true postmodernism, a story that is neither pagan nor modernist, but Christian. It is a story about the possibility of human formation for harmonious and charitable union with God. And this ancient story is truly postmodern because it is a story about the future, of what is to come after the present. At the same time, it partakes of the paradox which Lyotard locates in the word 'postmodern': 'the future (*post*) anterior (*modus*)' (Lyotard 1992, 24). The future now.

The postmodern work, according to Lyotard, is not governed by the past, and cannot be judged by present rules, precisely because it calls past rules into question. The rules that govern the work are made in its production. The writer or artist works 'without rules, and in order to establish the rules for what *will have been made*' (Lyotard 1992, 24). Thus the work is an event, ahead of its time. This is true of God's work, which cannot be governed by the past. It is always ahead of its time: *post-modern*. The Church is a postmodern event because it exists to establish the 'rule' of love for what will have been made: the peace and harmony of Christ's coming commonwealth.

It is only a story because it is only one way of telling the world – as Creation rather than Void, as Light rather than Darkness. The Church tells its story as best it can. Some like it and believe, and others don't. The Church moves on and tells it somewhere else. At the end of the world it's a matter of telling different stories. When the postmodernist culture of late capitalism tells us that the end of human striving arrives when society is indistinguishable from a market, when everything can be bought and sold and the good life is a matter of efficient management, then it's a difference between having the kingdom of God now, shopping on a Sunday, or still waiting, hoping and praying, for the return of one who loves us for what will have been made.

BIBLIOGRAPHY

Altizer, T. J. J. (1966), *The Gospel of Christian Atheism* (London: Collins)

Altizer, T. J. J., and W. Hamilton (1966), *Radical Theology and the Death of God* (Harmondsworth: Penguin Books)

Anderson, G. H., and T. F. Stransky, ed. (1979), *Mission Trends No. 4: Liberation Theologies* (Grand Rapids, MI: Wm B. Eerdmans)

Armstrong, A. H. (1986), 'The Ancient and Continuing Pieties', in *Classical Mediterranean Spirituality*, ed. A. H. Armstrong (London: Routledge & Kegan Paul), pp. 66–101

Arthur, J., and B. Lloyd (1982), *Sex and Gender* (Harmondsworth: Penguin Books)

Assmann, H. (1976), *Theology for a Nomad Church* (Maryknoll, NY: Orbis Books)

Auerbach, E. (1968), *Mimesis: The Representation of Reality in Western Literature* (Princeton, NJ: Princeton University Press)

Beierwaltes, W. (1986), 'The Love of Beauty and the Love of God', in *Classical Mediterranean Spirituality*, ed. A. H. Armstrong (London: Routledge & Kegan Paul), pp. 293–313

Berry, R. J. (1984), 'Sex', in *Free to Be Different*, ed. J. R. W. Stott (Basingstoke: Marshall, Morgan & Scott)

idem (1988), *God and Evolution* (London: Hodder & Stoughton)

Boff, L. (1979), *The Maternal Face of God: The Feminine and Its Religious Expressions* (San Francisco: Harper & Row)

Brearley, M. (1989), 'Matthew Fox: Creation Spirituality for the Aquarian Age', *Christian Jewish Relations* 22, pp. 37–49

Brow, R. (1989), 'The Taming of a New Age Prophet', *Christianity Today*, 16 June, pp. 28–30

Brown, C. (1984), *Miracles and the Critical Mind* (Grand Rapids, MI: Wm B. Eerdmans; Exeter: Paternoster Press)

Brown, P. (1990), *The Body and Society: Men, Women and Sexual Renunciation in Early Christianity* (London: Faber & Faber)

Bultmann, R. (1953), 'New Testament and Mythology', in *Kerygma and Myth: A Theological Debate*, ed. H. W. Bartsch (London: SPCK)

Butler, J. (1736), *The Analogy of Religion, Natural and Revealed, to the Constitution and Course of Nature*, in *The Works of Joseph Butler*, ed. W. E. Gladstone, vol. 1 (Oxford: Clarendon Press, 1896)

Chopp, R. (1986), *The Praxis of Suffering* (Maryknoll, NY: Orbis Books)

Christ, P., and J. Plaskow, ed. (1979), *Womanspirit Rising: A Feminist Reader in Religion* (San Francisco: Harper & Row)

Clark, E. (1983), *Women in the Early Church* (Delaware: Michael Glazier)

Coakley, S. (1990), 'Creaturehood Before God: Male and Female', *Theology* 93 (September–October), pp. 343–54

idem (1992), 'Mariology and "Romantic Feminism": A Critique', in *Women's Voices: Essays in Contemporary Feminist Theology*, ed. T. Elwes (London: Marshall Pickering)

Coulson, C. A. (1955), *Science and Christian Faith* (London: Oxford University Press)

Cupitt, D. (1980), *Taking Leave of God* (London: SCM Press)

idem (1984), *The Sea of Faith* (London: BBC Publications)

idem (1987), *The Long-Legged Fly: A Theology of Language and Desire* (London: SCM Press)

idem (1990), *Creation Out of Nothing* (London: SCM Press)

idem (1991), *What is a Story?* (London: SCM Press)

idem (1992), *The Time Being* (London: SCM Press)

D'Costa, G. (1986a), 'The Pluralist Paradigm in the Christian Theology of Religions', *Scottish Journal of Theology* 39, pp. 211–24

idem (1986b), *Theology and Religious Pluralism: The Challenge of Other Religions* (Oxford: Basil Blackwell)

idem (1987), *John Hick's Theology of Religions* (New York: University Press of America)

Daly, M. (1985), *Beyond God the Father: Toward a Philosophy of Women's Liberation* (Boston: Beacon Press)

Davidson, J. D., and W. Rees-Mogg (1992), *The Great Reckoning: How the World Will Change in the Depression of the 1990s* (London: Sidgwick & Jackson)

Descartes, R. (1641), *Meditations*, in *Descartes' Philosophical Writings*, ed. & trans. N. K. Smith (London: Macmillan, 1952)

Dostoyevsky, F. (1880), *The Brothers Karamazov*, trans. D. Magarshack (Harmondsworth: Penguin Books, 1982)

Elwes, T., ed. (1992), *Women's Voices: Essays in Contemporary Feminist Theology* (London: Marshall Pickering)

Ferreira, M. J. (1986), *Scepticism and Reasonable Doubt* (Oxford: Clarendon Press)

Fox, M. (1972), *On Becoming a Musical, Mystical Bear: Spirituality American Style*, 2nd ed. (New York: Harper & Row)

idem (1976), *Whee! We, Wee All the Way Home: A Guide to the New Sensual Spirituality* (Wilmington, NC: Consortium)

idem (1979), *A Spirituality Named Compassion* (Minneapolis, MN: Winston Press)

idem (1980), *Breakthrough: Meister Eckhart's Creation Spirituality in New Translation* (Garden City, NY: Doubleday & Co.)

idem (1981), *Whee! We, Wee All the Way Home: A Guide to the New Sensual Spirituality*, 2nd ed. (Santa Fe: Bear & Co.)

idem (1983), *Original Blessing: A Primer in Creation Spirituality* (Santa Fe: Bear & Co.)

idem (1984), 'Creation-Centered Spirituality from Hildegard of Bingen to Julian of Norwich: 300 Years of an Ecological Spirituality in the West', in *Cry of the Environment: Rebuilding the Christian Creation Tradition*, ed. P. N. Joranson and K. Butigan (Santa Fe: Bear & Co.), pp. 85–106

idem (1987), *Hildegard of Bingen's Book of Divine Works* (Santa Fe: Bear & Co.)

idem (1988), *The Coming of the Cosmic Christ: The Healing of Mother Earth and the Birth of a Global Renaissance* (San Francisco: Harper & Row) (1991), *Creation Spirituality: Liberating Gifts for the Peoples of the Earth* (San Francisco: HarperCollins)

idem (1992), *Sheer Joy: Conversations with Thomas Aquinas on Creation Spirituality* (San Francisco: HarperCollins)

Fox, M., and B. Swimme (1982), *Manifesto! For a Global Civilization* (Santa Fe: Bear & Co.)

Frazer, J. G. (1907), *Adonis, Attis, Osiris: Studies in Oriental Religion* (London: Macmillan)

Freire, P. (1972), *Pedagogy of the Oppressed* (Harmondsworth: Penguin Books)

Goldstein, V. S. (1960), 'The Human Situation – A Feminine View', *Journal of Religion* 40, pp. 100–12

Goodall, M., and J. Reader (1992), 'Why Matthew Fox Fails to Change the World', in *The Earth Beneath: A Critical Guide to Green Theology*, ed. I. Ball, M. Goodall, C. Palmer, and J. Reader (London: SPCK), pp. 104–19

Goulder, M. D., and J. Hick (1983), *Why Believe in God?* (London: SCM Press)

Gutiérrez, G. (1973), *A Theology of Liberation: History, Politics and Salvation* (Maryknoll, NY: Orbis Books)

Hadden, J. (1969), *The Gathering Storm in the Churches* (Garden City, NY: Doubleday)

Hampson, D. (1990), *Theology and Feminism* (Oxford: Basil Blackwell)

Hardy, D. W. (1989), 'Created and Redeemed Sociality', in *On Being the Church: Essays on the Christian Community*, ed. C. E. Gunton and D. W. Hardy (Edinburgh: T. & T. Clark), pp. 21–47

Harris, M. J. (1985), *Easter in Durham* (Exeter: Paternoster Press)

Harrison, Verna E. F. (1990), 'Male and Female in Cappadocian Theology', *Journal of Theological Studies* 41 (October), pp. 441–71

Hartshorne, C. (1983), *Man's Vision of God and the Logic of Theism* (Chicago: Shoe String Press)

Harvey, D. (1989), *The Condition of Postmodernity: An Enquiry Into the Origins of Cultural Change* (Oxford: Basil Blackwell)

Hayter, M. (1987), *The New Eve in Christ: The Use and Abuse of the Bible in the Debate About Women in the Church* (London: SPCK)

Heschel, A. J. (1966), *The Earth is the Lord's/The Sabbath: Its Meaning for Modern Man* (New York: Harper & Row)

Hick, J., ed. (1977), *The Myth of God Incarnate* (London: SCM Press)

Hooper, W., ed. (1979), *They Stand Together: The Letters of C. S. Lewis to Arthur Greeves (1914–1963)* (London: Collins)

Hopko, T. (1982), 'On the Male Character of Christian Priesthood', in *Women and the Priesthood*, ed. K. Ware, G. Barrois, and T. Hopko (New York: St Vladimir's Press)

House of Bishops (1986), *The Nature of Christian Belief: A Statement and Exposition by the House of Bishops of the General Synod of the Church of England* (London: Church House Publishing)

Hume, D. (1748), 'Of Miracles', section 10 of *An Enquiry Concerning Human Understanding*, in *Enquiries: Concerning Human*

Understanding and Concerning the Principles of Morals, ed. L. A. Selby-Bigge, 2nd ed. (Oxford: Clarendon Press, 1902)

Huxley, A. (1958), *The Perennial Philosophy* (London: Fontana)

Jameson, F. (1991), *Postmodernism or the Cultural Logic of Late Capitalism* (London: Verso)

Jencks, C. (1977), *The Language of Post-Modern Architecture* (London: Academy Editions)

Jenson, R. W. (1982), *The Triune Identity: God According to the Gospel* (Philadelphia: Fortress Press) (1992), 'The Hauerwas Project', *Modern Theology* 8.3, pp. 285–95

Jüngel, E. (1983), *God as the Mystery of the World: On the Foundation of the Theology of the Crucified One in the Dispute Between Theism and Atheism*, trans. D. L. Guder (Edinburgh: T. & T. Clark)

Kant, I. (1787), *Critique of Pure Reason*, trans. N. K. Smith (London: Macmillan, 1933)

idem (1788), *Critique of Practical Reason*, trans. L. W. Beck (Indianpolis: Bobbs-Merrill, 1956)

Kasper, W. (1976), *Jesus the Christ* (London: Burns & Oates)

Kierkegaard, S. (1850), *Training in Christianity*, trans. W. Lowrie (Princeton, NJ: Princeton University Press, 1967)

idem (1941), *Concluding Unscientific Postscript*, trans. D. F. Swenson and W. Lowrie (Princeton, NJ: Princeton University Press)

Kirk, J. A. (1979), *Liberation Theology: An Evangelical View from the Third World* (Basingstoke: Marshall, Morgan & Scott)

Kuhn, T. S. (1970), *The Structure of Scientific Revolutions*, 2nd ed. (Chicago: University of Chicago Press)

Künneth, Walter (1965), *The Theology of the Resurrection*, trans. James W. Leitch (London: SCM Press)

Lampe, G. W. H. (1971), *God as Spirit* (Oxford: Clarendon Press)

Le Corbusier (1927), *Towards a New Architecture*, trans. Frederick Etchells (London: The Architectural Press)

Le Doeuff, M. (1987), 'Ants and Women, or Philosophy Without Boundaries', in *Contemporary French Philosophy*, ed. A. Phillips Griffiths (Cambridge: Cambridge University Press)

Levine, L. W. (1977), *Black Culture and Black Consciousness: Afro-American Folk Thought from Slavery to Freedom* (Oxford: Oxford University Press)

Lewis, C. S. (1943), *The Abolition of Man: Or Reflections on Education with Special Reference to the Teaching of English in the Upper Forms of Schools* (London: Collins Fount, 1978)

idem (1946), *The Great Divorce: A Dream* (London: Collins Fount, 1977)

idem (1971), *Undeceptions: Essays on Theology and Ethics* (London: Geoffrey Bles)

idem (1977a), *Fern-Seed and Elephants and Other Essays on Christianity*, ed. W. Hooper (London: Collins Fount)

idem (1977b), *Miracles: A Preliminary Study* (London: Collins Fount)

Lewontin, R. C. (1985), Chapter 1 in *Population and Biology*, ed. N. Keyfitz (Liege: Ordina)

Lindbeck, G. A. (1984), *The Nature of Doctrine: Religion and Theology in a Postliberal Age* (London: SPCK)

Loughlin, G. (1988), 'Sec-Saying/Say-Seeing', *Theology* 91, pp. 201–9

idem (1992), 'Christianity at the End of the Story or the Return of the Master-Narrative', *Modern Theology* 8.4, pp. 365–84

Lovejoy, A. O. (1936), *The Great Chain of Being: A Study of the History of an Idea* (Cambridge, MA: Harvard University Press)

Lyotard, J-F. (1984), *The Postmodern Condition: A Report on Knowledge*, trans. G. Bennington and B. Massumi (Minneapolis, MN: University of Minnesota Press)

idem (1992), *The Postmodern Explained to Children: Correspondence 1982–1985* (London: Turnaround)

McFague, S. (1987), *Models of God* (Philadelphia: Fortress Press)

McGrath, A. E. (1984), '*Homo Assumptus?* A Study in the Christology of *Via Moderna* with Particular Reference to William of Ockham', *Ephemerides Theologicae Lovanienses* 60, pp. 283–97

idem (1986), *The Making of Modern German Christology* (Oxford: Basil Blackwell)

MacIntyre, A. (1985), *After Virtue: A Study in Moral Theory*, 2nd ed. (London: Duckworth)

MacKay, D. M. (1979a), *Freedom of Action in a Mechanistic Universe* (Cambridge: Cambridge University Press)

idem (1979b), *Human Science and Human Dignity* (London: Hodder & Stoughton)

Macmurray, J. (1961), *Persons in Relation* (London: Faber & Faber)

Mandel, E. (1978), *Late Capitalism* (London: Verso)

228   Different Gospels

Marriage, A. (1989), *Life-Giving Spirit: Responding to the Feminine in God* (London: SPCK)

Marx, K., and F. Engels (1975), *The Holy Family or Critique of Critical Criticism*, trans. R. Dixon and C. Dutt, 2nd ed. (Moscow: Progress)

Medawar, P. (1984), *The Limits of Science* (New York: Harper & Row)

Midgley, M. (1985), *Evolution as a Religion* (London: Methuen)

idem (1988), 'On Not Being Afraid of Natural Sex Difference', in *Feminist Perspectives in Philosophy*, ed. M. Griffiths and M. Whitford (London: Macmillan)

Míguez Bonino, J. (1975), *Doing Theology in a Revolutionary Situation*, ed. William H. Lazareth (Philadelphia: Fortress Press). Also published as *Revolutionary Theology Comes of Age* (London: SPCK, 1975)

Milbank, J. (1990), *Theology and Social Theory* (Oxford: Basil Blackwell)

idem (1991), ''Postmodern Critical Augustinianism': A Short *Summa* in Forty-Two Responses to Unasked Questions', *Modern Theology* 7.3, pp. 225–37

Miller, W. L. (1954), 'Piety Along the Potomac', *The Reporter*

idem (1955), 'The Gospel of Norman Vincent Peale', *Union Seminary Quarterly Review*

Millett, K. (1969), *Sexual Politics* (New York: Ballantine Books)

Miranda, J. P. (1977), *Being and the Messiah: The Message of St John* (Maryknoll, NY: Orbis Books)

Moltmann, J. (1974), *The Crucified God: The Cross of Christ as the Foundation and Criticism of Christian Theology*, trans. R. A. Wilson and J. Bowden (London: SCM Press)

idem (1976), ''On Latin American Liberation Theology': An Open Letter to José Míguez Bonino', *Christianity and Crisis* 36 (29 March)

Monod, Jacques (1971), *Chance and Necessity* (London: Collins)

Nebelsick, H. R. (1984), 'Article Review: Iain Paul, *Science, Theology and Einstein*', *Scottish Journal of Theology* 37, pp. 237–42

Neurath, O. (1973), *Empiricism and Sociology*, ed. M. Neurath and R. S. Cohen (Dordrecht: D. Reidel)

Newbigin, L. (1989), *The Gospel in a Pluralist Society* (London: SPCK)

Newman, B. (1992), 'Romancing the Past: A Critical Look at Matthew Fox and the Medieval "Creation Mystics"', *Touchstone* 5, pp. 5-10

Niebuhr, H. R. (1929), *The Social Sources of Denominationalism* (Cleveland: World Publishing, 1965)

Nietzsche, F. (1966), *Beyond Good and Evil: Prelude to a Philosophy of the Future*, trans. W. Kaufmann (New York: Random House)

Oddie, W. (1984), *What Will Happen to God?* (London: SPCK)

Ogden, S. M. (1966), *The Reality of God and Other Essays* (New York: Harper & Row)

Osborn, L. H. (1992), *Angels of Light? The Challenge of New Age Spirituality* (London: Darton, Longman & Todd)

idem (1993), *Guardians of Creation: Nature in Theology and Christian Life* (Leicester: Inter-Varsity Press)

Pannenberg, W. (1968), *Jesus: God and Man*, trans. L. L. Wilkins and D. A. Priebe (London: SCM Press)

Peters, E. (1989), 'Matthew Fox and the Vatican Wolves', *Dialog* 28, pp. 137-42

Polanyi, M. (1969), *Knowing and Being* (London: Routledge & Kegan Paul)

Polkinghorne, J. (1983), *The Way the World Is* (London: SPCK)

Raboteau, A. J. (1978), *Slave Religion: The Invisible Institution in the Ante-Bellum South* (Oxford: Oxford University Press)

Rahner, K. (1961-81), *Theological Investigations* (London: Darton, Longman & Todd)

Raschke, C. (1980), *The Interruption of Eternity: Modern Gnosticism and the Origins of the New Religious Consciousness* (Chicago: Nelson-Hall)

Reardon, B. (1980), *Religious Thought in the Victorian Age* (London: Longman)

Richardson, A., and J. Bowden, ed. (1983), *New Dictionary of Christian Theology* (London: SCM Press)

Robinson, J. A. T. (1963), *Honest to God* (London: SCM Press)

Rogerson, J. W. (1985), 'Using the Bible in the Debate About Abortion', in *Abortion and the Sanctity of Human Life*, ed. J. H. Channer (Exeter: Paternoster Press)

Ruether, R. R. (1984), *Sexism and God-Talk: Toward a Feminist Theology* (London: SCM Press)

idem (1990), 'Matthew Fox and Creation Spirituality: Strengths and Weaknesses', *The Catholic World*, July-August, pp. 168-72

Santmire, H. P. (1985), *The Travail of Nature: The Ambiguous Ecological Promise of Christian Theology* (Philadelphia: Fortress Press)

Schleiermacher, F. D. (1821), *The Christian Faith* (Edinburgh: T. & T. Clark, 1928)

Sen, A. (1990), 'More Than 100 Million Women Are Missing', *New York Review of Books* 37 (20 December), pp. 61–6

Smail, T. (1992), 'The Liberating Lord', *Anglicans for Renewal*, 48 (Spring)

Snow, C. P. (1975), *The Two Cultures* (Cambridge: Cambridge University Press)

Soskice, J. Martin (1985), *Metaphor and Religious Language* (Oxford: Clarendon Press)

Stamp, K. (1956), *The Peculiar Institution: Slavery in the Ante-Bellum South* (New York: Alfred Knopf)

Starhawk (1979), *The Spiral Dance: A Rebirth of the Ancient Religion of the Great Goddess* (San Francisco: Harper & Row)

Steiner, G. (1991), *Real Presences: Is There Anything* in *What We Say?* (London: Faber & Faber)

Storkey, E. (1988), *What's Right with Feminism?* (London: SPCK)

Sykes, S. (1990), 'Richard Hooker and the Ordination of Women to the Priesthood', in *After Eve: Women, Theology and the Christian Tradition*, ed. J. Martin Soskice (London: Marshall Pickering)

Taylor, M. C. (1982), *Deconstructing Theology* (Atlanta, GA: Scholars Press)

idem (1984), *Erring: A Postmodern A/theology* (Chicago: University of Chicago Press)

idem (1987), *Altarity* (Chicago: University of Chicago Press)

Thorpe, W. H. (1978), *Purpose in a World of Chance* (Oxford: Oxford University Press)

Tillich, P. (1964), 'The Struggle Between Space and Time', in *Theology of Culture* (New York: Oxford University Press), pp. 30–9

idem (1968), *Systematic Theology*, combined volume (Welwyn: J. Nisbet & Co.)

Torrance, T. F. (1969), *Theological Science* (Oxford: Oxford University Press)

Troeltsch, E. (1972), *The Absoluteness of Christianity and the History of Religion* (London: SCM Press)